Build systems with Go
Everything a Gopher must know

Juan M. Tirado

Build systems with Go

by Juan M. Tirado

Copyright ©2021

ISBN: 9798502040150

Independently published

Cover by Juan M.Tirado

Gopher Gotham image by Egon Elbre (@egonelbre)

All rights reserved. No part of this work may be reproduced or transmitted in any form or by any means, electronic or mechanical, including photocopying, recording or by any information storage or retrieval system, without the prior written permission of the copyright owner.

This book has been entirely written using LaTeX.

Notes to this version

The reception of version v0.1.0 exceeded all my expectations. The book was #1 for one month in the category of new releases. This is an amazing achievement for a single-person self-published book. Thank you all for your exceptional support, comments, and suggestions. Version v0.2.0 is the first revision after the initial release. Many explanations have been revisited searching for a trade-off between conciseness and utility. Extra figures have been added, and a new chapter about Cgo has been included.

Revision History:

- **v0.2.0**: 2021-05-05 New Cgo chapter, revisited and enhanced explanations, typos, and readers' suggestions. Mentions to changes in Go 1.16.

- **v0.1.0**: 2021-03-29 First version.

Contents

Preface   11

I   The Go language   17

1   First steps with Go   21
    1.1   Save the world with Go!!!   21
    1.2   Passing arguments to our program   22
    1.3   Summary   25

2   The basics   27
    2.1   Packages and imports   27
    2.2   Variables, constants, and enums   29
    2.3   Functions   33
    2.4   Pointers   36
    2.5   nil and zero values   37
    2.6   Loops and branches   37
    2.7   Errors   42
    2.8   Defer, panic, and recover   43
    2.9   Init functions   46
    2.10   Summary   47

3   Arrays, slices, and maps   49
    3.1   Arrays   49
    3.2   Slices   50

3.3 Maps	54
3.4 Summary	56

4 Structs, methods, and interfaces — 57
    4.1 Structs . . . 57
    4.2 Methods . . . 62
    4.3 Interfaces . . . 65
    4.4 Summary . . . 69

5 Reflection — 71
    5.1 reflect.Type . . . 71
    5.2 reflect.Value . . . 75
    5.3 Creating functions on the fly . . . 78
    5.4 Tags . . . 80
    5.5 The three laws of reflection . . . 82
    5.6 Summary . . . 84

6 Concurrency — 85
    6.1 Goroutines . . . 85
    6.2 Channels . . . 87
    6.3 Select . . . 93
    6.4 WaitGroup . . . 96
    6.5 Timers, tickers, and timeouts . . . 98
    6.6 Context . . . 100
    6.7 Once . . . 106
    6.8 Mutexes . . . 108
    6.9 Atomics . . . 109
    6.10 Summary . . . 112

7 Input/Output — 113
    7.1 Readers and writers . . . 113
    7.2 Reading and Writing files . . . 116
    7.3 Standard I/O . . . 119
    7.4 Summary . . . 122

8 Encodings — 123
    8.1 CSV . . . 123
    8.2 JSON . . . 125
    8.3 XML . . . 129
    8.4 YAML . . . 133
    8.5 Tags and encoding . . . 136
    8.6 Summary . . . 140

9 HTTP — 141
- 9.1 Requests — 141
- 9.2 HTTP Server — 147
- 9.3 Cookies — 150
- 9.4 Middleware — 153
- 9.5 Summary — 157

10 Templates — 159
- 10.1 Filling templates with structs — 159
- 10.2 Actions — 161
- 10.3 Functions — 163
- 10.4 HTML — 166
- 10.5 Summary — 167

11 Testing — 169
- 11.1 Tests — 169
- 11.2 Examples — 178
- 11.3 Benchmarking — 181
- 11.4 Coverage — 183
- 11.5 Profiling — 185
- 11.6 Summary — 190

12 Modules and documentation — 191
- 12.1 Modules — 191
- 12.2 Documentation — 195
- 12.3 Summary — 197

13 Cgo — 199
- 13.1 Use C code from Go — 199
- 13.2 Exchanging variables — 201
- 13.3 Exchanging arrays and structs — 204
- 13.4 Linking libraries — 209
- 13.5 Calling Go functions from C — 210
- 13.6 Summary — 216

II Building systems — 217

14 Protocol buffers — 221
- 14.1 The proto file — 221
- 14.2 Complex messages — 225
- 14.3 Importing other proto definitions — 226

14.4 Nested types 228
14.5 Type Any 230
14.6 Type Oneof 231
14.7 Maps 233
14.8 JSON 235
14.9 Summary 236

15 gRPC   **237**
15.1 Basic concepts 237
15.2 Definition of services 238
15.3 Creating a server 241
15.4 Creating clients 242
15.5 Streaming 244
15.6 Transcoding 256
15.7 Interceptors 261
15.8 Summary 267

16 Logging with Zerolog   **269**
16.1 The log package 269
16.2 Zerolog basics 270
16.3 Zerolog settings 275
16.4 Zerolog advanced settings 279
16.5 Summary 285

17 Command Line Interface   **287**
17.1 The basics 287
17.2 Arguments and Flags 289
17.3 Commands 295
17.4 Advanced features 300
17.5 Summary 308

18 Relational databases   **309**
18.1 SQL in Go 309
18.2 GORM 315
18.3 Manipulate data 322
18.4 Summary 331

19 NoSQL databases   **333**
19.1 Cassandra and GoCQL 333
19.2 Summary 347

20 Kafka — **349**
- 20.1 The basics — 349
- 20.2 Using the Confluent client — 351
- 20.3 Using the Segmentio client — 357
- 20.4 Using the Kafka REST API — 362
- 20.5 Summary — 369

PREFACE

Welcome and thank you for reading these lines.

Since I started programming in Go, I have always enjoyed its extraordinary commitment to simplicity. It is difficult to find another language that can make complex things so easily. That is the beauty of this language. Years have passed by and Go is no longer the new kid on the block, it has already become a mature language surrounded by a rich ecosystem of libraries, projects, and tools. Talking about Go is no longer talking about that fancy language that makes your life easier. Go is the gravity centre of a continuously growing ecosystem of amazing solutions maintained by a devoted community of developers.

Go was originally designed to simplify the building of complex systems. However, when a developer decides to learn Go most of the learning resources simply explain the language. This book goes one step further by exploring tools, libraries, and projects from the Go ecosystem you can use to build ready-for-production systems. Everything a gopher must know in a single book.

I hope you find this book useful.

WHO SHOULD READ THIS BOOK?

This book is oriented to new Go adopters and developers with programming experience in other languages. The first part of this book covers the Go language from its basics to more advanced concepts. The second part assumes these concepts to be known by the reader and explores how to use them with other tools to build systems. If you are new to Go you can start from the beginning. However, if you have some experience you can start with the second part and revisit any basic concept if needed. Or you can simply go and check the chapters at your convenience.

STRUCTURE OF THIS BOOK

This book is structured to easily find those pieces you may find more interesting for your work. However, if you are an absolute beginner or you do not feel very comfortable with all the concepts explained in this book you can always start from the beginning. Whatever your use case is, these are the contents of this book.

- **Part I: The Go language**
  The first part explores the language from the very basics to advanced tools offered by the standard library.

- **Chapter 1: First steps with Go**
  This Chapter is specifically written to motivate newbies to run their first Go program.

- **Chapter 2: The basics**
  This Chapter explains all the Go basics including syntax, variables, types, pointers, functions, and execution flow.

- **Chapter 3: Arrays, slices, and maps**
  Go includes powerful native data structures such as arrays and maps. This Chapter extends previous concepts and shows the reader how to write her first data processing solutions.

- **Chapter 4: Structs, methods, and interfaces**
  This Chapter describes how Go defines advanced data structures, their associated methods, and interfaces.

- **Chapter 5: Reflection**
  By exploring how Go uses reflection, the reader can understand the many possibilities of manipulating in-memory data structures.

- **Chapter 6: Concurrency**
  Concurrency is not an easy topic. However, this Chapter demonstrates how Go help developers to design complex solutions effortless. This Chapter covers goroutines, channels, concurrency statements, contexts and more.

- **Chapter 7: Input/Output**
  Any program requires to write or read data to and from different sources. This Chapter explains through examples how Go provides I/O support.

- **Chapter 8: Encodings**
  The Go standard library offers by default solutions to work with encodings such as CSV, JSON or XML. This Chapter, explains how to use these encodings and others not available by default.

- **Chapter 9: HTTP**
  This Chapter explains how we can implement our own HTTP clients and servers, and how to deal with requests, cookies, headers or middleware.

- **Chapter 10: Templates**
  Templates are pieces of data than can be filled programmatically. This Chapter explains how to define, customize, and use them.

- **Chapter 11: Testing**
  This Chapter will show the reader how simple it is to execute testing routines and benchmarks in Go. Additionally, it will introduce the reader how to run coverage tests and execution profiles.

- **Chapter 12: Modules and documentation**
  This Chapter explains how to manage dependencies in Go and how to document code.

- **Chapter 13: Cgo**
  Go can operate C structs and functions using Cgo. This Chapter describes how any Go program can use C code and how we can execute Go functions from any program written in C.

- **Part II: Building systems**
  The second part of the book is oriented to those readers who feel comfortable with the language and want to explore solutions from the Go ecosystem that can be used to build sophisticated systems.

- **Chapter 14: Protocol buffers**
  This Chapter reviews what is the protocol buffer serialization format and how to use it with Go.

- **Chapter 15: gRPC**
  Read this Chapter if you need of a fast, modular, and easy-to-deploy message protocol in your system. This Chapter explains how to define services, servers, clients, streaming, and interceptors.

- **Chapter 16: Logging with Zerolog**
  This Chapter shows the reader how to log a program using the powerful Zerolog library.

- **Chapter 17: Command Line Interface**
  Complex programs require complex command line interfaces. This Chapters, shows the developer how to define and integrate the Cobra library in their projects to obtain professional CLIs with minimal effort.

- **Chapter 18: Relational databases**
  This Chapter introduces how the standard library can be used to manipulate and query data from SQL databases. Additionally, it explores how to use the GORM library for ORM solutions.

- **Chapter 19: NoSQL databases**
  NoSQL database solutions are quite common and the Go ecosystem offers solutions to work with them. This Chapter, explains how to operate with Apache Cassandra using the GoCQL client.

- **Chapter 20: Kafka**
  This Chapter reviews the basics of Apache Kafka and overviews three different solutions to interact with this streaming platform.

CONVENTIONS

This book is built around self-contained examples. These examples are minimalist pieces of code that help the reader becoming familiar with the explained concepts. Examples are small enough to bring the reader an idea of how a real program looks like. Some examples may print something to help the reader, in that case, the expected output is shown for the reader's convenience.

This is how an example looks like.

Title of this example.

```
1 In the left side
2 of this box,
3 you can find
4 the code for
5 this example
```

```
This box contains the
output.
```

```
The output can be here instead of beside the code.
```

Additional tips and notes can be found across the book.

> ⚠ This is a warning note.

> ? This is a curiosity or tip with additional information.

The code

This book contains a large number of examples fully available at the author's GitHub repository under the Apache license:

  `https://github.com/juanmanuel-tirado/savetheworldwithgo`

Feel free to fork the repository at your convenience. If you find any issue or have any comment regarding the code, please let the author know.

About the author

Juan M. Tirado has been programming half of his life. He holds a Ph. D. in computer science and has been a researcher at the UC3M, INRIA, and the University of Cambridge. He is interested in how data can be leveraged to enhance large scale distributed systems. With a background between a systems architect and a data scientist, he helps companies to design and implement data-driven solutions. In his free time, he enjoys music, mountaineering, and tapas.

You can follow the author at:

- Website: `https://jmtirado.net/`
- LinkedIn: `https://www.linkedin.com/in/juan-tirado`
- Medium: `https://juanmanuel-tirado.medium.com/`
- Twitter: @jmtirado

Some words of gratitude

This book is a one-person project carried out with a lot of effort and great illusion. If you have found this book useful, the author would appreciate you spread the word and tell your friends and colleagues. Your comments and/or suggestions are always welcome to help in improving this book.

Part I
The Go language

Image by Egon Elbre (@egonelbre)

1. FIRST STEPS WITH GO

This chapter will show you how to write, compile and execute your first program in Go. For this, you need a working Go installation. Follow the steps for your platform described in the official documentation[1]. Next, take any plain text editor of your choice: NotePad, Nano, Vim, etc. You will need one of them to write down the code. If you prefer to use more sophisticated tools such as GoLand, Atom or Visual Studio Code the following examples still apply. However, I recommend you follow the current explanation if this is your first time with Go.

1.1. SAVE THE WORLD WITH GO!!!

If you are familiar with any computer language you already know what comes next: a *Hello World!* program. This is just a program that will print a message in your console output. Traditionally this is the first approach to any programming language. And this is still the case although we have changed the message.

Example 1.1: Save the world with Go!!!

```go
package main

import "fmt"

func main() {
    fmt.Println("Save the world with Go!!!")
}
```

```
Save the world with Go
!!!
```

The above code has the basic components of a Go program. First, we set the name of the package that contains our code (line 1). In line 2, we import the library required to invoke our

---
[1] https://golang.org/doc/install

`Println` function. The logic of our program is contained between brackets in a function called `main` between lines 5 and 7. The statement in line 6 prints our message using the standard output.

Go must be compiled before execution. This is, we need to run our code through a compiler to generate executable code for our platform. The result from the compilation process is an executable file. Depending on your platform this file will be different. To compile our program, we only need to write down the code above in any text editor, save it as *main.go* and compile it. To compile the code only run the *go build* command.

Example 1.2: Compilation with go build.

```
>> go build main.go
>> ls
main main.go
>> ./main
Save the world with Go!!!
```

If you run the code above in a Unix-compatible terminal you should get the same result. As you can see, the process is straight forward for this example. The `go build` command generates an executable file named `main`. This file can be executed (notice that ./ runs any executable file) displaying our message.

1.2. PASSING ARGUMENTS TO OUR PROGRAM

Now that we already know how to print a message, it would be nice if we could add some information from the outside. For example, what about computing the sum of two numbers? The idea is to pass two numbers to our program and tell the user what is the resulting sum.

First, we need to know how we can pass arguments to our program. This can be done using the `os.Args` variable. The example below is taken from here[2].

Example 1.3: Passing arguments.

```go
package main

import (
    "fmt"
    "os"
)

func main() {

    argsWithProg := os.Args
    argsWithoutProg := os.Args[1:]
```

---

[2]https://gobyexample.com/command-line-arguments

CHAPTER 1. FIRST STEPS WITH GO 23

```
12
13      arg := os.Args[3]
14
15      fmt.Println(argsWithProg)
16      fmt.Println(argsWithoutProg)
17      fmt.Println(arg)
18  }
```

There is a bunch of interesting things in this code. We have declared and initialized three variables called `argsWithProg`,`argsWithoutProg`, and `arg`. These variables contain all the arguments passed to our program, the arguments without the program name, and the argument in the third position respectively. If we compile and run the program like shown in the previous example we can understand how arguments passing works.

Example 1.4: Passing arguments output

```
>>> ./main Save the world with Go
[./main Save the world with Go]
[Save the world with Go]
world
```

The `os.Args` method returns an array (do not worry, this is explained in Chapter 3) containing all the arguments passed to the program including the name of the executable file. The variable `ArgsWithoutProg` has our input message (Save the world with Go). We removed the name of the program with the index `os.Args[1:]`. As mentioned before, this will be explained in more detail in the corresponding Chapter. In Go, arrays are indexed from 0 to $n-1$ with n the array length. Finally, in `arg` we get the argument at position 3 returning the word `world`.

Now that we explored how we can pass arguments to a program, we can do something with these parameters.

Example 1.5: Sum two numbers passed by arguments.

```
1  package main
2
3  import (
4       "fmt"
5       "os"
6       "strconv"
7  )
8
9  func main() {
10
11      argsWithProg := os.Args
12
13      numA, err := strconv.Atoi(argsWithProg[1])
14      if err != nil {
```

```
15        fmt.Println(err)
16        os.Exit(2)
17     }
18     numB, err := strconv.Atoi(argsWithProg[2])
19     if err != nil {
20        fmt.Println(err)
21        os.Exit(2)
22     }
23     result := numA + numB
24     fmt.Printf("%d + %d = %d\n", numA, numB, result)
25 }
```

We can only run mathematical operations with numbers. This is a problem because arguments are passed as strings of characters. Fortunately, we can use the `strconv.Atoi` function to convert a number from a string representation into an integer number. This may result in some conversion errors. For example:

- "42" → 42
- "-33" → -33
- "4.2" → This is a conversion error because we are not expecting floating numbers.
- "thirteen" → This is a conversion error because this is a textual representation of a number.

Is for this reason that `strconv.Atoi` returns two parameters. The first one is the integer number we can extract from the string. The second one is an error variable that will be filled in case there is an error. To know if there was a problem during the conversion process we can check if the error variable was filled or not. This is done in lines 14 and 19 with `if` statements. If the `err` variable contains some value (`!=nil`), we print the error and exit the program with `os.Exit(2)`.

If everything is correct, we compute the sum of `numA` and `numB` variables and print the result. To make it more appealing, we add some additional formatting to our output in line 24. You do not need to fully understand the meaning of `fmt.Printf` but you can guess that we are filling a string with `numA`, `numB`, and `result` values.

Now we can compile it and run like we did before:

Example 1.6: Sum numbers output.

```
>>> ./sum 2 2
2 + 2 = 4
>>> ./sum 42 -2
42 + -2 = 40
>>> ./sum 2 2.2
strconv.Atoi: parsing "2.2": invalid syntax
>>> ./sum 2 two
strconv.Atoi: parsing "two": invalid syntax
```

And voilà! our little calculator is ready. We can sum two numbers and detect when the input cannot be converted into an integer. However, there is one potential issue? What happens if we do not have any arguments? Consider this as an improvement exercise.

1.3. SUMMARY

In this Chapter, we showed how to write a Go program, compile it, and execute it. Additionally, we extended a basic example to include arguments passing and perform some mathematical operations, error control, and mathematical operations. If you feel comfortable with the content of this Chapter, consider exploring the basics of Go as presented in Chapter 2.

2. THE BASICS

This Chapter introduces the basics of Go. Like any programming language, Go uses variables, control loops, and data structures to create programs. You may find this Chapter not long enough to cover all the basics of a programming language. This is one of the greatest advantages of Go, its simplicity. The content of this Chapter reviews all the concepts a Go adopter must know to dive into the language.

2.1. PACKAGES AND IMPORTS

If you have already read Chapter 1 you will have noticed that every piece of code starts with a **package** statement. Go programs are organized into packages. A **package** is a group of one or more source files which code is accessible from the same **package**. Additionally, a **package** can be exported and used in other packages.

The **package** main is a special case that informs the Go compiler to consider that package as the entry point for an executable file. Actually, the **package** main is expected to have a main function in order to be compiled.

A **package** can be imported into other packages using the keyword **import**. The line **import** "fmt" makes the fmt package available to the source file. When importing a package, Go checks the GOPATH and GOROOT environment variables. The GOPATH points to the Go workspace and it is defined during the installation[1]. Similarly, GOROOT points to a custom Go installation. This variable should not be required unless a custom installation is done. The Go compiler will first check the GOROOT and then the GOPATH when importing a package.

---

[1] https://golang.org/cmd/go/#hdr-GOPATH_environment_variable

2.1.1. IMPORT THIRD-PARTY PACKAGES

Programs may require additional packages that are developed by third-parties. For example, the implementation of a database driver. Go is dramatically different importing third-party code when compared to other languages. Go forces code transparency by only compiling source code. This means that in order to import third-party packages, the source code must be locally available. Before import any third-party package you can use the Go command-line tool to download the code.

For example, to get the Mongo driver which is available at http://go.mongodb.org/mongo-driver we execute:

Example 2.1: Third-party package download using `go get`.
```
>>> go get -v go.mongodb.org/mongo-driver
get "go.mongodb.org/mongo-driver": found meta tag get.metaImport{Prefix:"go.
   mongodb.org/mongo-driver", VCS:"git", RepoRoot:"https://github.com/mongodb/
   mongo-go-driver.git"} at //go.mongodb.org/mongo-driver?go-get=1
go.mongodb.org/mongo-driver (download)
package go.mongodb.org/mongo-driver: no Go files in /XXXX/src/go.mongodb.org/
   mongo-driver
```

This downloads the source code from the external repository into our environment. Afterwards, we can import the code using `import "go.mongodb.org/mongo-driver/mongo"`. In some cases, the package name may not be very convenient. If required we can use an alias like shown below:

```
package main

import (
    myalias "go.mongodb.org/mongo-driver/mongo"
)
//...
client, err := myalias.NewClient(...))
//....
```

> ❓ Using `go get` to download third-party code is not a scalable solution. Fortunately, Go modules facilitate the acquisition of packages and their versioning for any project. Go modules are explained in Chapter 12.

2.2. VARIABLES, CONSTANTS, AND ENUMS

Variables are the cornerstone of any programming language. This Section explores Go variables and special cases such as constants and enums.

2.2.1. VARIABLES

Go is a strong statically typed language. This means that the type of the variable must be fixed at compilation time. Go syntax permits different alternatives when declaring variables as shown in Example 2.2.

Example 2.2: Declaration of variables.

```
package main

import "fmt"

func main() {

    var a int
    a = 42

    var aa int = 100

    b := -42

    c := "this is a string"

    var d, e string
    d, e = "var d", "var e"

    f, g := true, false

    fmt.Println(a)
    fmt.Println(aa)
    fmt.Println(b)
    fmt.Println(c)
    fmt.Println(d)
    fmt.Println(e)
    fmt.Println(f)
    fmt.Println(g)

}
```

```
42
100
-42
this is a string
var d
var e
true
false
```

The basic construction of a variable is formed by the reserved word **var** followed by the variable name and its type. For example, `var a int` declares variable `a` of type `int`. Notice that this declares a variable with no value. The type and the value can be set in one line as shown in the example with `var aa int = 100`. Similarly, using the `:=` we can declare and assign a value to the variable. However, the type will be inferred by the compiler. In our example, `b := -42` has type `int` while `c := "this is a string"` is a string. Finally, we can declare and assign values to several variables in one line like in `f, g := true, false`.

2.2.2. BASIC TYPES

Go comes with the set of basic types described in Table 2.1.

Type	Description
`bool`	Boolean (*true* or *false*)
`string`	String of characters
`int, int8, int16, int32, int64`	Signed integers
`uint, uint8, uint16, uint32, uint64, uintptr`	Unsigned integers
`byte`	Byte, similar to uint8
`rune`	Unicode code point
`float32, float64`	Floating numbers
`complex64, complex128`	Complex numbers

Table 2.1: Basic types

Integer numbers `int` and `uint` are platform-dependant and may vary from 32 to 64 bits. Using types such as `uint8` or `int16` set the variable size. For floating and complex numbers it is required to set the type size.

If you are familiar with other languages you may find the `rune` type something weird. This type is simply a character represented using UTF-8 which requires 32 bits instead of the classic 8 bits used in ASCII. Actually, `rune` is simply an alias for `int32`[2].

Example 2.3: Variables declaration

```
1 package main
2
3 import "fmt"
4
5 func main() {
```

---

[2]Actually, `rune` could be an alias for `uint32` instead of `int32`.

CHAPTER 2. THE BASICS

```
 6      var aBool bool = true
 7      var aString string = "yXXXy"
 8      var aComplex complex64 = 5i
 9      var aRune rune = '€'
10
11      fmt.Println(aBool)
12      fmt.Println(aString)
13      fmt.Println(aComplex)
14      fmt.Println(aRune)
15      fmt.Printf("%U\n",aRune)
16      fmt.Printf("%c\n",aRune)
17  }
```

```
true
yXXXy
(0+5i)
8364
U+20AC
€
```

Example 2.3 shows how variables from different types are declared, assigned and printed. Running the code prints the variable values. The `rune` type requires special attention. By simply printing the variable we get the integer value 8364. However, the UTF-8 representation is U+20AC (format using `\%U`). A printable representation of the Euro symbol (€) is obtained with the `\%c` format.

2.2.3. CONSTANTS

A constant is a value defined at compilation time that cannot be changed. Apart from the impossibility of setting new values, constants are similar to variables.

Example 2.4: Constants declaration

```
 1  package main
 2
 3  import (
 4      "fmt"
 5      "reflect"
 6  )
 7
 8  const (
 9      Pi = 3.14
10      Avogadro float32 = 6.022e23
11  )
12
13  func main() {
14      fmt.Println("What is the value of Pi? Pi is", Pi)
15      fmt.Println(reflect.TypeOf(Pi))
16      fmt.Println("Avogadro's Number value is", Avogadro)
17      fmt.Println(reflect.TypeOf(Avogadro))
18  }
```

```
What is the value of Pi
? Pi is 3.14
float64
Avogadro's Number value
 is 6.022e+23
float32
```

Example 2.4 defines π and Avogadro's number. A constant can be defined in the same places a variable can be defined. Like variables, the type of a constant can be inferred. In our example, we defined `Pi` constant without type and `Avogadro` as **float32**. By default Go will select the largest available type. Is for this reason that `Pi` is a **float64** number even when a **float32** would be large enough[3].

2.2.4. ENUMS

Enums (enumerates) is a data type consisting of constant values. Classic examples are the days of the week, the months of the year, the states of a system, etc. Enums are intrinsically related to the `iota` keyword.

Example 2.5: Enums declaration

```
 1  package main
 2
 3  import "fmt"
 4
 5  type DayOfTheWeek uint8
 6
 7  const (
 8      Monday DayOfTheWeek = iota
 9      Tuesday
10      Wednesday
11      Thursday
12      Friday
13      Saturday
14      Sunday
15  )
16
17
18  func main() {
19
20      fmt.Printf("Monday is %d\n", Monday)
21      fmt.Printf("Wednesday is %d\n", Wednesday)
22      fmt.Printf("Friday is %d\n", Friday)
23
24  }
```

```
Monday is 0
Wednesday is 2
Friday is 4
```

The code above defines an enum with the days of the week from Monday to Sunday. We have declared a **type** called DayOfTheWeek which is represented using **uint8** (an unsigned byte). Items from the same enumerate are expected to have consecutive values. In our example Monday is zero, Tuesday is one, Wednesday is two, etc. This is what `iota`

---

[3]We can check the type of a variable using `reflect.TypeOf`. Visit Chapter 5 for more details.

does. It assigns consecutive values starting from 0 to the items of the enum. Notice that after the `iota` statement all the variables belong to the same type (`DayOfTheWeek`).

2.3. FUNCTIONS

Functions are a basic concept in Go. A function encapsulates a piece of code that performs certain operations or logic that is going to be required by other sections of the code. A function is the most basic solution to reuse code.

A function receives none or several parameters and returns none or several values. Functions are defined by keyword `func`, the arguments with their types, and the types of the returned values.

In example 2.6, the `sum` function returns the sum of two `int` arguments `a` and `b`.

Example 2.6: Function with two arguments.

```
1  package main
2
3  import "fmt"
4
5  func sum(a int, b int) int {
6      return a + b
7  }
8
9  func main() {
10     result := sum(2,2)
11     fmt.Println(result)
12 }
```

```
4
```

It is possible to return multiple values like shown in example 2.7.

Example 2.7: Function returning several values.

```
1  package main
2
3  import "fmt"
4
5  func ops(a int, b int) (int, int) {
6      return a + b, a - b
7  }
8
9  func main() {
10     sum, subs := ops(2,2)
11     fmt.Println("2+2=",sum, "2-2=",subs)
```

```
2+2= 4 2-2= 0
10+2= 12
```

```go
12      b, _ := ops(10,2)
13      fmt.Println("10+2=",b)
14 }
```

Functions can receive an undetermined number of arguments. These are called variadic functions. Example 2.8 declares a function to compute the sum of several numbers. Variadic arguments are identified with ... before the type. These arguments must have the same type and can be treated as an array. How to iterate arrays is explained in more detail in section 3.2.2.

Example 2.8: Variadic function

```go
1 package main
2
3 import "fmt"
4
5 func sum(nums ...int) int {
6     total := 0
7     for _, a := range(nums) {
8         total = total + a
9     }
10    return total
11 }
12
13 func main(){
14     total := sum(1,2,3,4,5)
15     fmt.Println("The first five numbers sum is",total)
16 }
```

```
The first five numbers
sum is 15
```

Functions can receive other functions as arguments. In Example 2.9, the function `doit` expects a function and two integers as parameters. Notice that the `operator` argument is a function where we specify the type of its arguments and returned values. When using the `doit` function we can modify its behavior changing the `operator` argument. In this case, we can sum and multiply numbers using the corresponding functions.

Example 2.9: Functions as arguments.

```go
1 package main
2
3 import "fmt"
4
5 func doit(operator func(int,int) int, a int, b int) int {
6     return operator(a,b)
7 }
```

CHAPTER 2. THE BASICS

```
 8
 9 func sum(a int, b int) int {
10     return a + b
11 }
12
13 func multiply(a int, b int) int {
14     return a * b
15 }
16
17 func main() {
18     c := doit(sum, 2, 3)
19     fmt.Println("2+3=", c)
20     d := doit(multiply, 2, 3)
21     fmt.Println("2*3=", d)
22 }
```

```
2+3= 5
2*3= 6
```

Go permits anonymous functions, and these functions can be closures. A closure is a function that can refer to variables outside its body. This can be particularly useful to define inline functions or to solve complex problems like those that require recursion.

In Example 2.10, the function `accumulator` defines a closure function that is bounded to variable `i`. Statements `a := accumulator(1)` and `b := accumulator(2)` create two functions with different starting `i` variables. For this reason, for the same number of iterations outputs for `a` and `b` differ.

Example 2.10: Functions closure.

```
 1 package main
 2
 3 import "fmt"
 4
 5 func accumulator(increment int) func() int {
 6     i:=0
 7     return func() int {
 8         i = i + increment
 9         return i
10     }
11 }
12
13 func main() {
14
15     a := accumulator(1)
16     b := accumulator(2)
17
18     fmt.Println("a","b")
19     for i:=0;i<5;i++ {
20         fmt.Println(a(),b())
21     }
```

```
a b
1 2
2 4
3 6
4 8
5 10
```

2.4. Pointers

Go works with arguments as values or references. When working with references we talk about pointers. A pointer addresses a memory location instead of a value. In Go pointers are identified following the C notation with a star. For a type `T`, `*T` indicates a pointer to a value of type `T`.

Example 2.11, has two functions `a` and `b` that set an incoming argument to zero. The code in the `main` function simply declares a variable `x` and call these functions. Notice that `a` does not change `x` value because it receives values as arguments. This is `a` works with a copy of variable `x`. However, function `b` sets `x` to zero because it receives a pointer to the variable. The operator `&` returns the pointer to the variable, which is of type `*int`. See how this operator returns the memory address of variable `x` with `fmt.Println(&x)`.

Example 2.11: Passing values and references to a function.

```go
package main

import "fmt"

func a (i int){
    i = 0
}

func b (i *int) {
    *i = 0
}

func main() {
    x := 100

    a(x)
    fmt.Println(x)
    b(&x)
    fmt.Println(x)

    fmt.Println(&x)
}
```

```
100
0
0xc00001c0a0
```

How to decide when to use a pointer or a value depends on the use case. If a value is intended to be modified in different parts of the code, passing pointers seems reasonable.

2.5. NIL AND ZERO VALUES

A really important concept in Go is the zero value. When a variable is created and not initialized, the compiler automatically assigns it a default value. This value depends on the variable type. The keyword `nil` specifies a particular value for every non-initialized type. Notice that `nil` is not an undefined value like in other programming languages, `nil` is a value itself.

The output from Example 2.12 shows the zero value for various types. In general zero will be the zero value for numeric types such as `int` or `float`. Something similar occurs to `bool` although, 0 is considered to be `false`. In the case of `string` the empty string (`""`) is the zero value, not the numeric zero (0). For pointers, functions and other types `nil` is the default value.

Example 2.12: Zero values during initialization.

```
1  package main
2
3  import "fmt"
4
5  func main() {
6
7      var a int
8      fmt.Println(a)
9
10     var b *int
11     fmt.Println(b)
12
13     var c bool
14     fmt.Println(c)
15
16     var d func()
17     fmt.Println(d)
18
19     var e string
20     fmt.Printf("[%s]",e)
21 }
```

```
0
<nil>
false
<nil>
[]
```

2.6. LOOPS AND BRANCHES

No program is complete without control flow. Like in any other programming language, Go offers a set of constructions to define loops and branches.

2.6.1. IF/ELSE

The `if` statement permits the definition of branch executions using boolean expressions with the following construction.

```
if condition {
    // ...
} else if condition {
    // ...
} else {
    // ...
}
```

Compared with other more verbose programming languages Go does not require parenthesis around the defined condition, only the braces.

Example 2.13 emulates tossing a coin and tell us if we get head or tail.

Example 2.13: `if/else` example.

```
 1 package main
 2
 3 import (
 4     "fmt"
 5     "math/rand"
 6     "time"
 7 )
 8
 9 func main() {
10     rand.Seed(time.Now().UnixNano())
11     x := rand.Float32()
12
13     if x < 0.5 {
14         fmt.Println("head")
15     } else {
16         fmt.Println("tail")
17     }
18 }
```

```
head
```

In the example, we generate a random number using the `rand.Float32()` function. The x variable goes from 0 to 1 then, when x is less than 0.5 we get head, otherwise tail. The code in line 10 is just an initialization of the random generator. We set the initial random seed with the CPU time to get a different x value in every execution.

CHAPTER 2. THE BASICS

> ❓ If you are familiar with other programming languages you may be wondering how is the ternary operator. Something like the one you can find in C: `condition ? statement : statement`. There is no such thing in Go. Those operators do not follow the simplicity concepts from Go.

2.6.2. SWITCH

The `switch` operator is particularly useful when you want to take action for several values of the same variable.

For example, the program described in Example 2.14 takes a number and prints the name of the corresponding finger. This is done by enumerating the values we want to control and adding the corresponding statement before we define the next value that requires a different statement. Finally, we set the special case `default` that is reached when the value is not controlled by any case.

Example 2.14: switch example.

```go
package main

import "fmt"

func main() {
    var finger int = 1

    switch finger {
    case 0:
        fmt.Println("Thumb")
    case 1:
        fmt.Println("Index")
    case 2:
        fmt.Println("Middle")
    case 3:
        fmt.Println("Ring")
    case 4:
        fmt.Println("Pinkie")
    default:
        fmt.Println("Humans usually have no more than five fingers")
    }
}
```

```
Index
```

Branching with `switch` is very versatile. You do not always need to define the variable you want to check. You can simply start checking your cases and even you can use conditionals instead of constants.

Example 2.15 prints the quartile a random number belongs to. Compared with the previous example, we use conditions instead of constant values for the cases so we do not specify the variable to be observed in the `switch` statement. Notice that this is an alternative way to use the `if/else` logic.

Example 2.15: `switch`.

```go
package main

import (
    "fmt"
    "math/rand"
    "time"
)

func main() {

    rand.Seed(time.Now().UnixNano())
    x := rand.Float32()

    switch {
    case x < 0.25:
        fmt.Println("Q1")
    case x < 0.5:
        fmt.Println("Q2")
    case x < 0.75:
        fmt.Println("Q3")
    default:
        fmt.Println("Q4")
    }
}
```

> (?) When several cases share the same logic, they can be stacked.
>
> ```go
> switch {
> case 0:
> case 1:
>     // statement for 0 and 1
> default:
>     // default statement
> }
> ```

CHAPTER 2. THE BASICS

> ❓ Using `default` in every `switch` is a good practice to avoid errors and unexpected behaviours.

2.6.3. FOR LOOPS

In Go the `for` construct permits to iterate depending on conditions and data structures. Iterations through structures are explained with further detail in Chapter 3.

Example 2.16: `for` loop example.

```go
package main

import (
    "fmt"
)

func main() {

    x := 5

    counter := x

    for counter > 0 {
        fmt.Println(counter)
        counter--
    }

    for i:=0; i < x; i++ {
        fmt.Print(i)
    }
    fmt.Println()

    for {
        if x % 2 != 0 {
            fmt.Printf("%d is odd\n", x)
            x++
            continue
        }
        break
    }

    for {
        fmt.Println("Never stop")
        break
    }
```

```
5
4
3
2
1
01234
5 is odd
Never stop
```

```
37
38  }
```

Example 2.16, shows four ways to construct a **for** loop. The first (line 14), iterates while a condition is satisfied. The loop prints all the numbers from x to 1 (5, 4, 3, 2, 1). The second loop (line 19) is very similar to a for loop declared in C/C++. We declare a variable `i`, a condition to be satisfied, and how the variable is going to be modified in every iteration. The output contains the numbers between 0 and x with zero included.

The third loop (line 24), has no conditions. In order to stop the loop we can use **break** and **continue**. They stop the loop and jump to the next iteration respectively. This particular loop will stop the execution if x is an even number by skipping the **if** branch. If the number is odd, x is modified and the **continue** statement jumps to the next iteration skipping the final **break** that will be reached in the next iteration. Consider that this is an artefact to demonstrate different flavours of a **for** construction and may not have a real practical sense.

Finally, in line 33 there is an infinite **for** loop. These loops are used to declare processes or operations that must be active for an undefined period (e.g. servers waiting for connections). The final **break** was added to avoid confusion during testing executions.

> **?** **Go has no *while* loops.** Actually, all the logic of a *while* construct can be achieved using **for**.

2.7. ERRORS

All error handling operations in Go are based on the type **error**. An **error** variable stores a message with some information. In situations where an error can occur, the usual way to proceed is to return a filled **error** informing about its cause. This can be done using the `errors.New` function.

Assume that there is a situation that may lead to an error, for example accessing a non-indexed item from a collection. In Example 2.17, the function `GetMusketeer` returns the name of one of the Four Musketeers. Unfortunately, we cannot control the requested musketeer. If the `id` argument is outside the limits of the collection, we have an error. Notice that the signature function returns (**string, error**) types. The usual way to proceed in these situations is to fill the error with some information and assign the zero value to the return value.

Example 2.17: Example of error handling.

CHAPTER 2. THE BASICS

```go
1  package main
2
3  import (
4      "errors"
5      "fmt"
6      "math/rand"
7      "time"
8  )
9
10 var Musketeers = []string{
11     "Athos", "Porthos", "Aramis", "D'Artagnan",
12 }
13
14 func GetMusketeer(id int) (string, error){
15     if id < 0 || id >= len(Musketeers) {
16         return "", errors.New(
17             fmt.Sprintf("Invalid id [%d]",id))
18     }
19     return Musketeers[id], nil
20 }
21
22 func main() {
23     rand.Seed(time.Now().UnixNano())
24     id := rand.Int() % 6
25
26     mosq, err := GetMusketeer(id)
27     if err == nil {
28         fmt.Printf("[%d] %s",id, mosq)
29     } else {
30         fmt.Println(err)
31     }
32 }
```

```
Invalid id [4]
...
[3] D'Artagnan
...
[0] Athos
```

> **?** Go has not `try`/`catch`/`except` idiom. According to the Go Faq, this was decided to remove convoluted code expressions.

2.8. DEFER, PANIC, AND RECOVER

The `defer` statement pushes a function onto a list. This list of functions is executed when the surrounding function ends. This statement is specially designed to ensure the correctness of the execution after the function ends. In particular, `defer` is useful to clean up resources allocated to a function.

Notice how in Example 2.18 the messages generated by `defer` statements are printed only after the main function ends. As can be extracted from the output, deferred functions are executed in inverse order as they were declared.

Example 2.18: defer.

```
1  package main
2
3  import "fmt"
4
5  func CloseMsg() {
6      fmt.Println("Closed!!!")
7  }
8
9  func main() {
10     defer CloseMsg()
11
12     fmt.Println("Doing something...")
13     defer fmt.Println("Certainly closed!!!")
14     fmt.Println("Doing something else...")
15
16 }
```

```
Doing something...
Doing something else...
Certainly closed!!!
Closed!!!
```

The built-in function `panic` stops the execution flow, executes deferred functions and returns control to the calling function. This occurs for all functions until the program crashes. A call to `panic` indicates a situation that goes beyond the control of the program. Example 2.19, calls `panic` in the middle of a loop. The first deferred function to be executed is from `something`, then from `main()`. Observe that the panic message is printed in the last step and the last statement from `main` is never reached.

Example 2.19: panic.

```
1  package main
2
3  import "fmt"
4
5  func something() {
6      defer fmt.Println("closed something")
7      for i:=0;i<5;i++ {
8          fmt.Println(i)
9          if i > 2 {
10             panic("Panic was called")
11         }
12     }
13 }
14
15 func main () {
16     defer fmt.Println("closed main")
```

```
0
1
2
3
closed something
closed main
panic: Panic was called
```

CHAPTER 2. THE BASICS

```
17      something()
18      fmt.Println("Something was finished")
19  }
```

It may occur that under certain conditions when **panic** is invoked, the control flow can be restored. The **recover** built-in function used inside a deferred function can be used to resume normal execution. The scenario presented in Example 2.20 recovers the execution control after the panic inside function `something`. Calling **panic(i)** executes the deferred function where the recover is different from **nil**. The returned value is the parameter of the **panic** function. Observe that in this case the `main` function finished and we could print the final message.

Example 2.20: recover.

```
1  package main
2
3  import "fmt"
4
5  func something() {
6      defer func() {
7          r := recover()
8          if r != nil{
9              fmt.Println("No need to panic if i=",r)
10         }
11     }()
12     for i:=0;i<5;i++ {
13         fmt.Println(i)
14         if i > 2 {
15             panic(i)
16         }
17     }
18     fmt.Println("Closed something  normally")
19 }
20
21 func main () {
22     defer fmt.Println("closed main")
23
24     something()
25     fmt.Println("Main was finished")
26 }
```

```
0
1
2
3
No need to panic if i=
3
Main was finished
closed main
```

2.9. INIT FUNCTIONS

Now that we understand what are variables, functions, and imports we can better understand how Go starts a program execution. We have mentioned that every program in Go must have a `main` package with a `main` function to be executed. However, this imposes some limitations for certain solutions such as libraries. Imagine we import a library into our code. A library is not designed to be executed, it only offers data structures, methods, functions, etc. Libraries probably do not even have a `main` package. If this library requires some initial configuration before invoked (initialize variables, detect the operating system, etc.) there must be a way to run this configuration without a `main` function.

Go defines `init` functions that are executed once per package. When we import a package the Go runtime follows this order:

1. Initialize imported packages recursively.

2. Initialize and assign values to variables.

3. Execute `init` functions.

The output from Example 2.21 shows how the initialization follows the order described above. The `xSetter` function is invoked first, followed by `init`, and the `main` function.

Example 2.21: Go runtime initialization order.

```
1  package main
2
3  import "fmt"
4
5  var x = xSetter()
6
7  func xSetter() int{
8      fmt.Println("xSetter")
9      return 42
10 }
11
12 func init() {
13     fmt.Println("Init function")
14 }
15
16 func main() {
17     fmt.Println("This is the main")
18 }
```

```
xSetter
Init function
This is the main
```

The `init` function has no arguments neither returns any value. A package can have several `init` functions and they cannot be invoked from any part of the code.

Go does not allow importing a package if this is not used inside the code. However, we may only be interested in running the `init` functions of a package. This is what Go calls the side effects of a package. This is usually done in packages that perform some bootstrapping or registration operation. The special `import _` statement only calls the `init` functions of a package not requiring it to be used inside the code.

Example 2.22 imports package `a` to use its side effects. Observe that this package has two `init` functions that are executed before the `init` of the importing package.

Example 2.22: Main using `import _`
```
1  package main
2
3  import (
4      "fmt"
5      _ "a"
6  )
7
8  func init() {
9      fmt.Println("Init from my program")
10 }
11
12 func main() {
13     fmt.Println("My program")
14 }
```

Example 2.23: Package with `init` functions.
```
1  package a
2
3  import "fmt"
4
5  func init() {
6      fmt.Println("Init 1 from
           package a")
7  }
8
9  func init() {
10     fmt.Println("Init 2 from
           package a")
11 }
```

```
Init 1 from package a
Init 2 from package a
Init from my program
My program
```

2.10. Summary

This Chapter overviews Go basics by introducing concepts such as packages, variables or errors. First, we explain how to use owned and third-party packages. We provide an overview of variables, constants and enums to explain how they are used inside of functions. Flow control is explained and how to manage errors with special control functions. Understanding this Chapter is necessary to continue with the next Chapter 3 where we explore advanced data structures.

3

ARRAYS, SLICES, AND MAPS

So far we have introduced the basics about variables and how to define a workflow using branches and loops. However, we have not explored data structures. Go offers other powerful data structures that are extensively used: arrays, slices, and maps. Arrays and maps are common to other programming languages. Slices are a particular Go construct. In this Chapter we explore these data structures and provide examples of how they can be used.

3.1. ARRAYS

By definition, an array is an indexed sequence of elements with a given length. Like any other Go variable, arrays are typed and their size is fixed.

Example 3.1 shows different ways to declare arrays. Variable a (line 7) declares an array of integers of size 5. By default, this array is filled with zeros. Notice that printing the array returns the sequence of numbers between brackets. We can assign values to the array in a single line like in the case of b. Similarly, c is declared as a 5 integers array with only three values assigned.

Example 3.1: Arrays declaration

```
1  package main
2
3  import "fmt"
4
5  func main() {
6
```

```
 7      var a[5] int
 8      fmt.Println(a)
 9
10      b := [5]int{0,1,2,3,4}
11      fmt.Println(b)
12
13      c := [5]int{0,1,2}
14      fmt.Println(c)
15
16  }
```

```
[0 0 0 0 0]
[0 1 2 3 4]
[0 1 2 0 0]
```

Every array has a `len` function that returns the array length. For example, `len(a)` will return 5 for the previous example.

3.2. SLICES

We have said that arrays have a fixed size. This makes them not very flexible in certain scenarios. Go offers a type called `slice` defined as a "descriptor for a contiguous segment of an underlying array and provides access to a numbered sequence elements from that array"[1]. In other words, a `slice` is a reference to an array. The `slice` itself does not store any data but offers a view of it. Table 3.1 describes available ways to select slices.

Index	Selected element(s)
a[0]	Element at position 0
a[3:5]	Elements from position 3 to 4
a[3:]	All the elements starting at position 3
a[:3]	All the elements from the start till position 2
a[:]	All the elements

Table 3.1: Examples of slices selections

> ⚠ Arrays and slices items are indexed from 0 to $n - 1$ with n the length of the array.

Example 3.2 and its output shows how to obtain different slices from a given array.

Example 3.2: Slices indexing.

---

[1] https://golang.org/ref/spec#Slice_types

CHAPTER 3. ARRAYS, SLICES, AND MAPS

```go
package main

import (
    "fmt"
)

func main(){
    a := [5]string{"a","b","c","d","e"}

    fmt.Println(a)
    fmt.Println(a[:])
    fmt.Println(a[0])
    fmt.Println(a[0],a[1],a[2],a[3],a[4])
    fmt.Println(a[0:2])
    fmt.Println(a[1:4])
    fmt.Println(a[:2])
    fmt.Println(a[2:])
}
```

```
[a b c d e]
[a b c d e]
a
a b c d e
[a b]
[b c d]
[a b]
[c d e]
```

In Go most of the time, we work with **slice** rather than arrays. Working with arrays or slices is very similar and does not require additional effort from the programmer. Example 3.3 uses `reflect.TypeOf` to print the type of different objects.

Example 3.3: Type differences between array, slice, and item.

```go
package main

import (
    "fmt"
    "reflect"
)

func main() {
    a := [5]string{"a","b","c","d","e"}

    fmt.Println(reflect.TypeOf(a))
    fmt.Println(reflect.TypeOf(a[0:3]))
    fmt.Println(reflect.TypeOf(a[0]))
}
```

```
[5]string
[]string
string
```

You can check below that the output from this program differs for every statement. The difference is subtle but very important. `[5]string` is an array with a fixed size of five elements. However, `[]string` is a **slice** without a defined size.

3.2.1. LENGTH AND CAPACITY

We have mentioned that a `slice` has no fixed size because it is a view of an undergoing storage array. An important difference between an array and a `slice` is the concept of capacity. While an array allocates a fixed amount of memory that is directly related to its length, a `slice` can reserve a larger amount of memory that does not necessarily have to be filled. The filled memory corresponds to its length, and all the available memory is the capacity. Both values are accessible using functions `len` and `cap`.

Example 3.4: Differences between length and capacity

```go
package main

import "fmt"

func main() {

    a := []int{0,1,2,3,4}

    fmt.Println(a, len(a), cap(a))

    b := append(a,5)
    fmt.Println(b, len(b), cap(b))
    b = append(b,6)
    fmt.Println(b, len(b), cap(b))

    c := b[1:4]
    fmt.Println(c, len(c), cap(c))

    d := make([]int,5,10)
    fmt.Println(d, len(d), cap(d))
    // d[6]=5 --> This will fail

}
```

```
[0 1 2 3 4] 5 5
[0 1 2 3 4 5] 6 10
[0 1 2 3 4 5 6] 7 10
[1 2 3] 3 9
[0 0 0 0 0] 5 10
```

Example 3.4 prints the length and capacity of various variables. Let this example serve to introduce **make** and **append** built-in functions. Variable a is an array and therefore, its length and capacity are the same. However, b which is an slice built by appending number 5 to a has different length and capacity. If a second **append** is done length changes, but capacity does not change.

Variable c shows how creating a new slice from an existing one, does not necessarily inherit its length and capacity. c only has three elements with capacity 9. This occurs because we are selecting elements of slice b starting at index 1 which results in a `slice` with the original capacity minus one. Finally, variable d is built using the **make** function.

CHAPTER 3. ARRAYS, SLICES, AND MAPS

This function takes a slice type, its length and capacity as arguments. If no capacity is set, this will be the same as the length.

The last statement from the example (line 21) illustrates a situation that triggers a runtime error. The element at position 6 is requested in a slice with capacity 10 and length 5. Any element with a position equal to or greater than length cannot be accessed independently of the slice capacity.

3.2.2. ITERATION

The most common operation you can find in a `slice` is the iteration through its items. Any `for` loop is a good candidate to do this. Go simplifies iterations through collections with the `range` clause to.

Example 3.5: `slice` iteration using the `range` clause.

```
1  package main
2
3  import "fmt"
4
5  func main(){
6      names := []string{
7          "Jeremy", "John", "Joseph",
8      }
9
10     for i:=0;i<len(names);i++{
11         fmt.Println(i,names[i])
12     }
13
14     for position, name := range names {
15         fmt.Println(position,name)
16     }
17 }
```

```
0 Jeremy
1 John
2 Joseph
0 Jeremy
1 John
2 Joseph
```

Example3.5 prints all the items of a collection of strings using two approaches. The first one (line 10), declares an index variable `i` to increment the index of the item to be retrieved. The second approach (line 14) using `range` prints the same output in a less verbose way. For arrays and slices, `range` returns the index of the item and the item itself for every iteration of the loop. The iteration is always done incrementally from index 0 to index n-1.

> ⚠ Notice that the item from the `slice` returned by `range` is a copy of the item. Therefore, modifying this variable inside the loop will not modify the iterated

array.

The next piece of code shows how when modifying the item returned by `range` we cannot modify the `slice` we are iterating through. A correct approach to modify the iterated `slice` is to access the original variable with the corresponding index.

```go
names := []string{"Jeremy", "John", "Joseph"}

for _, name := range(names) {
    // name is a copy
    name = name + "_changed"
}
fmt.Println(names)

for position, name := range(names) {
    // this modifies the original value
    names[position] = name + "_changed"
}
fmt.Println(names)
```

3.3. MAPS

A `map` is a construct that maps a key with a value. Keys are intended to be unique and can be of any type that implements `==` and `!=` operators.

Example 3.6 shows how to instantiate a map that stores string keys and integer values. Maps are defined by `map[K]V` where K is the key type and V is the value type. By default, uninitialized maps are `nil`.

Notice that the statement `ages["Jesus"]=33` (line 10) which is intended to set the value 33 for the key `"Jesus"` is intended to fail. This is because any `map` needs to be instantiated. This can be done using the `make` builtin function (line 12). For `map` the `make` function expects the map type (`map[K]V`) and optionally an initial size. This size is optional as the size can be modified during runtime. Finally, maps can also be initialized by indicating key-value pairs as shown in line 16.

Example 3.6: map creation.

```go
package main

import "fmt"
```

CHAPTER 3. ARRAYS, SLICES, AND MAPS

```go
 4
 5 func main() {
 6     var ages map[string]int
 7     fmt.Println(ages)
 8
 9     // This fails, ages was not initialized
10     // ages["Jesus"] = 33
11
12     ages = make(map[string]int,5)
13     // Now it works because it was initialized
14     ages["Jesus"] = 33
15
16     ages = map[string]int{
17         "Jesus": 33,
18         "Mathusalem": 969,
19     }
20     fmt.Println(ages)
21 }
```

```
map[]
0 false
33 true
map[Jesus:33 Mathusalem
:969]
```

Items from a `map` can be retrieved using any key type value like appears on Example 3.7 (`birthdays["Jesus"]`). Actually, this operation returns two items, one with the expected value and `true` if the item was found. In case, the key was not found, the value would be `nil`.

Example 3.7: map access operations.

```go
 1 package main
 2
 3 import "fmt"
 4
 5 func main() {
 6     birthdays := map[string]string{
 7         "Jesus": "12-25-0000",
 8         "Budha": "563 BEC",
 9     }
10     fmt.Println(birthdays, len(birthdays))
11
12     xmas, found := birthdays["Jesus"]
13     fmt.Println(xmas, found)
14
15     delete(birthdays, "Jesus")
16     fmt.Println(birthdays, len(birthdays))
17
18     _, found = birthdays["Jesus"]
19     fmt.Println("Did we find when its Xmas?", found)
20
21     birthdays["Jesus"]="12-25-0000"
22     fmt.Println(birthdays)
```

```
map[Budha:563 BEC Jesus
:12-25-0000] 2
12-25-0000 true
map[Budha:563 BEC] 1
Did we find when its Xmas?
false
map[Budha:563 BEC Jesus
:12-25-0000]
```

```
23
24 }
```

New items can be added like in `birthdays["Jesus"]="12-25-0000"`. Additionally, items can be removed using the built-in function **delete**.

3.3.1. ITERATION

To iterate a **map** we would require the collection of keys. Fortunately, the **range** built-in function offers a simple solution to iterate through all the key-value pair of any **map**. The rules explained for slices apply in the case of maps. For every iteration **range** returns the current key and value.

Example 3.8: map iteration using range.

```
 1 package main
 2
 3 import "fmt"
 4
 5 func main(){
 6     sales := map[string]int {
 7         "Jan": 34345,
 8         "Feb": 11823,
 9         "Mar": 8838,
10         "Apr": 33,
11     }
12
13     fmt.Println("Month\tSales")
14     for month, sale := range sales {
15         fmt.Printf("%s\t\t%d\n",month,sale)
16     }
17 }
```

```
Month  Sales
Jan    34345
Feb    11823
Mar    8838
Apr    33
```

> ⚠ The function **range** does not guarantee the same order for consecutive iterations.

3.4. SUMMARY

This Chapter shows how to declare, manipulate, and iterate through arrays, slices, and maps. These three native structures are extremely versatile and widely used in any Go program. The next Chapter exposes the tools Go offers to define their own data structures.

4. Structs, methods, and interfaces

In 1976 Niklaus Wirth published "Algorithms + Data Structures = Programs" [16]. It became a seminal book and its title is the best summary of what a computer program can be. Previous chapters explained the necessary items to define algorithms (branches, loops, variables, etc.). In this Chapter, we dig into how Go works with data structures.

4.1. Structs

If you are familiar with languages such as C/C++ you will find structs a relatively known construct. In a few words, a **struct** is a sequence of elements named fields. Each field has a name and a type.

In Example 4.1 we have a struct named Rectangle which represents the geometric figure with Height and Width fields. A **struct** can be instantiated in different ways. Not passing any argument (line 11) initializes every field in the **struct** with the zero value. Initial values can be set passing them as arguments in the same order they were declared (line 14). Additionally, we can set what value corresponds to what field using the field name (line 17). In this way, we do not need to set all the fields (line 20). Missing fields are set to their default value.

Example 4.1: Structure definition for a rectangle.

```
1 package main
2
```

```
3  import "fmt"
4
5  type Rectangle struct{
6      Height int
7      Width  int
8  }
9
10 func main() {
11     a := Rectangle{}
12     fmt.Println(a)
13
14     b := Rectangle{4,4}
15     fmt.Println(b)
16
17     c := Rectangle{Width: 10, Height: 3}
18     fmt.Println(c)
19
20     d := Rectangle{Width: 7}
21     fmt.Println(d)
22 }
```

```
{0 0}
{4 4}
{3 10}
{0 7}
```

This flexibility creating structs can be inconvenient. In Example 4.2, `a` is a rectangle with no `Width` field value. In this case, it does not make any sense to a rectangle with a width of zero. One possible solution is to define a `NewRectangle` function that requires all the necessary arguments to create this **struct**. Notice, that this function returns a pointer to the **struct** instead of a value.

Example 4.2: Struct constructor.

```
1  package main
2
3  import "fmt"
4
5  type Rectangle struct{
6      Height int
7      Width  int
8  }
9
10 func NewRectangle(height int, width int) *Rectangle {
11     return &Rectangle{height, width}
12 }
13
14 func main() {
15     a := Rectangle{Height: 7}
16     fmt.Println(a)
17
18     r := NewRectangle(2,3)
```

```
{7 0}
&{2 3}
{2 3}
```

CHAPTER 4. STRUCTS, METHODS, AND INTERFACES

```
19      fmt.Println(r)
20      fmt.Println(*r)
21 }
```

> ⚠ In Go it does not exist the concept of a constructor like in other languages. A **struct** is a very flexible construct that can be defined in many ways. When working with structs it is very important to take into consideration fields zero values and how these values may impact the code. In many cases, it is a good practice to define constructors, especially when certain values are not valid.
>
> ```
> func NewRectangle(height int, width int) (*Rectangle, error) {
>     if height <= 0 || width <= 0 {
>         return nil, errors.New("params must be greater than zero")
>     }
>     return &Rectangle{height, width}, nil
> }
> ...
> r, err := NewRectangle(2,0)
> if err != nil {
>     ...
> }
> ```

4.1.1. ANONYMOUS STRUCTS

Go permits the definition of anonymous structs like the one shown in Example 4.3 (line 15). Compared with a regular struct like `Circle` printing the struct brings a similar result. However, we cannot print its name as we do with type `Circle`. The fields from the anonymous function can be modified like done with regular structs. Notice that these anonymous structures can be compared with other structures if and only if they have the same fields (line 26).

Example 4.3: Anonymous struct.

```
1 package main
2
3 import (
4     "fmt"
5     "reflect"
6 )
7
```

```
{x:1 y:2 radius:3}
struct { x int; y int; radius int }
{x:10 y:10 radius:3}
main.Circle
{x:3 y:2 radius:3}
{x:10 y:10 radius:3}
struct { x int; y int; radius int }
```

```go
 8  type Circle struct {
 9      x int
10      y int
11      radius int
12  }
13
14  func main() {
15      ac := struct{x int; y int; radius int}{1,2,3}
16      c := Circle{10,10,3}
17
18      fmt.Printf("%+v\n", ac)
19      fmt.Println(reflect.TypeOf(ac))
20      fmt.Printf("%+v\n",c)
21      fmt.Println(reflect.TypeOf(c))
22
23      ac.x=3
24      fmt.Printf("%+v\n", ac)
25
26      ac = c
27      fmt.Printf("%+v\n", ac)
28      fmt.Println(reflect.TypeOf(ac))
29  }
```

4.1.2. Nested structs

Structs can be nested to incorporate other structs definition. Example 4.4 defines a `Circle` type using a `Coordinates` type. Obviously, instantiating a `Circle` requires the instantiation of a `Coordinate` type.

Example 4.4: Nested structs.

```go
 1  package main
 2
 3  import "fmt"
 4
 5  type Coordinates struct {
 6      x int
 7      y int
 8  }
 9
10  type Circle struct {
11      center Coordinates
12      radius int
13  }
14
15  func main() {
```

```
{center:{x:1 y:2} radius:3}
```

4.1.3. EMBEDDED STRUCTS

To embed a struct in other structs, this has to be declared as a nameless field. In Example 4.5 by embedding the `Coordinates` struct in the `Circle` type we make fields `x` and `y` directly accessible. The coordinates instance can also be accessed like the `Coordinates` field.

Example 4.5: Embedded structs.

```go
package main

import "fmt"

type Coordinates struct {
    x int
    y int
}

type Circle struct {
    Coordinates
    radius int
}

func main() {
    c := Circle{Coordinates{1, 2}, 3}
    fmt.Printf("%+v\n", c)
    fmt.Printf("%+v\n", c.Coordinates)
    fmt.Println(c.x, c.y)
}
```

```
{Coordinates:{x:1 y:2} radius:3}
{x:1 y:2}
1 2
```

> ⚠ Embedding structs can be done only if the compiler find no ambiguities. Considering the following code:
>
> ```go
> // ...
> type A struct { fieldA int }
>
> type B struct { fieldA int }
> ```

```
type C struct {
    A
    B
}
// ...
a := A{10}
b := B{20}
c := C{a,b}
// --> Ambiguos access
// fmt.Println(c.fieldA)
fmt.Println(c.A.fieldA,c.B.fieldA)
```

Because `fieldA` may belong to different structs, this access is ambiguous triggering an error during compilation. We have to specify which struct this field belongs to.

4.2. Methods

In the object-oriented world, a method is defined as a procedure associated with a class. In Go there is not such a thing as classes. However, Go defines methods as a special function with a receiver. The receiver sets the type that can invoke that function.

Assume we work with the `Rectangle` type and we want to add some operations such as computing the surface. In Example 4.6, the method `Surface() int` is a function with the receiver `(r Rectangle)`. This means that any type `Rectangle` can invoke this method. Inside the method, the fields `Height` and `Width` from the current instance `R` are accessible.

Example 4.6: Definition of methods for a `Rectangle` type.

```go
package main

import "fmt"

type Rectangle struct{
    Height int
    Width  int
}

func (r Rectangle) Surface() int {
    return r.Height * r.Width
}

func main() {
    r := Rectangle{2,3}
```

```
rectangle {2 3} has surface 6
```

```
16      fmt.Printf("rectangle %v has surface %d",r, r.Surface())
17 }
```

Receivers are very important because they define the type "receiving" the logic inside the method. In Example 4.7, we define two methods with the same logic. Method `Enlarge` receives a value of type `Rectangle` and method `EnlargeP` receives a type `*Rectangle`. If you follow the output, you can see how `Enlarge` does not modify any field of the original variable, while `EnlargeP` does. This happens because the `EnlargeP` receives the pointer to `rect` whereas, `Enlarge` receives a copy.

Example 4.7: Value and pointer receivers.

```
1  package main
2
3  import "fmt"
4
5  type Rectangle struct{
6      Height int
7      Width  int
8  }
9
10 func (r Rectangle) Enlarge(factor int) {
11     r.Height = r.Height * factor
12     r.Width = r.Width * factor
13 }
14
15 func (r *Rectangle) EnlargeP(factor int) {
16     r.Height = r.Height * factor
17     r.Width = r.Width * factor
18 }
19
20 func main() {
21     rect := Rectangle{2,2}
22     fmt.Println(rect)
23
24     rect.Enlarge(2)
25     fmt.Println(rect)
26
27     rect.EnlargeP(2)
28     fmt.Println(rect)
29 }
```

```
{2 2}
{2 2}
{4 4}
```

> In Example 4.7, the `EnlargeP` method requires a pointer. However, we invoke

the method with `rect.EnlargeP(2)` and `rect` is not a pointer. This is possible because the Go interpreter translates this into `(&rect).EnlargeP(2)`.

> ⚠ **If a method can have value or pointer receivers, which one should you use?**
>
> Generally, using pointers is more efficient because it reduces the number of copies. However, in some situations you may be more comfortable with value receivers. In any case, you should be consistent and do not mix them.

4.2.1. EMBEDDED METHODS

When a struct is embedded into other structs its methods are made available to the second one. This acts as some sort of inheritance in Go. In Example 4.8, the type `Box` embeds the type `Rectangle`. Observe how the method `Volume` can directly invoke the `Surface` method from `Rectangle` to compute the volume of the box.

Example 4.8: Embedded methods.

```go
package main

import "fmt"

type Rectangle struct {
    Height int
    Width  int
}

func (r Rectangle) Surface() int {
    return r.Height * r.Width
}

type Box struct {
    Rectangle
    depth int
}

func (b Box) Volume() int {
    return b.Surface() * b.depth
}

func main() {
    b := Box{Rectangle{3,3}, 3}
    fmt.Printf("%+v\n",b)
    fmt.Println("Volume", b.Volume())
```

```
{Rectangle:{Height:3 Width:3} depth:3}
Volume 27
```

27 `}`

> ⚠ Remember that embedded methods only work if there is no ambiguity in its definition. Consider the following example:
>
> ```go
> type A struct {}
> func (a A) Hi() string {
>     return "A says Hi"
> }
>
> type B struct {}
> func (b B) Hi() string {
>     return "B says Hi"
> }
>
> type Greeter struct{
>     A
>     B
> }
>
> func (g Greeter) Speak() string {
>     // return g.Hi() --> This method belongs to A or B?
>     return g.A.Hi() + g.B.Hi()
> }
> ```
>
> Invoking method `Hi` in `Greeter` is not possible because the compiler cannot determine which type `A` or `B` is the owner. This has to be solved by specifying the method owner.

4.3. Interfaces

An `interface` is a collection of methods with any signature. Interfaces do not define any logic or value. They simply define a collection of methods to be implemented. A type `A` implements an interface `I` if and only if all the methods from `I` are implemented in `A`.

Example 4.9: Interface declaration

```go
1  package main
2
3  import "fmt"
```

```go
type Animal interface {
    Roar() string
    Run() string
}

type Dog struct {}

func (d Dog) Roar() string {
    return "woof"
}

func (d Dog) Run() string {
    return "run like a dog"
}

type Cat struct {}

func (c *Cat) Roar() string {
    return "meow"
}

func (c *Cat) Run() string {
    return "run like a cat"
}

func RoarAndRun(a Animal) {
    fmt.Printf("%s and %s\n", a.Roar(), a.Run())
}

func main() {
    myDog := Dog{}
    myCat := Cat{}

    RoarAndRun(myDog)
    RoarAndRun(&myCat)
}
```

```
woof and run like a dog
meow and run like a cat
```

Example 4.9 declares the `Animal` **interface** with two methods `Roar` and `Run`. Next we have `Dog` and `Cat` types that define these methods. Automatically both types are considered to implement interface `Animal`. Function `RoarAndRun` receives an `Animal` type, so we can invoke the `Roar` and `Run` methods independently of the final argument type.

Notice that method receivers from `Dog` and `Cat` are different. Because all the methods of the **interface** must be implemented in order to consider a type to implement **interface** of type `Animal`, certain combinations in the example can fail. For example:

```
RoarAndRun(myDog) // --> It works
```

CHAPTER 4. STRUCTS, METHODS, AND INTERFACES

```
RoarAndRun(&myDog) // --> It does not work
```

However, if we try to invoke `RoarAndRun` for a `Cat` type (not a pointer) we find that it fails.

```
RoarAndRun(&myCat) // --> It works
RoarAndRun(myCat)  // --> It does not work
```

`RoarAndRun(myCat)` does not work because the receivers of the methods in the `Cat` type are pointers while we pass an argument by value. In case the method assigns a new value to any field, this cannot be reflected in the original caller because it is a copy. This difference may have an impact on your code. We have already seen that methods with pointer receivers can modify the values in the invoking struct (Example 4.7).

We can see this in Example 4.10 where `Person` implements `Greeter`. However, instantiating `p{}` does not return a `Greeter` type. Why? Because the method `SayHello` has a pointer receiver. This limits this method to `*Person` type. This may have an impact on your code if those types that implement interfaces are not consistently defined using pointers or values.

Example 4.10: Interface declaration

```
 1 package main
 2
 3 import "fmt"
 4
 5 type Greeter interface {
 6     SayHello() string
 7 }
 8
 9 type Person struct{
10     name string
11 }
12
13 func (p *Person) SayHello() string {
14     return "Hi! This is me "+ p.name
15 }
16
17 func main() {
18
19     var g Greeter
20
21     p := Person{"John"}
22     // g = p --> Does not work
23     g = &p
```

```
Hi! This is me John
```

```
24       fmt.Println(g.SayHello())
25  }
```

> ⚠ You may consider implementing an interface using methods with pointer and value receivers simultaneously to be able to work with both flavors. Something like
>
> ```
> func (p *Person) SayHello() string {
>     return "Hi! This is me "+ p.name
> }
> // ...
> func (p Person) SayHello() string {
>     return "Hi! This is me "+ p.name
> }
> ```
>
> This is some sort of method overloading and is not allowed in Go.

4.3.1. EMPTY INTERFACE

A special case of **interface** is the empty interface **interface{}**. This interface has no methods and it is implemented by any type. This **interface** is particularly useful for those situations where we cannot know the data type beforehand. As shown in Example 4.11 an empty **interface** can be assigned any value.

Example 4.11: Using the empty interface.

```
 1  package main
 2
 3  import "fmt"
 4
 5  func main() {
 6      var aux interface{}
 7
 8      fmt.Println(aux)
 9
10      aux = 10
11      fmt.Println(aux)
12
13      aux = "hello"
14      fmt.Println(aux)
15  }
```

```
<nil>
10
hello
```

The empty interface is a very ambiguous context for a typed language like Go. In many situations, it is necessary to know the underlying data type of the interface. Otherwise, it is not possible to know how to proceed with that data. A practical way to find the variable type is using a `switch` statement. Example 4.12 fills a slice of empty interfaces with an integer, a string, and a boolean. The `switch` statement can extract the type of value in runtime. This can be used to define how to operate with the value. In the example, we modify a print statement accordingly to the type. Notice that "`%T`" in the print statement gets the name of the value type.

Example 4.12: Explore the type of an empty interface.

```go
package main

import "fmt"

func main() {

    aux := []interface{}{42, "hello", true}

    for _, i := range aux {
        switch t := i.(type) {
        default:
            fmt.Printf("%T --> %s\n", t, i)
        case int:
            fmt.Printf("%T --> %d\n", t, i)
        case string:
            fmt.Printf("%T --> %s\n", t, i)
        case bool:
            fmt.Printf("%T --> %v\n", t, i)
        }
    }
}
```

```
int --> 42
string --> hello
bool --> true
```

> **(?) Go cannot be fully considered an object-oriented language.** Actually, concepts such as classes or hierarchy of classes do not exist. Similar functionality can indeed be obtained using the current language definition. However, we cannot say Go is an object-oriented language.

4.4. SUMMARY

This Chapter introduces the concepts of struct, methods, and interfaces used in Go. These concepts are fundamental pieces of the Go language and will appear across different sections of this book. Additionally, we explained certain situations that may seem weird to early adopters such as the difference between value and pointer receivers in methods.

5. REFLECTION

In programming, reflection is the ability of a program to examine, introspect and modify its structure and behavior [11]. In other words, this is a form of metaprogramming. Reflection is an extremely powerful tool for developers and extends the horizon of any programming language. Unfortunately, this comes with additional complexity.

In this Chapter, we introduce the `reflect`[1] package and explain through examples how to explore, introspect and modify our code in run-time. We split this explanation into two sections, according to how Go organizes the reflection package. Finally, we introduce how Go uses tags to enhance fields information.

5.1. REFLECT.TYPE

A starting point to understand reflection in Go, is to remember the concept of empty interface `interface{}` seen in Section 4.3.1. The empty interface can contain whatever type. For example:

```
unknown := interface{}
a := 16
unknown = a
```

This code works because `interface{}` accepts everything, therefore we can say that everything is an empty interface. This is very important because the function `reflect.TypeOf` is the main entrypoint for code introspection and receives and empty interface as argument. Observe Example 5.1 and how it obtains the type of variables `a` and `b`.

---
[1] https://golang.org/pkg/reflect/

Example 5.1: reflect.TypeOf with basic types.

```go
package main

import (
    "fmt"
    "reflect"
)

func main() {
    var a int32 = 42
    var b string = "forty two"

    typeA := reflect.TypeOf(a)
    fmt.Println(typeA)

    typeB := reflect.TypeOf(b)
    fmt.Println(typeB)
}
```

```
int32
string
```

The function `TypeOf` returns type `Type` with a set of methods to for code introspection. Example 5.2 explores a struct with two fields. Notice that we can navigate through the fields of any type, accessing its name and type.

Example 5.2: reflect.TypeOf with structs.

```go
package main

import (
    "fmt"
    "reflect"
)

type T struct {
    A int32
    B string
}

func main() {
    t := T{42, "forty two"}

    typeT := reflect.TypeOf(t)
    fmt.Println(typeT)

    for i:=0;i<typeT.NumField();i++{
        field := typeT.Field(i)
        fmt.Println(field.Name,field.Type)
    }
```

```
main.T
A int32
B string
```

CHAPTER 5. REFLECTION

```
23 }
```

Beyond type exploration, we can check if a type implements an interface. This can be done using the `Implements` method as shown in Example 5.3. This is a good example of how interfaces work in Go. The method `Add` has a pointer receiver (`*Calculator`) for that reason, the `main.Calculator` type does not implement the `Adder` interface.

Example 5.3: `reflect.TypeOf` with structs.

```
 1 package main
 2
 3 import (
 4     "fmt"
 5     "reflect"
 6 )
 7
 8 type Adder interface{
 9     Add (int, int) int
10 }
11
12 type Calculator struct{}
13
14 func(c *Calculator) Add(a int, b int) int {
15     return a + b
16 }
17
18 func main() {
19
20     var ptrAdder *Adder
21     adderType := reflect.TypeOf(ptrAdder).Elem()
22
23     c := Calculator{}
24
25     calcType := reflect.TypeOf(c)
26     calcTypePtr := reflect.TypeOf(&c)
27
28     fmt.Println(calcType, calcType.Implements(adderType))
29     fmt.Println(calcTypePtr, calcTypePtr.Implements(adderType))
30 }
```

```
main.Calculator false
*main.Calculator true
```

Using `reflect.Type` we can explore any kind of struct, with any number of fields and types. Example 5.4 uses a recursive type inspector that prints the structure of any given type. The inspector iterates through the struct fields even if they are other structs. This is done obtaining the `Kind` of the field and comparing it with a struct (`f.Type.Kind()==reflect.Struct`). You can check how this code, does not skip unexported fields.

Example 5.4: Recursive struct inspector.

```go
package main

import (
    "fmt"
    "reflect"
    "strings"
)

type T struct {
    B int
    C string
}

type S struct {
    C string
    D T
    E map[string]int
}

func printerReflect(offset int, typeOfX reflect.Type) {
    indent := strings.Repeat(" ",offset)
    fmt.Printf("%s %s: %s {\n",indent, typeOfX.Name(), typeOfX.Kind())
    if typeOfX.Kind() == reflect.Struct {
        for i:=0;i<typeOfX.NumField();i++{
            innerIndent := strings.Repeat(" ",offset+4)
            f := typeOfX.Field(i)
            if f.Type.Kind() == reflect.Struct {
                printerReflect(offset+4, f.Type)
            } else {
                fmt.Printf("%s %s: %s\n",innerIndent, f.Name, f.Type)
            }
        }
    }
    fmt.Printf("%s }\n", indent)
}

func main() {

    x := S{"root",
        T{42, "forty two"},
        make(map[string]int),
    }

    printerReflect(0, reflect.TypeOf(x))
}
```

```
S: struct {
    C: string
    T: struct {
        B: int
        C: string
    }
    E: map[string]int
}
```

5.2. REFLECT.VALUE

We have seen how `reflect.Type` permits code introspection. However, the `reflect.Type` type cannot access field values. This functionality is reserved to the `reflect.Value` type. Actually, from a `reflect.Value` type we can access its `reflect.Type` type. Example 5.5 uses the same variables from Example 5.1. Notice that in this case we can print the variables current value.

Example 5.5: `reflect.ValueOf`.

```
1  package main
2
3  import (
4      "fmt"
5      "reflect"
6  )
7
8  func main() {
9      var a int32 = 42
10     var b string = "forty two"
11
12     valueOfA := reflect.ValueOf(a)
13     fmt.Println(valueOfA.Interface())
14
15     valueOfB := reflect.ValueOf(b)
16     fmt.Println(valueOfB.Interface())
17 }
```

```
42
forty two
```

In order to know what type implements a value, we can be compare it with the `Kind` type returned by method `Kind()`. The type `Kind` is a number representing one of the types available in Go (**int32**, **string**, **map**, etc.). This can be combined with a **switch** statement as shown in Example 5.6 to identify what type are we working with.

Example 5.6: **switch** using `reflect.Kind`.

```
1  package main
2
3  import (
4      "fmt"
5      "reflect"
6  )
7
8  func ValuePrint(i interface{}) {
9      v := reflect.ValueOf(i)
10     switch v.Kind() {
```

```
Int32 with value 42
String with value forty two
```

```
11      case reflect.Int32:
12          fmt.Println("Int32 with value", v.Int())
13      case reflect.String:
14          fmt.Println("String with value", v.String())
15      default:
16          fmt.Println("unknown type")
17      }
18  }
19
20  func main() {
21      var a int32 = 42
22      var b string = "forty two"
23
24      ValuePrint(a)
25      ValuePrint(b)
26  }
```

Example 5.7 uses `reflect.Value` with a struct to print the field values. The reflected value of variable `t` is correctly printed. Similarly, we can print the value of every field in the struct. Notice the difference between printing `field.String()` and `field`. For numeric values `field.String()` returns a string like `<int32 Value>`. The string informs that there is an integer value in that field. However, `fmt.Println(field)` works as expected. This occurs because the function prints the corresponding value when it receives `Value` types.

Example 5.7: `reflect.ValueOf` with structs.

```
1  package main
2
3  import (
4      "fmt"
5      "reflect"
6  )
7
8  type T struct {
9      A int32
10     B string
11     C float32
12 }
13
14 func main() {
15     t := T{42, "forty two", 3.14}
16
17     valueT := reflect.ValueOf(t)
18     fmt.Println(valueT.Kind(), valueT)
19
20     for i:=0;i<valueT.NumField();i++{
21         field := valueT.Field(i)
```

```
struct {42 forty two 3.14}
int32 <int32 Value> 42
string forty two forty two
float32 <float32 Value> 3.14
```

```go
22        fmt.Println(field.Kind(), field.String(), field.Interface())
23    }
24 }
```

5.2.1. SETTING VALUES

Using `reflect.Value` we can set values on run-time. Every `Value` has methods `SetInt32`, `SetFloat32`, `SetString`, etc. that set the field to a **int32**, **float32**, **string**, etc. value. Example 5.8 sets the string fields from a struct to uppercase.

Example 5.8: Setting values using reflection.

```go
 1 package main
 2
 3 import (
 4     "fmt"
 5     "reflect"
 6     "strings"
 7 )
 8
 9 type T struct {
10     A string
11     B int32
12     C string
13 }
14
15 func main() {
16     t := T{"hello",42,"bye"}
17     fmt.Println(t)
18
19     valueOfT := reflect.ValueOf(&t).Elem()
20     for i:=0; i< valueOfT.NumField(); i++ {
21         f := valueOfT.Field(i)
22         if f.Kind() == reflect.String {
23             current := f.String()
24             f.SetString(strings.ToUpper(current))
25         }
26     }
27     fmt.Println(t)
28 }
```

```
{hello 42 bye}
{HELLO 42 BYE}
```

If the set operation is not valid, the operation will panic. For example, setting fields to a different type or trying to set unexported fields. In Example 5.9, the field `c` in unexported. Additional checking must be done using the `canSet()` method. Using this method we can skip unexported fields. Observe that the output has not modified c value.

Example 5.9: Setting values using reflection considering unexported fields.

```go
package main

import (
    "fmt"
    "reflect"
    "strings"
)

type T struct {
    A string
    B int32
    c string
}

func main() {
    t := T{"hello",42,"bye"}
    fmt.Println(t)

    valueOfT := reflect.ValueOf(&t).Elem()
    for i:=0; i< valueOfT.NumField(); i++ {
        f := valueOfT.Field(i)
        if f.Kind() == reflect.String {
            if f.CanSet() {
                current := f.String()
                f.SetString(strings.ToUpper(current))
            }
        }
    }

    fmt.Println(t)
}
```

```
{hello 42 bye}
{HELLO 42 bye}
```

5.3. CREATING FUNCTIONS ON THE FLY

In previous sections, we have explored how to inspect fields and modify values. Additionally, the `reflect` package permits the creation of new entities such as functions on the fly. This offers certain functionalities available in other programming languages. For example, the lack of generics in Go imposes some limitations although there is already a proposal at the moment of this writing[2].

---

[2]https://blog.golang.org/generics-proposal

CHAPTER 5. REFLECTION

Assume we want to write a function that generalizes the add operation. This function must sum numbers (integers and floats) and append strings. Given the current language definition, this is not possible. Check the code below. Go does not permit any kind of function overload. Every function must have a unique name. Similarly, the lack of generics makes it impossible to reuse the same code using the add operator (+) defined for every type.

```go
func Sum(a int, b int) int {...}

func Sum(a float32, b float32) float32 {...} // Not unique.

func Sum(a string, b string) string {...} // Not unique.
```

One interesting workaround is to use the `reflect.MakeFunc` function to build our own functions with different signatures. Example 5.10 builds an add function factory in `BuildAdder()`. This function receives the pointer to a function with two arguments of the same type and one output. The `MakeFunc` receives a function type and a function with a variable number of `Value` types inside an array, and returns an array of `Value`. We fill this function with a `switch` statement that implements the addition between the two arguments according to its type. Finally, we set this function to the original function (`fn.Set(newF)`.

Example 5.10: Using `reflect.MakeFunc` to create functions on run-time.

```
3
5.423
hello go
```

```go
1  package main
2
3  import (
4      "fmt"
5      "reflect"
6  )
7
8
9  func BuildAdder (i interface{}) {
10     fn := reflect.ValueOf(i).Elem()
11
12     newF := reflect.MakeFunc(fn.Type(), func(in []reflect.Value)[]reflect.Value
           {
13
14         if len(in) > 2 {
15             return []reflect.Value{}
16         }
17
18         a, b := in[0], in[1]
19
20         if a.Kind() != b.Kind() {
```

```go
21              return []reflect.Value{}
22          }
23
24          var result reflect.Value
25
26          switch a.Kind() {
27          case reflect.Int, reflect.Int8, reflect.Int16, reflect.Int32, reflect.
                Int64:
28              result = reflect.ValueOf(a.Int() + b.Int())
29          case reflect.Uint, reflect.Uint8, reflect.Uint16, reflect.Uint32,
                reflect.Uint64:
30              result = reflect.ValueOf(a.Uint() + b.Uint())
31          case reflect.Float32, reflect.Float64:
32              result = reflect.ValueOf(a.Float() + b.Float())
33          case reflect.String:
34              result = reflect.ValueOf(a.String() + b.String())
35          default:
36              result = reflect.ValueOf(interface{}(nil))
37          }
38          return []reflect.Value{result}
39      })
40      fn.Set(newF)
41  }
42
43  func main() {
44      var intAdder func(int64,int64) int64
45      var floatAdder func(float64, float64) float64
46      var strAdder func(string, string) string
47
48      BuildAdder(&intAdder)
49      BuildAdder(&floatAdder)
50      BuildAdder(&strAdder)
51
52      fmt.Println(intAdder(1,2))
53      fmt.Println(floatAdder(3.0,2.423))
54      fmt.Println(strAdder("hello"," go"))
55  }
```

5.4. Tags

Go provides powerful and versatile structs enrichment using tags. These tags can be interpreted on run-time using reflection which adds valuable information that can be employed for different purposes.

```go
type User struct {
```

CHAPTER 5. REFLECTION

```
    UserId string `tagA:"valueA1" tagB: "valueA2"`
    Email string `tagB:"value"`
    Password string `tagC: "v1 v2"`
    Others string `"something a b"`
}
```

The **struct** above declares four fields with different tags. Every tag becomes an attribute of the field that can be accessed later. Go permits tags to declare raw string literals like `"something a b"`. However, by convention tags follow a key-value schema separated by spaces. For example, the string `tagA:"valueA1"tagB:"valueA2"`, declares two tags `tagA` and `tagB` with values `valueA1` and `valueA2` respectively.

Example 5.11, uses `reflect.TypeOf` to access all the declared fields of the struct `User`. The type `Type` returned by `TypeOf` has functions to check the type name, number of fields, size, etc. Field information is stored in a type `StructField` that can be accessed using `Field()` and `FieldByName()` functions. For every `StructField` tags are stored in a `StructTag` type (`fieldUserId.Tag`). A `StructTag` contains all the available tags of a field.

Example 5.11: Access to field tags using reflect.

```
1  package main
2
3  import (
4      "fmt"
5      "reflect"
6  )
7
8  type User struct {
9      UserId string `tagA:"valueA1" tagB: "valueA2"`
10     Email string `tagB:"value"`
11     Password string `tagC:"v1 v2"`
12 }
13
14 func main() {
15     T := reflect.TypeOf(User{})
16
17     fieldUserId := T.Field(0)
18     t := fieldUserId.Tag
19     fmt.Println("StructTag is:",t)
20     v, _ := t.Lookup("tagA")
21     fmt.Printf("tagA: %s\n", v)
22
23     fieldEmail, _ := T.FieldByName("Email")
24     vEmail := fieldEmail.Tag.Get("tagB")
25     fmt.Println("email tagB:", vEmail)
26
27     fieldPassword, _ := T.FieldByName("Password")
```

```
StructTag is: tagA:"valueA1"
tagB: "valueA2"
tagA: valueA1
email tagB: value
Password tags: [tagC:"v1 v2"
]
v1 v2
```

```
28      fmt.Printf("Password tags: [%s]\n",fieldPassword.Tag)
29      fmt.Println(fieldPassword.Tag.Get("tagC"))
30 }
```

> ⚠ By convention tags must be declared like `key:"value"` strings. Notice that blank spaces in the string do not follow the convention. E.g.: `key: "value"` is not a valid declaration.

5.5. THE THREE LAWS OF REFLECTION

At this point, we have explored some actions we can carry out using reflection. Reflection is an extremely powerful tool although it can become extremely convoluted. Rob Pike enumerated the three laws of reflection [12] that govern Go. We reproduce and explain these three laws in this Section.

5.5.1. THE FIRST LAW OF REFLECTION

Reflection goes from interface value to reflection object.

We have explained that function `reflect.TypeOf` inspects any type. The signature of this function receives an empty interface by argument (`TypeOf(i interface{})`). However, we have already seen that print any type returned by this function like in the code below.

```
var a int32 = 42
fmt.Println(reflect.TypeOf(a))    // --> Prints int32
```

How is this possible? Variable `a` is stored into an empty interface before `TypeOf` is called. A similar process is done with `ValueOf`. The empty interface stores the underlying type and points to the corresponding value. That is why we can resolve the variable type or value.

5.5.2. THE SECOND LAW OF REFLECTION

Reflection goes from reflection object to interface value.

If the first law defines how we go from the interface to the value, the second law defines the inverse. For a `Value` type we can get the original interface using `func (v Value) Interface interface{}`. The code below will print 42 twice.

CHAPTER 5. REFLECTION

```
var a int32 = 42
v := reflect.ValueOf(a)
fmt.Println(v) // --> Prints 42
fmt.Println(v.Interface()) // --> Prints 42
```

What is the difference between printing `v` and `v.Interface()` if both outputs are the same? In the first case, we print a `Value`. In the second case, we print an `int32` variable. The reason why the first case prints the same is that `Println` states that in the case of `reflect.Value` types the output is the concrete value that this type holds. Then, why use `v.Interface()`? Simply because `v` is not the real value although some operations like `Println` can reach it.

5.5.3. THE THIRD LAW OF REFLECTION

To modify a reflection object, the value must be settable.

The third law may sound evident, you cannot set something if it is not settable. However, this is something difficult to see. The example below tries to set an integer.

```
var a int32 = 42
v := reflect.ValueOf(a)
v.SetInt(16) // <-- panic
```

The last instruction will panic. This is due to the settability of `v`. The value contained by `v` is not the original one, it is a copy. Notice that `reflect.ValueOf(a)` uses a copy of `a`. The value does not point to the original place where the 42 is stored, we need a pointer. However, the following will fail.

```
var a int32 = 42
v := reflect.ValueOf(&a)
v.SetInt(16) // --> panic
```

Now `v` is a pointer to an integer. If we set this value, we are trying to modify the pointer. What we are looking for is the content that is been pointed by this pointer. This is where we use the `Elem()` method.

```
var a int32 = 42
v := reflect.ValueOf(&a).Elem()
v.SetInt(16)
fmt.Println(v.Interface())
```

The settability of a field can be checked using the method `CanSet()` as discussed in Example 5.9.

5.6. Summary

In this Chapter, we explored how to use reflection in Go and how to use types, values, and tags. We enumerated the three laws of reflection and showed examples for each of the rules. Reflection is a powerful tool in advanced programming projects and will appear in different Chapters of this book. However, the developer must consider that code introspection comes with a cost in terms of performance, code readability, and maintenance. Is for this reason, that reflection is expected to be used in certain scenarios where it is the only solution for a given problem.

6. Concurrency

The title of this Chapter may sound intimidating. Concurrency is a tough topic in computer science that causes developer headaches. Fortunately, Go was designed with simplicity in mind. It facilitates the creation of concurrent programs, inter-thread communication, and other topics that in other languages require deep tech knowledge. At the end of this Chapter you will understand concepts such as goroutines, channels, and how they can be used to design sophisticated concurrent programs.

6.1. Goroutines

A Goroutine is a lightweight thread managed by the Go runtime. Goroutines are declared using the `go` statement followed by the function to be executed. Example 6.1 launches the `ShowIt` function in a goroutine that runs concurrently with the `main` function. Both functions print a message after sleeping (`time.Sleep`). The `main` function sleeps half the time of `ShowIt` that is why we have a ratio of two messages from one function versus the other. It is important to notice that although the loop in `ShowIt` is endless, the program execution terminates when the `main` function finishes. No goroutine will remain running when the `main` function finishes.

Example 6.1: Creation of goroutines.

```
1  package main
2
3  import (
4      "fmt"
5      "time"
```

```
 6 )
 7
 8 func ShowIt() {
 9     for {
10         time.Sleep(time.Millisecond * 100)
11         fmt.Println("Here it is!!!")
12     }
13 }
14
15 func main() {
16
17     go ShowIt()
18
19     for i := 0; i < 5; i++ {
20         time.Sleep(time.Millisecond * 50)
21         fmt.Println("Where is it?")
22     }
23 }
```

```
Where is it?
Where is it?
Here it is!!!
Where is it?
Where is it?
Here it is!!!
Where is it?
```

Goroutines are very lightweight with a very small memory demand (only 2Kb) when compared with a thread. We can expect to have several goroutines concurrently running. This can as easy as invoking the `go` statement when required. Example 6.2 creates three goroutines that print a number after sleeping for a given time. The output shows the proportion of messages we expect depending on the sleeping time. Observe that multiple executions of this program may not return the same output. Why? Because the goroutines initialization time may vary and because we are using the console output which may is a single output for multiple routines.

Example 6.2: Creation of multiple goroutines.

```
 1 package main
 2
 3 import (
 4     "time"
 5     "fmt"
 6 )
 7
 8 func ShowIt(t time.Duration, num int) {
 9     for {
10         time.Sleep(t)
11         fmt.Println(num)
12     }
13 }
14
15 func main() {
16     go ShowIt(time.Second, 100)
17     go ShowIt(time.Millisecond*500,10)
```

```
1
10
1
1
100
10
1
```

```
18      go ShowIt(time.Millisecond*250,1)
19
20      time.Sleep(time.Millisecond*1200)
21 }
```

6.2. Channels

Channels are a mechanism that provides communication for concurrently running functions. A channel can send or receive elements of a specified type.

Channels are instantiated using the `make` built-in function. Example 6.3 `make(chan int)` instantiates a channel that can send or receive integers. In this particular example, the `generator` function runs in a goroutine that computes the sum of the first five integers and sends it through the `channel`. Meanwhile, the main function waits until something is sent through the channel with `result := <- ch`. Notice that this last operation is blocking and will not be completed until something is sent through the channel.

Example 6.3: Goroutine using reading channels.

```
1  package main
2
3  import (
4      "fmt"
5      "time"
6  )
7
8  func generator(ch chan int) {
9      sum := 0
10     for i:=0;i<5;i++ {
11         time.Sleep(time.Millisecond * 500)
12         sum = sum + i
13     }
14     ch <- sum
15 }
16
17 func main() {
18
19     ch := make(chan int)
20
21     go generator(ch)
22
23     fmt.Println("main waits for result...")
24     result := <- ch
25
26     fmt.Println(result)
```

```
main waits for result
...
10
```

```
27 }
```

We can enhance this example using the channel in both directions: reading and writing. In Example 6.4, `generator` receives the number of elements to iterate through the channel. The function will be blocked until the number is received. You can observe this by manipulating the sleep time in the main function before sending the `n` value through the channel.

Example 6.4: Goroutine using read/write channels.

```go
package main

import (
    "fmt"
    "time"
)

func generator(ch chan int) {
    fmt.Println("generator waits for n")
    n := <- ch
    fmt.Println("n is",n)
    sum := 0
    for i:=0;i<n;i++ {
        sum = sum + i
    }
    ch <- sum
}

func main() {

    ch := make(chan int)

    go generator(ch)

    fmt.Println("main waits for result...")
    time.Sleep(time.Second)
    ch <- 5
    result := <- ch

    fmt.Println(result)
}
```

```
main waits for result
...
generator waits
n is 5
10
```

Channels can be used to read or write. However, observe that the arrow statement `<-` always goes from the right to the left.

```
ch <- 5 // send 5 through channel
n := <- ch // initialize n with value from channel
<- ch // wait until something is sent through ch
```

6.2.1. BUFFERED CHANNELS

Channels can be buffered or unbuffered. The statement `make(chan int)` generates an unbuffered channel. Unbuffered channels have no capacity, this means that both sides of the channel must be ready to send and receive data. On the other side, buffered channels can be declared with `make(chan int, 10)` where 10 is the buffer size. In this case, the channel can store values independently of the readiness of sender and receiver.

In Example 6.5, two functions and the `main` send data to the same channel. Due to the code workflow, the main writes to the channel when nobody is listening which triggers the error `fatal error: all goroutines are asleep - deadlock!`. In this case, a buffered channel can store messages until the receivers are ready to consume the messages. This example only needs a one-element buffer. However, you can check how removing the size value in the `make` statement returns an unbuffered channel.

Example 6.5: Channel buffering.

```
1  package main
2
3  import (
4      "fmt"
5      "time"
6  )
7
8  func MrA(ch chan string) {
9      time.Sleep(time.Millisecond*500)
10     ch <- "This is MrA"
11 }
12
13 func MrB(ch chan string) {
14     time.Sleep(time.Millisecond*200)
15     ch <- "This is MrB"
16 }
17
18 func main() {
19     //ch := make(chan string)
20     ch := make(chan string, 1)
21
22     ch <- "This is main"
23
24     go MrA(ch)
```

```
This is main
This is MrB
This is MrA
```

```
25      go MrB(ch)
26
27      fmt.Println(<-ch)
28      fmt.Println(<-ch)
29      fmt.Println(<-ch)
30 }
```

> ⚠ Like slices, buffered channels have `len` and `cap` functions. We could think of using these functions to avoid sending data to full channels.
>
> ```
> if len(ch) == cap(ch) {
>     // channel was full, now we don't know
> } else {
>     // channel was free, now we don't know
> }
> ```
>
> However, this code is not very reliable because the checked condition was true before the current statement. In these situations, a `select` clause is more convenient as explained below.

6.2.2. Close

When a channel is not going to be used anymore, it can be terminated with the built-in function `close`. If a closed channel is used, it causes a runtime panic. Receivers can know if a channel was closed using a multi-value receive operation (`x, ok := <- ch`). The first returned is a value sent through the channel, the second is a boolean indicating whether the reception was correct or not. This second value can be used to identify closed channels.

In Example 6.6, a goroutine sends numbers through a channel. Once it has finished, the channel is closed. The receiver (`main` function) runs an endless loop consuming the elements sent through the channel. When the channel is closed, the `found` variable becomes `false` and we know that the channel was closed.

Example 6.6: `close` function in channels.

```
1 package main
2
3 import (
4     "fmt"
5     "time"
```

```go
 6 )
 7
 8 func sender(out chan int) {
 9     for i:=0;i<5;i++ {
10         time.Sleep(time.Millisecond * 500)
11         out <- i
12     }
13     close(out)
14     fmt.Println("sender finished")
15 }
16
17 func main() {
18
19     ch := make(chan int)
20
21     go sender(ch)
22
23     for {
24         num, found := <- ch
25         if found {
26             fmt.Println(num)
27         } else {
28             fmt.Println("finished")
29             break
30         }
31     }
32 }
```

```
0
1
2
3
4
finished
```

6.2.3. Consuming data with range

Normally, we cannot know beforehand the number of values that are going to be sent through a channel. We can use to block the execution and wait for values until the channel is closed. Check how in Example 6.7 the loop in the main function consumes data from the channel until this is closed independently of the number of generated values.

Example 6.7: Channel consumption using range.

```go
1 package main
2
3 import "fmt"
4 func generator(ch chan int) {
5     for i:=0;i<5;i++{
6         ch <- i
7     }
8     close(ch)
```

```go
 9 }
10
11 func main() {
12     ch := make(chan int)
13
14     go generator(ch)
15
16     for x := range(ch) {
17         fmt.Println(x)
18     }
19     fmt.Println("Done")
20 }
```

```
0
1
2
3
4
Done
```

6.2.4. CHANNELS DIRECTION

The data flow direction in a channel can be specified.

```go
ch := make(chan int)      // sender and receiver
ch := make(<- chan int)   // receiver
ch := make(chan <- int)   // sender
```

This provides better type-safety and permits better utilization of channels. In Example 6.8, we define `sender` and `receiver` functions to send and receive values respectively. Because channel directions are set, if `receiver` tries to send data using the channel an error at compilation time will appear. And similarly, `sender` cannot read data from the channel.

Example 6.8: Channels direction.

```go
 1 package main
 2
 3 import (
 4     "fmt"
 5     "time"
 6 )
 7
 8 func receiver(input <- chan int) {
 9     for i := range input {
10         fmt.Println(i)
11     }
12 }
13
14 func sender(output chan <- int, n int) {
15     for i:=0;i<n;i++ {
16         time.Sleep(time.Millisecond * 500)
```

```
0
1
4
9
Done
```

```go
17            output <- i * i
18        }
19        close(output)
20 }
21
22
23 func main() {
24
25     ch := make(chan int)
26
27     go sender(ch, 4)
28     go receiver(ch)
29
30     time.Sleep(time.Second*5)
31     fmt.Println("Done")
32 }
```

6.3. Select

The `select` statement is somehow similar to the `switch` statement. From a set of send/receive operations, it blocks the execution until one operation is ready. Example 6.9, executes two different goroutines that send values through two different channels. See how the `select` statement can group the receive operations in a single statement. Inside the `select`, cases are evaluated in the same order they are defined. If two or more cases are ready then, a pseudo-random uniform selection chooses the next one. The `select` statement is executed only for a single operation, to keep on waiting for more messages it has to be iteratively executed like in a loop.

Example 6.9: select.

```go
1 package main
2
3 import (
4     "fmt"
5     "strconv"
6     "time"
7 )
8
9 func sendNumbers(out chan int) {
10     for i:=0; i < 5; i++ {
11         time.Sleep(time.Millisecond * 500)
12         out <- i
13     }
```

```
14        fmt.Println("no more numbers")
15  }
16
17  func sendMsgs(out chan string) {
18      for i:=0; i < 5; i++ {
19          time.Sleep(time.Millisecond * 300)
20          out <- strconv.Itoa(i)
21      }
22      fmt.Println("no more msgs")
23  }
24
25  func main() {
26      numbers := make(chan int)
27      msgs := make(chan string)
28
29      go sendNumbers(numbers)
30      go sendMsgs(msgs)
31
32      for i:=0;i<10;i++ {
33          select {
34          case num := <- numbers:
35              fmt.Printf("number %d\n", num)
36          case msg := <- msgs:
37              fmt.Printf("msg %s\n", msg)
38          }
39      }
40  }
```

```
msg 0
number 0
msg 1
msg 2
number 1
msg 3
number 2
msg 4
no more msgs
number 3
number 4
```

`select` accepts multi-value reception (`x, ok := <- ch`). This feature can be used to know if a channel is ready for reception or not. Example 6.10, extends the previous example to stop data reception when both channels are closed. Remember that in multi-value reception, the second value turns `false` when the channel is closed. Compared with the previous example, now we do not need to know beforehand the number of messages to be received. We can wait until the channels are closed.

Example 6.10: `select` with multi values.

```
1  package main
2
3  import (
4      "fmt"
5      "strconv"
6      "time"
7  )
8
9  func sendNumbers(out chan int) {
10     for i:=0; i < 5; i++ {
```

CHAPTER 6. CONCURRENCY

```
11              time.Sleep(time.Millisecond * 500)
12              out <- i
13          }
14          fmt.Println("no more numbers")
15          close(out)
16      }
17
18      func sendMsgs(out chan string) {
19          for i:=0; i < 5; i++ {
20              time.Sleep(time.Millisecond * 300)
21              out <- strconv.Itoa(i)
22          }
23          fmt.Println("no more msgs")
24          close(out)
25      }
26
27      func main() {
28          numbers := make(chan int)
29          msgs := make(chan string)
30
31          go sendNumbers(numbers)
32          go sendMsgs(msgs)
33
34          closedNums, closedMsgs := false, false
35
36          for !closedNums || !closedMsgs {
37              select {
38              case num, ok := <- numbers:
39                  if ok {
40                      fmt.Printf("number %d\n", num)
41                  } else {
42                      closedNums = true
43                  }
44              case msg, ok := <- msgs:
45                  if ok {
46                      fmt.Printf("msg %s\n", msg)
47                  } else {
48                      closedMsgs = true
49                  }
50              }
51          }
52      }
```

```
msg 0
number 0
msg 1
msg 2
number 1
msg 3
number 2
msg 4
no more msgs
number 3
number 4
no more numbers
```

The **select** statement is blocking. The execution will be blocked until at least one of the declared communications is ready. This can be changed by adding a **default** case which is executed when none of the communications is ready. It can be used to avoid errors when channels are not ready. In Example 6.11, we use an unbuffered channel that is never going to be ready. Using the **default** case, we can control this situation and run without panic. As an exercise, you can use a buffered channel to check how the execution changes.

Example 6.11: Non-blocking `select` using `default` cases.

```go
package main

import "fmt"

func main() {
    ch := make(chan int)
    //ch := make(chan int,1)

    select {
    case i := <-ch:
        fmt.Println("Received", i)
    default:
        fmt.Println("Nothing received")
    }

    select {
    case ch <- 42:
        fmt.Println("Send 42")
    default:
        fmt.Println("Nothing sent")
    }

    select {
    case i := <-ch:
        fmt.Println("Received", i)
    default:
        fmt.Println("Nothing received")
    }
}
```

```
Nothing received
Nothing sent
Nothing received
```

6.4. WAITGROUP

Normally, when working with several goroutines we have to wait until their completion. In order to facilitate this, Go offers the `WaitGroup` type in the `sync` package. This type has three methods `Add`, `Done`, and `Wait`. A `WaitGroup` works like a counter with the number of goroutines we are waiting to be finished. Every time a goroutine finishes, the `Done` method decreases the counter. The `Wait` method blocks the execution until the counter reaches zero.

Example 6.12, defines an example of consumer/producer with a function generating

CHAPTER 6. CONCURRENCY

tasks (random numbers) that are consumed by other goroutines. The `WaitGroup` variable `wg` is instantiated and incremented to 3 elements (`wg.Add(3)`). Notifying `wg` about completion is up to the goroutines. For this, we pass the `wg` by reference so they can notify their completion. Notice, that this is done with **defer** `wg.Done()` to ensure that the notification is sent. Finally, `wg.Wait()` waits until all the goroutines are finished.

Example 6.12: `WaitGroup` and several goroutines.

```go
package main

import (
    "fmt"
    "math/rand"
    "sync"
    "time"
)

func generator(ch chan int, wg *sync.WaitGroup) {
    defer wg.Done()
    for i:=0;i<5;i++ {
        time.Sleep(time.Millisecond*200)
        ch <- rand.Int()
    }
    close(ch)
    fmt.Println("Generator done")
}

func consumer(id int, sleep time.Duration,
    ch chan int, wg *sync.WaitGroup) {
    defer wg.Done()
    for task := range(ch) {
        time.Sleep(time.Millisecond*sleep)
        fmt.Printf("%d - task[%d]\n",id,task)
    }
    fmt.Printf("Consumer %d done\n",id)
}

func main() {
    rand.Seed(42)

    ch := make(chan int,10)
    var wg sync.WaitGroup
    wg.Add(3)

    go generator(ch,&wg)
    go consumer(1,400,ch,&wg)
    go consumer(2,100,ch,&wg)

```

```
2 - task
[3440579354231278675]
2 - task
[5571782338101878760]
1 - task[6087471365438564111]
2 - task
[1926012586526624009]
Generator done
Consumer 2 done
1 - task[404153945743547657]
Consumer 1 done
```

```
41        wg.Wait()
42 }
```

Similar behaviour can be obtained using channels. However, this approach is highly recommended in scenarios where several goroutines block the execution flow and their termination can be determined by the goroutines themselves.

6.5. TIMERS, TICKERS, AND TIMEOUTS

In concurrent scenarios time management becomes really important. During the execution several events may occur with different periods or timelines. For single events to occur in the future the `time` package offers the `Timer` type. A `Timer` has a channel `c` that triggers a signal after a given time. Similarly, the `Ticker` type triggers a signal for channel `c` for a given period.

Example 6.13: Timer and Ticker.

```
 1 package main
 2
 3 import (
 4     "fmt"
 5     "time"
 6 )
 7
 8 func worker(x *int) {
 9     for {
10         time.Sleep(time.Millisecond * 500)
11         *x = *x + 1
12     }
13 }
14
15 func main() {
16     timer := time.NewTimer(time.Second * 5)
17     ticker := time.NewTicker(time.Second)
18
19     x := 0
20     go worker(&x)
21
22     for {
23         select {
24         case <- timer.C:
25             fmt.Printf("timer -> %d\n", x)
26         case <- ticker.C:
27             fmt.Printf("ticker -> %d\n", x)
28         }
```

```
ticker -> 2
ticker -> 3
ticker -> 5
ticker -> 7
timer  -> 9
ticker -> 9
ticker -> 11
```

```
29            if x>=10 {
30                break
31            }
32        }
33 }
```

Example 6.13, checks the value of x over time using a Timer and a Ticker. The worker increases x by one every 500 milliseconds. The **select** statement can be used here to react when timer and ticker send an event. ticker will wake up every second finding x to be increased by two. Notice that worker sleeps for half second in every iteration. For timer there will be a single operation after five seconds. Notice, that worker could be implemented using a Ticker instead of time.Sleep.

Example 6.14: Timer and Ticker management.

```
1 package main
2
3 import (
4     "fmt"
5     "time"
6 )
7
8 func reaction(t *time.Ticker) {
9     for {
10        select {
11        case x := <-t.C:
12            fmt.Println("quick",x)
13        }
14    }
15 }
16
17 func slowReaction(t *time.Timer) {
18    select {
19    case x := <-t.C:
20        fmt.Println("slow", x)
21    }
22 }
23
24 func main() {
25     quick := time.NewTicker(time.Second)
26     slow := time.NewTimer(time.Second * 5)
27     stopper := time.NewTimer(time.Second * 4)
28     go reaction(quick)
29     go slowReaction(slow)
30
31     <- stopper.C
32     quick.Stop()
```

```
33
34      stopped := slow.Stop()
35      fmt.Println("Stopped before the event?",stopped)
36 }
```

```
quick 2021-01-13 19:56:59.2428 +0100 CET m=+1.004374708
quick 2021-01-13 19:57:00.240984 +0100 CET m=+2.002541186
quick 2021-01-13 19:57:01.240728 +0100 CET m=+3.002267097
quick 2021-01-13 19:57:02.241683 +0100 CET m=+4.003202851
Stopped before the event? true
```

Timers and tickers can be managed using `Stop()` and `Reset()` methods. Invoking the `Stop` method closes the channel and terminates the triggering of new events. In the case of timers, the method returns **true** if the invocation was triggered before the event was triggered.

In Example 6.14 we define two events, `quick` using a `Ticker` every second, and `slow` using a `Timer` triggered after 5 seconds. The third `Timer stopper` is set to 4 seconds. When the `stopper` timer is reached we stop `quick` and `slow`. Observe that `quick.Stop` has no returned value. In the case of `slow.Stop`, **true** value is returned as the timer was not triggered yet.

6.6. Context

Working with APIs or between processes requires additional control logic such as cancellations, timeouts or deadlines. If we send a request to an API, we wait a while for completion. Afterwards, we can assume the request expired. The `Context` type from the `context` package[1], offers constructions to deal with these situations.

The `Context` interface defines the elements of a common context in Go:

```
type Context interface {
    Deadline() (deadline time.Time, ok bool)
    Done() <-chan struct{}
    Err() error
    Value(key interface{}) interface{}
}
```

The `Deadline()` method returns the deadline for the context and **false** if no deadline was set. The `Done()` method returns a channel that is closed when the operations in the

[1]https://golang.org/pkg/context

context are completed. This channel is closed depending on a `cancel` function, a deadline or a timeout. `Err()` returns and **error** if any. Finally, `Value()` stores key-value pairs of elements that belong to the context.

A `Context` can be built using an empty context (`context.Background()`) or a previously defined context. Go provides four types of contexts with their corresponding initialization functions. These contexts are `WithCancel()`, `WithTimeout()`, `WithDeadline()`, and `WithValue()`.

6.6.1. WITHCANCEL

The function `context.WithCancel()` returns a context, and a `CancelFunc` type. This type, forces the context to be done. In Example 6.15, function `setter` is run simultaneously in several goroutines to increase a shared counter variable. This function receives a context by argument. In the `main` function the `cancel` function from the context is invoked informing about its termination. All the goroutines receive the message by checking the `Done()` method.

Example 6.15: Context WithCancel.

```
1  package main
2
3  import (
4      "context"
5      "fmt"
6      "sync/atomic"
7      "time"
8  )
9
10 func setter(id int, c *int32, ctx context.Context) {
11     t := time.NewTicker(time.Millisecond*300)
12     for {
13         select {
14         case <- ctx.Done():
15             fmt.Println("Done", id)
16             return
17         case <- t.C:
18             atomic.AddInt32(c, 1)
19         }
20     }
21 }
22
23 func main() {
24     ctx, cancel := context.WithCancel(context.Background())
25
26     var c int32 = 0
```

```
Final check:   15
Done 1
Done 3
Done 2
Done 4
Done 0
```

```
27      for i:=0;i<5;i++ {
28          go setter(i, &c, ctx)
29      }
30
31      time.Sleep(time.Second * 1)
32      fmt.Println("Final check: ", c)
33
34      cancel()
35      time.Sleep(time.Second)
36  }
```

Normally, the `cancel()` function is executed using **defer** to ensure that the context is terminated.

6.6.2. WithTimeout

Timeouts are a very common approach to avoid allocating resources for a long time. The `context.WithTimeout` function receives a `time.Duration` argument setting how much time to wait until the context is done. Example 6.16 iteratively executes a goroutine that takes an incrementally longer time to finish. The context is finished before we can run the fifth iteration. The **select** statement blocks the execution until we receive a new number or the context is done. Observe that in the case the context reaches the timeout, the `Err()` method is filled with the corresponding message.

Example 6.16: Context WithTimeout.

```
1  package main
2
3  import (
4      "context"
5      "fmt"
6      "time"
7  )
8
9  func work(i int, info chan int) {
10     t := time.Duration(i*100)*time.Millisecond
11     time.Sleep(t)
12     info <- i
13 }
14
15 func main() {
16     d := time.Millisecond * 300
17
18     ch := make(chan int)
19     i:=0
```

```
Received 0
Received 1
Received 2
Received 3
Done!!
context deadline
exceeded
```

```
20      for {
21          ctx, cancel := context.WithTimeout(context.Background(), d)
22          go work(i, ch)
23          select {
24          case x := <- ch:
25              fmt.Println("Received",x)
26          case <- ctx.Done():
27              fmt.Println("Done!!")
28          }
29          if ctx.Err()!=nil{
30              fmt.Println(ctx.Err())
31              return
32          }
33          cancel()
34          i++
35      }
36  }
```

> ⚠ **When working with contexts inside loops, cancel functions should not be deferred.** Remember that `defer` executes when the function returns, therefore all the resources allocated are not released until then.
>
> If there is a number of contexts declared inside a loop
>
> ```
> for ... {
>     ctx, cancel = context.WithCancel(context.Backgroun())
>     // defer cancel()   ---> release when the function returns
>     ...
>     cancel()
> }
> ```

6.6.3. WithDeadline

Similar to a timeout, this kind of context has an absolute termination time set. When the deadline is reached, the context is finished. Example 6.17, uses various goroutines to modify a shared variable. The context is set to expire after three seconds. Notice that this approach is similar to use a context with a timeout. We block the execution until the context is done (`<-ctx.Done()`). From the output, we can observe how the goroutines are informed about the context termination. Not all the done messages are printed because the program terminates before the goroutines have time to print the message.

Example 6.17: Context `WithDeadline`.

```go
package main

import (
    "context"
    "fmt"
    "sync/atomic"
    "time"
)

func accum(c *uint32, ctx context.Context) {
    t := time.NewTicker(time.Millisecond*250)
    for {
        select {
        case <- t.C:
            atomic.AddUint32(c, 1)
        case <- ctx.Done():
            fmt.Println("Done context")
            return
        }
    }
}

func main() {
    d := time.Now().Add(time.Second*3)
    ctx, cancel := context.WithDeadline(context.Background(), d)
    defer cancel()

    var counter uint32 = 0

    for i:=0;i<5;i++ {
        go accum(&counter, ctx)
    }

    <- ctx.Done()
    fmt.Println("counter is:", counter)
}
```

```
Done context
counter is: 57
Done context
Done context
```

6.6.4. WITHVALUE

A context can be defined by the information it contains. The `context.WithValue` function receives key and value arguments not returning a cancel function. In Example 6.18, we use a context with key `"action"` to define the action to be performed by a calculator function.

Example 6.18: Context `WithValue`.

```go
package main

import (
    "context"
    "errors"
    "fmt"
)

func main() {

    f := func(ctx context.Context, a int, b int) (int, error) {

        switch ctx.Value("action") {
        case "+":
            return a + b, nil
        case "-":
            return a - b, nil
        default:
            return 0, errors.New("unknown action")
        }
    }

    ctx := context.WithValue(context.Background(), "action", "+")
    r, err := f(ctx, 22, 20)
    fmt.Println(r, err)
    ctx2 := context.WithValue(context.Background(), "action", "-")
    r, err = f(ctx2, 22, 20)
    fmt.Println(r, err)
}
```

```
42 <nil>
2 <nil>
```

As it can be extracted from the example, these contexts are not attached to temporal restrictions and their termination can be determined by other factors such as an invalid authentication token.

6.6.5. PARENT CONTEXTS

When creating a new context this can use the empty `context.Background` or it can use another existing context. This can be used to stack different restrictions and generate more complex contexts. Example 6.19 combines a timeout context with a context with values. While the value selects what action to be performed, the timeout sets the time to wait until completion. Check that for the `"slow"` action the message is not printed because it takes longer than the timeout limit.

Example 6.19: Context WithValue.

```go
1  package main
2
3  import (
4      "context"
5      "fmt"
6      "time"
7  )
8
9  func calc(ctx context.Context) {
10     switch ctx.Value("action") {
11     case "quick":
12         fmt.Println("quick answer")
13     case "slow":
14         time.Sleep(time.Millisecond*500)
15         fmt.Println("slow answer")
16     case <- ctx.Done():
17         fmt.Println("Done!!!")
18     default:
19         panic("unknown action")
20     }
21 }
22
23 func main() {
24     t := time.Millisecond*300
25     ctx, cancel := context.WithTimeout(context.Background(), t)
26     qCtx := context.WithValue(ctx, "action", "quick")
27     defer cancel()
28
29     go calc(qCtx)
30     <-qCtx.Done()
31
32     ctx2, cancel2 := context.WithTimeout(context.Background(), t)
33     sCtx := context.WithValue(ctx2, "action", "slow")
34     defer cancel2()
35
36     go calc(sCtx)
37     <-sCtx.Done()
38     fmt.Println("Finished")
39 }
```

```
quick answer
Finished
```

6.7. ONCE

In certain scenarios, it only makes sense to execute certain operations once. If several goroutines can execute these operations, the `sync.Once` type ensures that they are only run once. Its method `Do` receives a function by an argument that is executed a single time. This type is very useful to use with initialization functions.

CHAPTER 6. CONCURRENCY

Example 6.20 starts five goroutines that try to initialize a value. However, the initialization time for each one is random. Using `Once` we can register the first goroutine to be started. When the `Do` method is invoked, the other goroutines simply continue the program flow.

Example 6.20: Single actionable variable using Once.

```go
package main

import (
    "fmt"
    "math/rand"
    "sync"
    "time"
)

var first int

func setter(i int, ch chan bool, once *sync.Once) {
    t := rand.Uint32() % 300
    time.Sleep(time.Duration(t)*time.Millisecond)
    once.Do(func(){
        first = i
    })
    ch <- true
    fmt.Println(i,"Done")
}

func main() {
    rand.Seed(time.Now().UnixNano())

    var once sync.Once

    ch := make(chan bool)
    for i:=0;i<10;i++ {
        go setter(i, ch, &once)
    }

    for i:=0;i<10;i++{
        <- ch
    }
    fmt.Println("The first was", first)
}
```

```
2 Done
3 Done
1 Done
4 Done
0 Done
The first was 2
```

6.8. Mutexes

Race conditions occur when a variable is accessed by two or several goroutines concurrently. To ensure the correctness of the program, we can set mutual exclusion areas that force goroutines to wait until no goroutine is operating in that area. The type `Mutex` and its methods `Lock()` and `Unlock()` restrict the access to code regions. When a goroutine attempts to operate in a code region it must acquire the mutex by invoking the `Lock` method. After the operations in the mutual exclusion finish, the `Unlock` method returns the control of the region and other goroutines can enter.

Example 6.21 shows a common scenario with three goroutines accessing a common variable x. The writer fills the map variable x by multiplying values from the previous index by a given factor. Observe that the two writers modify x with different frequencies. To make it concurrent safe a mutual exclusion area is defined around `x[i]=x[i-1]*factor`. The output shows how when the reader prints the current x value, sometimes the values correspond to modifications done by the first or second goroutine.

Example 6.21: Mutex.

```
package main

import (
    "fmt"
    "sync"
    "time"
)

func writer(x map[int]int, factor int, m *sync.Mutex) {
    i := 1
    for {
        time.Sleep(time.Second)
        m.Lock()
        x[i] = x[i-1] * factor
        m.Unlock()
        i++
    }
}

func reader(x map[int]int, m *sync.Mutex) {
    for {
        time.Sleep(time.Millisecond*500)
        m.Lock()
        fmt.Println(x)
        m.Unlock()
    }
}
```

```
map[0:1]
map[0:1 1:2]
map[0:1 1:3]
map[0:1 1:3 2:6]
map[0:1 1:3 2:9]
map[0:1 1:3 2:9 3:18]
map[0:1 1:3 2:9 3:27]
map[0:1 1:3 2:9 3:27 4:54]
```

```
28
29  func main() {
30      x := make(map[int]int)
31      x[0]=1
32
33      m := sync.Mutex{}
34      go writer(x, 2, &m)
35      go reader(x, &m)
36
37      time.Sleep(time.Millisecond * 300)
38      go writer(x, 3, &m)
39
40      time.Sleep(time.Second*4)
41  }
```

The `Lock` method blocks the thread execution. This means that the longer the exclusion area, the longer is the wait. The size of the mutual exclusion area must be small enough to permit the correctness of the execution.

6.9. ATOMICS

The package `sync/atomic` defines a set of functions for atomic operations. Atomics use low-level atomic memory primitives outperforming mutexes when used correctly. However, as stated in the Go reference, these functions must be used with care and only for low-level applications. For other applications, the `sync` package offers better tools (`WaitGroup`, `Mutex`, etc.).

Atomics offer functions for specific native types. See Table 6.1 for a description of the available functions for type `int32`. Similar functions are available for `uint32`, `int64`, `uint64`, and `uintptr`.

Function	Description
`AddInt32(addr *int32, delta int32) (new int32)`	Add a delta value
`CompareAndSwapInt32(addr *int32, old, new int32) (swapped bool)`	If value at *addr is equal to old, swap with new
`LoadInt32(addr *int32) (val int32)`	Safe load
`StoreInt32(addr *int32, val int32)`	Safe store
`SwapInt32(addr *int32, new int32) (old int32)`	Swap value at *addr with new

Table 6.1: Atomic operations available for the `int32` type.

Working with atomics is similar to work with mutexes, we ensure safe reading and writing operations for shared variables. Example 6.22 shows how two goroutines concurrently modify the shared `counter` variable and how this is accessed to be printed. Notice how `atomic.AddInt32` ensures safe concurrent writings without the need for a mutual exclusion area. On the other side, to ensure a safe read we use `atomic.LoadInt32`.

Example 6.22: Atomic access to variable.

```go
package main

import (
    "fmt"
    "sync/atomic"
    "time"
)

func increaser(counter *int32) {
    for {
        atomic.AddInt32(counter,2)
        time.Sleep(time.Millisecond*500)
    }
}

func decreaser(counter *int32) {
    for {
        atomic.AddInt32(counter, -1)
        time.Sleep(time.Millisecond*250)
    }
}

func main() {
    var counter int32 = 0

    go increaser(&counter)
    go decreaser(&counter)

    for i:=0;i<5;i++{
        time.Sleep(time.Millisecond*500)
        fmt.Println(atomic.LoadInt32(&counter))
    }
    fmt.Println(atomic.LoadInt32(&counter))
}
```

```
0
1
2
0
2
2
```

Atomic operations are designed only for the native types shown in Table 6.1. Fortunately, Go offers the type `Value` that can load and store any type by using the empty interface `interface{}`. Example 6.23 shows a case with a shared variable of type struct. The `Value` type comes with the `Load()` and `Store()` functions that permit to safely read and write our **struct**. In this example, `updater` sets new values to the shared variable and one `observer` checks its content. By invoking `monitor.Load`, the observer loads the latest stored version of the struct. To ensure concurrent writing, a mutual exclusion region must be defined. Observe that the fields of the `Monitor` type are not modified atomically and this may lead to concurrency problems if no mutex is used.

Example 6.23: Atomic access to `Value` type.

```go
package main

import (
    "fmt"
    "sync"
    "sync/atomic"
    "time"
)

type Monitor struct {
    ActiveUsers int
    Requests    int
}

func updater(monitor atomic.Value, m *sync.Mutex) {
    for {
        time.Sleep(time.Millisecond*500)
        m.Lock()
        current := monitor.Load().(*Monitor)
        current.ActiveUsers += 100
        current.Requests += 300
        monitor.Store(current)
        m.Unlock()
    }
}

func observe(monitor atomic.Value) {
    for {
        time.Sleep(time.Second)
        current := monitor.Load()
        fmt.Printf("%v\n", current)
    }
}

func main() {
    var monitor atomic.Value
    monitor.Store(&Monitor{0,0})
    m := sync.Mutex{}

    go updater(monitor, &m)
    go observe(monitor)

    time.Sleep(time.Second * 5)
}
```

```
&{200 600}
&{300 900}
&{500 1500}
&{700 2100}
```

6.10. SUMMARY

This Chapter describes the set of tools Go offers to tackle concurrent problems. The simple but yet powerful design of Go makes it possible to easily design highly concurrent solutions in just a few lines of code. We explain how concurrent goroutines can synchronize each other using channels with various examples. Components from `sync` package such as `Once`, `Mutex`, and `atomic` are detailed and must be understood by newcomers. Finally, this Chapter makes an exhaustive explanation of different context types and how and where they can be used.

7
INPUT/OUTPUT

Data is not isolated into programs, it has to flow from and to other programs, systems or devices. Input/Output operations are expected to be present in most programs. Go provides basic interfaces in the `io` package that are extended by other packages such as `ioutils` or `os`. This Chapter explains the basics of I/O operations and provides examples of how to use them in Go.

7.1. READERS AND WRITERS

I/O operations can be summarized by readers and writers. Go defines the `Reader` and `Writer` interfaces in the `io` package[1]. A `Reader` must implement a read operation that receives a target byte array where the read data is stored, it returns the number of bytes read and error if any. A `Writer` takes a byte array to be written and returns the number of written bytes and error if any.

```
type Reader interface {
    Read(p []byte) (n int, err error)
}
```

```
type Writer interface {
    Write(p []byte) (n int, err error)
}
```

Example 7.1 shows a `Reader` implementation for strings. This reader fills the array `p` with as many characters as `len(p)` starting from the last read position stored in `from`. The first part in the `Read` method adds some error control. If all the characters from the string were processed, it returns EOF to indicate that no more characters are available. Notice that the `target` array is reused so in those iterations where the number of read characters

---
[1]https://golang.org/pkg/io

is smaller than the length of the array it will contain characters from previous calls.

Example 7.1: Implementation of a Reader interface.

```go
package main

import (
    "errors"
    "fmt"
    "io"
)

type MyReader struct {
    data string
    from int
}

func(r *MyReader) Read(p []byte) (int, error) {
    if p == nil {
        return -1, errors.New("nil target array")
    }
    if len(r.data) <= 0 || r.from == len(r.data){
        return 0, io.EOF
    }
    n := len(r.data) - r.from
    if len(p) < n {
        n = len(p)
    }
    for i:=0;i < n; i++ {
        b := byte(r.data[r.from])
        p[i] = b
        r.from++
    }
    if r.from == len(r.data) {
        return n, io.EOF
    }
    return n, nil
}

func main() {
    target := make([]byte,5)
    empty := MyReader{}
    n, err := empty.Read(target)
    fmt.Printf("Read %d: Error: %v\n",n,err)
    mr := MyReader{"Save the world with Go!!!",0}
    n, err = mr.Read(target)
    for err == nil {
        fmt.Printf("Read %d: Error: %v -> %s\n",n,err, target)
        n, err = mr.Read(target)
```

```
Read 0: Error: EOF
Read 5: Error: <nil> -> Save
Read 5: Error: <nil> -> the w
Read 5: Error: <nil> -> orld
Read 5: Error: <nil> -> with
Read 5: Error: EOF -> Go!!!
```

CHAPTER 7. INPUT/OUTPUT 115

```
46      }
47      fmt.Printf("Read %d: Error: %v -> %s\n",n,err, target)
48 }
```

Implementing a writer is similar to implementing a reader. Example 7.2 implements a writer designed with a limiting number of bytes to be written in each call. Go specifies that when the number of written bytes is smaller than the size of p an error must be filled. Additionally, we consider that an empty p corresponds to an EOF. Our writer will add the content of p to the current data string in batches. Observe that all iterations except the last one return an error due to the size limit.

Example 7.2: Implementation of a Writer interface.

```
1  package main
2
3  import (
4      "errors"
5      "io"
6      "fmt"
7  )
8
9  type MyWriter struct {
10     data string
11     size int
12 }
13
14 func (mw *MyWriter) Write(p []byte) (int, error) {
15     if len(p) == 0 {
16         return 0, io.EOF
17     }
18     n := mw.size
19     var err error = nil
20     if len(p) < mw.size {
21         n = len(p)
22     } else {
23         err = errors.New("p larger than size")
24     }
25     mw.data = mw.data + string(p[0:n])
26
27     return n, err
28 }
29
30 func main() {
31     msg := []byte("the world with Go!!!")
32
33     mw := MyWriter{"Save ",6}
34     i := 0
```

```
35      var err error
36      for err == nil && i < len(msg) {
37          n, err := mw.Write(msg[i:])
38          fmt.Printf("Written %d error %v --> %s\n", n, err, mw.data)
39          i = i + n
40      }
41  }
```

```
Written 6 error p larger than size --> Save the wo
Written 6 error p larger than size --> Save the world wi
Written 6 error p larger than size --> Save the world with Go!
Written 2 error <nil> --> Save the world with Go!!!
```

These examples are shown just to demonstrate how to work with these interfaces. Actually, the `io` package has more interfaces such as `ByteReader`, `ByteWriter`, `PipeReader`, `ReadSeeker`, etc. Before defining your interfaces, check the Go reference for existing ones or other types implementing these interfaces.

7.2. Reading and Writing files

We mentioned that the `io` package groups basic I/O operations and their interfaces. The package `io/util`[2] has implementations of these interfaces ready to be used. Example 7.3 writes a message into a file and then reads it. The function `ioutil.WriteFile` requires the file path, the content of the file to be written, and the file permissions. Notice that the file content is intended to be a byte array. If using strings, the casting is straight forward. On the other side, the `ioutil.ReadFile` function returns a byte of arrays with the content of the file. It is important to highlight that both functions may return errors and these have to be controlled.

Example 7.3: File writing and reading with `ioutil`.

```
1  package main
2
3  import (
4      "fmt"
5      "io/ioutil"
6  )
7
```

---

[2]https://golang.org/pkg/io/ioutil/

CHAPTER 7. INPUT/OUTPUT

```go
 8 func main() {
 9     msg := "Save the world with Go!!!"
10     filePath := "/tmp/msg"
11
12     err := ioutil.WriteFile(filePath,
13         []byte(msg), 0644)
14     if err != nil {
15         panic(err)
16     }
17
18     read, err := ioutil.ReadFile(filePath)
19     if err != nil{
20         panic(err)
21     }
22
23     fmt.Printf("%s\n", read)
24 }
```

```
Save the world with Go
!!!
```

The `ioutil` simplifies the steps to be carried out when working with files. It heavily uses the `os` package that provides an operating system independent interface. This package is closer to the operating system including additional entities such as file descriptors. This makes possible file manipulation at a lower level.

Example 7.4 writes the items of an array to a file using a loop instead of a single statement like in the previous example. First, we create a file at the desired path with `os.Create`. This function returns an open file descriptor with a large number of available methods[3]. Next, we can use any of the writing available methods to write our content. Finally, we to close the file to release the descriptor (`defer f.Close()`).

Example 7.4: File writing with os.

```go
 1 package main
 2
 3 import "os"
 4
 5 func main() {
 6     filePath := "/tmp/msg"
 7     msg := []string{
 8         "Rule", "the", "world", "with", "Go!!!"}
 9
10     f, err := os.Create(filePath)
11     if err != nil {
12         panic(err)
13     }
14     defer f.Close()
15
```

---

[3]https://golang.org/pkg/os/#File

```go
16      for _, s := range msg {
17          f.WriteString(s+"\n")
18      }
19  }
```

Using low-level functions we have better control of read and write operations. For example, we can read and write portions of files using the `Seek` method from the `File` type. This method indicates the offset to be used when writing or reading a file. In Example 7.5 `Seek` is used to modify given certain positions in the content of a file and then reads the modified content. After using `Seek`, we have to set the pointer to the first position of the file with `file.Seek(0,0)`, otherwise the read content would start at the last modified position.

Example 7.5: Utilization of file descriptors with os.

```go
1  package main
2
3  import (
4      "fmt"
5      "os"
6  )
7
8  func main() {
9      tmp := os.TempDir()
10     file, err := os.Create(tmp+"/myfile")
11     if err != nil {
12         panic(err)
13     }
14     defer file.Close()
15
16     msg := "Save the world with Go!!!"
17
18     _, err = file.WriteString(msg)
19     if err != nil {
20         panic(err)
21     }
22
23     positions := []int{4, 10, 20}
24     for _, i := range positions {
25         _, err := file.Seek(int64(i),0)
26         if err != nil {
27             panic(err)
28         }
29         file.Write([]byte("X"))
30     }
31     // Reset
32     file.Seek(0,0)
```

```
SaveXthe wXrld with Xo!!!
```

```
33      // Read the result
34      result := make([]byte,len(msg))
35      _, err = file.Read(result)
36      if err != nil {
37          panic(err)
38      }
39      fmt.Printf("%s\n",result)
40  }
```

7.3. Standard I/O

The standard I/O follows the same principles of writers and readers. The main difference is the utilization of os.Stdin, os.Stdout, and os.Stderr variables. These variables are open file descriptors to standard input, output, and error. Because they are variables of type File they offer some of the methods explained in the previous section.

Example 7.6 writes a message to the standard output using the os.Stdout variable. The result is similar to use fmt.Print. However, because we are using a file descriptor we can get the number of written bytes. Notice that the end of line "\n" is also a character.

Example 7.6: Writing to standard output with os.Stdout

```
1  package main
2
3  import (
4      "fmt"
5      "os"
6  )
7
8  func main() {
9      msg := []byte("Save the world with Go!!!\n")
10     n, err := os.Stdout.Write(msg)
11     if err != nil {
12         panic(err)
13     }
14     fmt.Printf("Written %d characters\n",n)
15 }
```

```
Save the world with Go!!!
Written 26 characters
```

Reading from standard input may look complicated because of the interaction with the keyboard. However, from the point of view of the operating system, this is like writing to a file. Example 7.7 reads a message from standard input and prints the same message in upper case. By pressing enter, we insert the EOF character that finishes the stream. This example uses a fixed size target array. At the time of printing the result, we have to select a slice as long as the number of read characters. The reader can check how by removing this limitation unreadable characters will be printed because the array has not been initialized.

Example 7.7: Reading from standard input with `os.Stdin`

```go
package main

import (
    "fmt"
    "os"
    "strings"
)

func main() {
    target := make([]byte, 50)
    n, err := os.Stdin.Read(target)
    if err != nil {
        panic(err)
    }
    msg := string(target[:n])
    fmt.Println(n, strings.ToUpper(msg))
}
```

```
>>> save the world with go!!!
26 SAVE THE WORLD WITH GO!!!
```

In the previous example, the size of the target array limits the amount of data that can be received from the standard input. When the input is larger than the available size the remainder will be lost. This can be solved using buffers. The `bufio`[4] package implements buffered readers and writers that are very useful when the amount of incoming or outgoing data is unknown or exceeds a reasonable size for in-memory solutions.

The Example 7.8 reads a string from the standard input and returns it transformed to uppercase like in the previous example. Buffered readers come with various helping functions and methods. The used `ReadString` returns the string from the beginning until the argument delimiter is found.

Example 7.8: Standard input reading using `bufio`.

```go
package main

import (
    "bufio"
    "fmt"
    "os"
    "strings"
```

---

[4]https://golang.org/pkg/bufio/

CHAPTER 7. INPUT/OUTPUT

```
 8  )
 9
10  func main() {
11      reader := bufio.NewReader(os.Stdin)
12      fmt.Print(">>> What do you have to say?\n")
13      fmt.Print("<<< ")
14      text, err := reader.ReadString('\n')
15      if err != nil {
16          panic(err)
17      }
18      fmt.Println(">>> You're right!!!")
19      fmt.Println(strings.ToUpper(text))
20  }
```

```
>>> What do you have to say?
<<< go rules
>>> You're right!!!
GO RULES
```

The `Scanner` type can be particularly useful if we have a stream that has to be split into certain pieces. Example 7.9 uses a scanner to read lines from the standard input until the total accumulated length of the input strings exceeds 15 characters. The delimiter can be customized defining a split function[5].

Example 7.9: Standard input reading using `bufio` scanners.

```
 1  package main
 2
 3  import (
 4      "bufio"
 5      "fmt"
 6      "os"
 7  )
 8
 9  func main() {
10      scanner := bufio.NewScanner(os.Stdin)
11      fmt.Println(">>> What do you have to say?\n")
12      counter := 0
13      for scanner.Scan() {
14          text := scanner.Text()
15          counter = counter + len(text)
16          if counter > 15 {
17              break
18          }
19      }
20      fmt.Println("that's enough")
21  }
```

```
>>> What do you have to say?

Rule the world
with
that's enough
```

Example 7.10 demonstrate how to use a `bufio.NewWriter` with the standard output. The program emulates a typing machine by printing the characters of a string with a

---
[5] https://golang.org/pkg/bufio/#Scanner

temporal sleep between each character. Notice that the `Flush()` method has to be invoked to force the buffer to be printed.

Example 7.10: Standard output writing.

```go
package main

import (
    "bufio"
    "os"
    "time"
)

func main() {
    writer := bufio.NewWriter(os.Stdout)

    msg := "Rule the world with Golang!!!"
    for _, letter := range msg {
        time.Sleep(time.Millisecond*300)
        writer.WriteByte(byte(letter))
        writer.Flush()
    }
}
```

```
Save the world with Go
!!!
```

7.4. Summary

This Chapter explores the simple and efficient approach Go follows to tackle input/output operations. We explain and demonstrate how writers and readers are the cornerstones of I/O and how `ioutils` and `os` packages offer solutions at a high or low level.

8. ENCODINGS

We can find popular formats such as CSV, JSON, XML or YAML that are used to represent data from a byte level to a human-readable format. Other formats such as base64 or PEM data serialization are oriented to facilitate machine to machine interaction. In Go, the package `encoding` offers a set of subpackages that facilitate the conversion from Go types to these formats and the other way around. Many concepts explained in this Chapter were already introduced in Chapter 7 when we explained readers and writers. In this Chapter, we explore CSV, JSON, and XML manipulation techniques. Additionally, we present how to work with YAML using the GO-yaml third-party package.

8.1. CSV

Comma Separated Values [9] (CSV) is a widely used format to represent tabular data. Go provides CSV read/write operators in the package `encoding/csv`. Every line from a CSV is defined as a CSV record and every record contains the items separated by commas.

In order to read CSV data we use a `Reader` type that converts CSV lines into CSV records. Example 8.1 shows how a `csv.Reader` processes a string with CSV content. Notice that CSV are partially typed and in the case of strings they have to quoted like in variable `in`. The `Read` method returns the next CSV record or error if any. Like in any other `Reader` an `EOF` error is reached when no more records are available. Every record is represented using a `[]string`.

Example 8.1: CSV reading.

```
1  package main
```

```go
 2
 3 import (
 4     "encoding/csv"
 5     "fmt"
 6     "io"
 7     "log"
 8     "strings"
 9 )
10
11
12 func main() {
13     in := `user_id,score,password
14 "Gopher",1000,"admin"
15 "BigJ",10,"1234"
16 "GGBoom",,"1111"
17 `
18     r := csv.NewReader(strings.NewReader(in))
19
20     for {
21         record, err := r.Read()
22         if err == io.EOF {
23             break
24         }
25         if err != nil {
26             log.Fatal(err)
27         }
28         fmt.Println(record)
29     }
30 }
```

```
[user_id score password]
[Gopher 1000 admin]
[BigJ 10 1234]
[GGBoom   1111]
```

Example 8.2 writes CSV records to standard output. Every CSV record is a string array that has to be passed to the `Write` method. Finally, the `Flush` method ensures that we send all the buffered data to the standard output.

The writing process follows a similar approach as shown in Example 8.2. Instead of converting from strings to CSV records, the writer works oppositely.

Example 8.2: CSV writing.

```go
1 package main
2
3 import (
4     "encoding/csv"
5     "os"
6 )
7
8 func main() {
9     out := [][]string{
```

```
10          {"user_id","score","password"},
11          {"Gopher","1000","admin"},
12          {"BigJ","10","1234"},
13          {"GGBoom","","1111"},
14      }
15      writer := csv.NewWriter(os.Stdout)
16      for _, rec := range out {
17          err := writer.Write(rec)
18          if err != nil {
19              panic(err)
20          }
21      }
22      writer.Flush()
23
24 }
```

```
user_id,score,password
Gopher,1000,admin
BigJ,10,1234
GGBoom,,1111
```

8.2. JSON

The JavaScript Object Notation [4] (JSON) is a light-weight data interchange format defined by ECMA in 1999. It has turned extremely popular because it is human readable and easy to parse. JSON processing operators are available at `encoding/json`. This package provides `Marhsal` and `Unmarshal` functions that convert types to a JSON representation in `[]byte`, and vice versa.

The `Marshal` function converts booleans, integers, floats, strings, arrays, and slices into its corresponding JSON representation. Example 8.3 shows the output generated after marshalling various types. Notice that the `Marshal` function returns a `[]byte` with the JSON representation of the input and `error` in case of failure.

Example 8.3: JSON marshalling.

```
1 package main
2
3 import (
4 "encoding/json"
5 "fmt"
6 )
7
8 func main() {
9     number, err := json.Marshal(42)
10    if err!=nil{
11        panic(err)
12    }
13    fmt.Println(string(number))
```

```
42
3.14
"This is a msg!!!"
[1,1,2,3,5,8]
{"one":1,"two":2}
```

```go
	float, _ := json.Marshal(3.14)
	fmt.Println(string(float))

	msg, _ := json.Marshal("This is a msg!!!")
	fmt.Println(string(msg))

	numbers, _ := json.Marshal([]int{1,1,2,3,5,8})
	fmt.Println(string(numbers))

	aMap, _ := json.Marshal(map[string]int{"one":1,"two":2})
	fmt.Println(string(aMap))
}
```

If a JSON is correctly formed, the `Unmarshal` function can convert it to a previously known type. Example 8.4 recovers JSON representations of `int` and `map[string]int`. The unmarshalling process requires a pointer to a type compatible with the data to be unmarshalled and returns an error if the process fails. Observe that the output from this example is the string representation of Go types, not JSON representations.

Example 8.4: JSON unmarshalling.

```go
package main

import (
"encoding/json"
"fmt"
)

func main() {

	aNumber, _ := json.Marshal(42)

	var recoveredNumber int = -1
	err := json.Unmarshal(aNumber, &recoveredNumber)
	if err!= nil {
		panic(err)
	}
	fmt.Println(recoveredNumber)


	aMap, _ := json.Marshal(map[string]int{"one":1,"two":2})

	recoveredMap := make(map[string]int)
	err = json.Unmarshal(aMap, &recoveredMap)
	if err != nil {
		panic(err)
```

```
42
map[one:1 two:2]
```

```
26      }
27      fmt.Println(recoveredMap)
28 }
```

Structs can also be used with `Marshal` and `Unmarshal` functions. Actually, Go provides special tags to help in this task. Fields can be tagged to indicate how they have to be transformed to JSON.

In Example 8.5, we define a database of users where users are represented with a `User` value. Every field is tagged with an expression that consists of

```
FieldName type `json:"JSONfieldName,omitempty"`
```

This tag defines how to name the field in the JSON object, and whether to omit it if the zero value is found. In our example, `userC` has no `Score`. When printing the marshalled representation (`dbJson`), notice that one score is missing. Furthermore, the `password` field is always missing. This happens because the field visibility does not allow exporting values. In this case, we could consider this a good practice to hide user passwords.

Example 8.5: Custom struct JSON marshalling.

```go
1  package main
2
3  import (
4      "bytes"
5      "encoding/json"
6      "fmt"
7  )
8
9  type User struct {
10     UserId   string `json:"userId,omitempty"`
11     Score    int    `json:"score,omitempty"`
12     password string `json:"password,omitempty"`
13 }
14
15 func main() {
16
17     userA := User{"Gopher", 1000, "admin"}
18     userB := User{"BigJ", 10, "1234"}
19     userC := User{UserId: "GGBoom", password: "1111"}
20
21     db := []User{userA, userB, userC}
22     dbJson, err := json.Marshal(&db)
23     if err != nil {
24         panic(err)
```

```
25      }
26
27      var recovered []User
28      err = json.Unmarshal(dbJson, &recovered)
29      if err != nil{
30          panic(err)
31      }
32      fmt.Println(recovered)
33
34      var indented bytes.Buffer
35      err = json.Indent(&indented, dbJson,"","    ")
36      if err != nil {
37          panic(err)
38      }
39      fmt.Println(indented.String())
40 }
```

```
[{"userId":"Gopher","score":1000},{"userId":"BigJ","score":10},{"userId":"GGBoom"}]
[
    {
        "userId": "Gopher",
        "score": 1000
    },
    {
        "userId": "BigJ",
        "score": 10
    },
    {
        "userId": "GGBoom"
    }
]
[{Gopher 1000 } {BigJ 10 } {GGBoom 0 }]
```

To improve the readability of our JSON output, this can be unmarshalled with indentation. The `Indent` function adds indentation and sends the output to a buffered type (line 35). Finally, the example shows the unmarshalled struct. In this case, the `score` is displayed even when it is the zero value. Observe, that the field omission only works during marshalling. In the unmarshalling process, omitted fields are simply set to the zero value.

8.3. XML

The Extensible Markup Language[15] (XML) is a markup language developed by the W3C back in 1998. Like JSON, it is human-readable and easy to parse. However, it is very verbose which limits its applicability in certain scenarios. The package `encoding/xml` provides functions to work with this format. The package works similarly to the `encoding/json` package explained in the previous section. They share the same interfaces from the `encoding` package. However, there are certain limitations for XML we will explain in the examples below.

Example 8.6 transforms various variables into their XML representation. The `Marhsal` function returns a `[]byte` with the representation and an error if any. The process is similar to the one described for the JSON format. A more detailed explanation about how the different types are converted into XML can be found in the package documentation [1].

Example 8.6: XML marshalling.

```go
package main

import (
    "encoding/xml"
    "fmt"
)

func main() {
    number, err := xml.Marshal(42)
    if err!=nil{
        panic(err)
    }
    fmt.Println(string(number))

    float, _ := xml.Marshal(3.14)
    fmt.Println(string(float))

    msg, _ := xml.Marshal("This is a msg!!!")
    fmt.Println(string(msg))

    numbers, _ := xml.Marshal([]int{1,2,2,3,5,8})
    fmt.Println(string(numbers))

    aMap, err := xml.Marshal(map[string]int{"one":1,"two":2})
    fmt.Println(err)
    fmt.Println("-",string(aMap),"-")
}
```

---

[1] https://golang.org/pkg/encoding/xml/#Marshal

```
<int>42</int>
<float64>3.14</float64>
<string>This is a msg!!!</string>
<int>1</int><int>2</int><int>2</int><int>3</int><int>5</int><int>8</int>
xml: unsupported type: map[string]int
- -
```

Notice that in the case of marshalling **map[string]int** we get an error. Unlike in Example 8.3 where we could marshal the same type into a properly formed JSON, we cannot directly do the same in XML. This is because there is not a single way of representing a map into XML. For this reason, the package implementation excludes the map **map** type from marshalling.

For this case, we have to define our marshaller. To do this, we can create a type that implements methods MarshalXML and UnmarshalXML. These methods will be invoked during marshal and unmarshal operations so we can control the XML representation of any type[2]. Example 8.7 defines the conversion for a **map[string]string** type using keys as element tags and values as data elements. The code does not control all the scenarios, but it may serve as a starting point for the reader to understand custom XML marshallers.

Example 8.7: XML unmarshalling.

```go
package main

import (
    "encoding/xml"
    "errors"
    "fmt"
)

type MyMap map[string]string

func (s MyMap) MarshalXML(e *xml.Encoder, start xml.StartElement) error {
    tokens := []xml.Token{start}

    for key, value := range s {
        t := xml.StartElement{Name: xml.Name{"", key}}
        tokens = append(tokens, t, xml.CharData(value), xml.EndElement{t.Name})
    }

    tokens = append(tokens, xml.EndElement{start.Name})

    for _, t := range tokens {
        err := e.EncodeToken(t)
```

---

[2]Check the package reference for other examples.

CHAPTER 8. ENCODINGS

```go
23            if err != nil {
24                return err
25            }
26        }
27
28        return e.Flush()
29 }
30
31 func (a MyMap) UnmarshalXML(d *xml.Decoder, start xml.StartElement) error {
32
33        key := ""
34        val := ""
35
36        for {
37
38            t, _ := d.Token()
39            switch tt := t.(type) {
40
41            case xml.StartElement:
42                key = tt.Name.Local
43            case xml.CharData:
44                val = string(tt)
45            case xml.EndElement:
46                if len(key) != 0{
47                    a[key] = val
48                    key,val = "", ""
49                }
50                if tt.Name == start.Name {
51                    return nil
52                }
53
54            default:
55                return errors.New(fmt.Sprintf("uknown %T",t))
56            }
57        }
58
59        return nil
60 }
61
62
63 func main() {
64
65        var theMap MyMap = map[string]string{"one": "1","two":"2","three":"3"}
66        aMap, _ := xml.MarshalIndent(&theMap, "", "    ")
67        fmt.Println(string(aMap))
68
69        var recoveredMap MyMap = make(map[string]string)
70
71        err := xml.Unmarshal(aMap, &recoveredMap)
72        if err != nil {
```

```
73        panic(err)
74    }
75
76    fmt.Println(recoveredMap)
77 }
```

```
<MyMap>
    <one>1</one>
    <two>2</two>
    <three>3</three>
</MyMap>
map[one:1 three:3 two:2]
```

Excluding situations like the one described in the previous example, type fields can be tagged to facilitate its XML conversion. Example 8.8 is very similar to Example 8.5. In both cases, we use the same User type with the same omit options. However, we have to create an additional type UsersArray which contains the array of users. As an exercise, check what happens when a []User type is directly passed to the marshal function.

Example 8.8: XML struct marshalling.

```
1  package main
2
3  import (
4      "encoding/xml"
5      "fmt"
6  )
7
8  type User struct {
9      UserId   string `xml:"userId,omitempty"`
10     Score    int    `xml:"score,omitempty"`
11     password string `xml:"password,omitempty"`
12 }
13
14 type UsersArray struct {
15     Users []User `xml:"users,omitempty"`
16 }
17
18 func main() {
19
20     userA := User{"Gopher", 1000, "admin"}
21     userB := User{"BigJ", 10, "1234"}
22     userC := User{UserId: "GGBoom", password: "1111"}
23
24     db := UsersArray{[]User{userA, userB, userC}}
```

```go
25      dbXML, err := xml.Marshal(&db)
26      if err != nil {
27          panic(err)
28      }
29
30      var recovered UsersArray
31      err = xml.Unmarshal(dbXML, &recovered)
32      if err != nil{
33          panic(err)
34      }
35      fmt.Println(recovered)
36
37      var indented []byte
38      indented, err = xml.MarshalIndent(recovered,"","    ")
39      if err != nil {
40          panic(err)
41      }
42      fmt.Println(string(indented))
43 }
```

```
{[{Gopher 1000 } {BigJ 10 } {GGBoom 0 }]}
<UsersArray>
    <users>
        <userId>Gopher</userId>
        <score>1000</score>
    </users>
    <users>
        <userId>BigJ</userId>
        <score>10</score>
    </users>
    <users>
        <userId>GGBoom</userId>
    </users>
</UsersArray>
```

8.4. YAML

YAML [18] (Yet Another Markup Language) is a data serialization language that is human-readable and easy to parse. It is a superset of JSON [17] although it uses indentation to indicate nested entities. This format has gained popularity as a default format for configuration files. Go does not offer any YAML support in the standard library. However, we can find third-party modules with all the necessary tools to use this format.

This section covers the utilization of go-yaml [3] to marshal and unmarshal YAML content. Before running this code in your environment remember to download the go-yaml code to your machine. Execute `go get gopkg.in/yaml.v2` to get the code. Refer to Section 2.1.1 for more details about importing third-party code or Chapter 12 to use go modules.

Go-yaml follows the same `marshal/unmarshal` approach we have already seen for JSON and XML formats. Example 8.9 prints some YAML encodings after using the `Marshal` function.

Example 8.9: YAML marshalling.

```go
package main

import (
    "gopkg.in/yaml.v2"
    "fmt"
)

func main() {
    number, err := yaml.Marshal(42)
    if err!=nil{
        panic(err)
    }
    fmt.Println(string(number))

    float, _ := yaml.Marshal(3.14)
    fmt.Println(string(float))

    msg, _ := yaml.Marshal("This is a msg!!!")
    fmt.Println(string(msg))

    numbers, _ := yaml.Marshal([]int{1,1,2,3,5,8})
    fmt.Println(string(numbers))

    aMap, _ := yaml.Marshal(map[string]int{"one":1,"two":2})
    fmt.Println(string(aMap))
}
```

```
42

3.14

This is a msg!!!

- 1
- 1
- 2
- 3
- 5
- 8

one: 1
two: 2
```

YAML can be decoded using the `Unmarshal` function as shown in Example 8.10.

Example 8.10: YAML unmarshalling.

```go
package main
```

---

[3] https://github.com/go-yaml/yaml

CHAPTER 8. ENCODINGS

```go
 2
 3 import (
 4     "fmt"
 5     "gopkg.in/yaml.v2"
 6 )
 7
 8 func main() {
 9
10     aNumber, _ := yaml.Marshal(42)
11
12     var recoveredNumber int = -1
13     err := yaml.Unmarshal(aNumber, &recoveredNumber)
14     if err!= nil {
15         panic(err)
16     }
17     fmt.Println(recoveredNumber)
18
19
20     aMap, _ := yaml.Marshal(map[string]int{"one":1,"two":2})
21
22     recoveredMap := make(map[string]int)
23     err = yaml.Unmarshal(aMap, &recoveredMap)
24     if err != nil {
25         panic(err)
26     }
27     fmt.Println(recoveredMap)
28 }
```

```
42
map[one:1 two:2]
```

Go-yaml accepts field tags following the same rules we have seen so far. The output from Example 8.11 shows the representation of the users' array after been encoded and the value of the filled structure.

Example 8.11: YAML struct marshalling.

```go
 1 package main
 2
 3 import (
 4     "fmt"
 5     "gopkg.in/yaml.v2"
 6 )
 7
 8 type User struct {
 9     UserId   string `yaml:"userId,omitempty"`
10     Score    int    `yaml:"score,omitempty"`
11     password string `yaml:"password,omitempty"`
12 }
13
```

```go
14  func main() {
15
16      userA := User{"Gopher", 1000, "admin"}
17      userB := User{"BigJ", 10, "1234"}
18      userC := User{UserId: "GGBoom", password: "1111"}
19
20      db := []User{userA, userB, userC}
21      dbYaml, err := yaml.Marshal(&db)
22      if err != nil {
23          panic(err)
24      }
25      fmt.Println(string(dbYaml))
26
27      var recovered []User
28      err = yaml.Unmarshal(dbYaml, &recovered)
29      if err != nil{
30          panic(err)
31      }
32      fmt.Println(recovered)
33  }
```

```
- userId: Gopher
  score: 1000
- userId: BigJ
  score: 10
- userId: GGBoom

[{Gopher 1000 } {BigJ 10 } {GGBoom 0 }]
```

8.5. TAGS AND ENCODING

In Section 5.4, we explained how Go provides field tags to enrich structs and how reflection can be used to analyse these tags. The encodings presented in this Chapter use tags to define how to marshal/unmarshal structs. Similarly, we can define our own tags to define new encoding solutions.

To show how we can leverage tags to define our encoding, let's assume that we have developed a solution that only works with strings. For some reason, this solution makes a strong distinction between lowercase and uppercase strings. Due to the nature of the problem, we have to constantly use the functions `strings.ToUpper` and `strings.ToLower` in our code. To eliminate redundant code, we decide to use an encoding solution to automatically convert our strings to uppercase or lowercase.

```go
type User struct {
    UserId string `pretty:"upper"`
    Email string `pretty:"lower"`
    password string `pretty:"lower"v
}

type Record struct {
    Name string `pretty:"lower"`
    Surname string `pretty:"upper"`
```

CHAPTER 8. ENCODINGS 137

```
    Age int `pretty:"other"`
}
```

For the structs above, we defined the tag key `pretty`, with values `upper` or `lower` that transform a string into uppercase or lowercase respectively. Our encoding is defined as follows:

1. Unexported fields such as `password` are ignored.
2. Only `lower` and `upper` are valid tag values.
3. Only strings are candidates to be encoded.
4. Every field is identified by its field name, and separated from the new value by a colon.
5. The fields are surrounded by brackets.
6. No recursion, or collections will be encoded.

With this definition we have that `User:{"John", "John@Gmail.com", "admin"}` is encoded as `{UserId:JOHN, Email:john@gmail.com}` and `Record{"John", "Johnson",33}` as `{Name:john, Surname:JOHNSON}`. As you can see, the output is a subset of JSON that only accepts strings.

Following the common interface for encodings we have already seen in this Chapter, we can define a custom function for our encoding. Example 8.12, defines how to process the field tags from any **interface** to return our encoding. What we do is to iterate through the fields of the **interface** and encode them when possible using the auxiliary function `encodeField`. The encoded fields are written to a buffer that contains the final output. Notice from the definition above, that not all the situations are permitted and this may generate errors.

Example 8.12: `Marshal` function for custom encoding using field tags (excerpt).

```
1  package main
2
3  import (
4      "bytes"
5      "encoding/json"
6      "errors"
7      "fmt"
8      "reflect"
9      "strings"
10 )
11
12 func Marshal(input interface{}) ([]byte, error) {
13     var buffer bytes.Buffer
```

```go
    t := reflect.TypeOf(input)
    v := reflect.ValueOf(input)

    buffer.WriteString("{")
    for i:=0; i < t.NumField();i++ {
        encodedField,err := encodeField(t.Field(i),v.Field(i))

        if err != nil {
            return nil, err
        }
        if len(encodedField) != 0 {
            if i >0 && i<= t.NumField()-1 {
                buffer.WriteString(", ")
            }
            buffer.WriteString(encodedField)
        }
    }
    buffer.WriteString("}")
    return buffer.Bytes(),nil
}

func encodeField(f reflect.StructField, v reflect.Value) (string, error) {

    if f.PkgPath!=""{
        return "",nil
    }

    if f.Type.Kind() != reflect.String {
        return "", nil
    }

    tag, found := f.Tag.Lookup("pretty")
    if !found {
        return "", nil
    }

    result := f.Name+":"
    var err error = nil
    switch tag {
    case "upper":
        result = result + strings.ToUpper(v.String())
    case "lower":
        result = result + strings.ToLower(v.String())
    default:
        err = errors.New("invalid tag value")
    }
    if err != nil {
        return "", err
    }
```

```
64        return result, nil
65 }
```

The `encodeField` function uses the `reflect` package to inspect the tags and field values. If we find the `pretty` tag and one of its values, we return the encoded value of the field. To do this there are some previous checks. The function `f.PkgPath` is empty for exported fields, therefore if non empty this is an unexported field and must not be encoded. With `f.Type.Kind()` we check the field type. `f.Tag.Lookup("pretty")` checks if this field has a `pretty` tag. Finally, a **switch** statement transforms the field value according to its tag value.

Example 8.13 continues the previous code and shows how our `Marshal` function can be used with different structs. Notice how fields such as `password` or `Age` are ignored in the encoding. We can combine our tags with other encoding formats such as JSON and check the different outputs.

Example 8.13: Marshal function for custom encoding using field tags (continues 8.12).

```
 1
 2 type User struct {
 3     UserId string `pretty:"upper"`
 4     Email string `pretty:"lower"`
 5     password string `pretty:"lower"`
 6 }
 7
 8 type Record struct {
 9     Name string `pretty:"lower" json:"name"`
10     Surname string `pretty:"upper" json:"surname"`
11     Age int `pretty:"other" json:"age"`
12 }
13
14
15 func main() {
16     u := User{"John", "John@Gmail.com", "admin"}
17
18     marSer, _ := Marshal(u)
19     fmt.Println("pretty user", string(marSer))
20
21     r := Record{"John", "Johnson",33}
22     marRec, _:= Marshal(r)
23     fmt.Println("pretty rec", string(marRec))
24
25     jsonRec, _ := json.Marshal(r)
26     fmt.Println("json rec",string(jsonRec))
27 }
```

```
pretty user {UserId:JOHN, Email:john@gmail.com}
pretty rec {Name:john, Surname:JOHNSON}
json rec {"name":"John","surname":"Johnson","age":33}
```

8.6. Summary

In this Chapter we explore different encoding formats available in Go. In particular, we explore CSV, JSON, XML and YAML. The simplicity of the marshal/unmarshal methods together with the utilization of fields tagging makes it possible to define how a struct has to be converted to different formats. Finally, we showed a use-case that permits the definition of a custom encoding using fields tagging.

9

HTTP

Since Tim Berners Lee came up with the idea of the World Wide Web, HTTP has been its foundation. A good understanding of HTTP is basic to exchange data, manipulate APIs or crawl the web. This Chapter, details the tools that Go provides all the necessary elements to manage HTTP constructs such as requests, cookies or headers. In particular, we explore the `net/http` package. This Chapter assumes you are familiar with HTTP and how it works.

9.1. REQUESTS

HTTP requests are actions to performed by an HTTP server at a given URL following the client-server paradigm. Go simplifies HTTP requests sending with functions `Get`, `Post`, and `PostForm`. By simply invoking these functions an HTTP request is sent.

9.1.1. GET

The simplest manner to send an GET request is using the `http.Get` function. This function returns an `http.Response` type with a filled error y any. Like defined in the HTTP protocol, the response has a `Header` type and a body encoded into a `Reader` type.

Example 9.1: GET request.

```
1  package main
2
3  import (
4      "bufio"
```

```go
5       "fmt"
6       "net/http"
7  )
8
9  func main() {
10
11      resp, err := http.Get("https://httpbin.org/get")
12      if err != nil {
13          panic(err)
14      }
15
16      fmt.Println(resp.Status)
17      fmt.Println(resp.Header["Content-Type"])
18
19      defer resp.Body.Close()
20      buf := bufio.NewScanner(resp.Body)
21
22      for buf.Scan() {
23          fmt.Println(buf.Text())
24      }
25  }
```

```
200 OK
[application/json]
{
  "args": {},
  "headers": {
    "Accept-Encoding": "gzip",
    "Host": "httpbin.org",
    "User-Agent": "Go-http-client/2.0",
    "X-Amzn-Trace-Id": "Root=1-6006ab94-3e51e02b509a1d3433bb59c1"
  },
  "origin": "111.111.111.111",
  "url": "https://httpbin.org/get"
}
```

Example 9.1, shows how to send a GET request to https://httpbin.org/get. This URL will return a basic response we can use to test our program. The response status is one of the values defined at the RFC7231 [10] (200 if everything went right). The header field is a map, therefore we can access values using the name of the header we are looking for like in resp.Header["Content-Type"]. The body of the response is a reader that has to be consumed. If you are not familiar with I/O operations check Chapter 7. A convenient way to consume this reader is using any of the functions from the bufio package.

> ⚠ **Do not forget to close** the reader when accessing the body (`resp.Body.Close()`).

9.1.2. POST

Sending a POST follows the same principles of GET requests. However, we are expected to send a body with the request and set the Content-type attribute in the header. Again, Go has a `Post` function that simplifies this operation as shown in Example 9.2. Notice that the POST body is expected to be an `io.Reader` type. In this example, we send a JSON body to the `https://httpbin.org/post` which simply returns the body we have sent. Notice that the second argument of `http.Post` indicates the content-type and the format or our body. Accessing the fields from the `Response` type can be done as explained in the previous example.

Example 9.2: POST request.

```go
package main

import (
    "bufio"
    "bytes"
    "fmt"
    "net/http"
)

func main() {
    bodyRequest := []byte(`"user": "john","email":"john@gmail.com"`)
    bufferBody := bytes.NewBuffer(bodyRequest)

    url := "https://httpbin.org/post"

    resp, err := http.Post(url, "application/json", bufferBody)
    if err != nil {
        panic(err)
    }
    defer resp.Body.Close()

    fmt.Println(resp.Status)
    bodyAnswer := bufio.NewScanner(resp.Body)
    for bodyAnswer.Scan() {
        fmt.Println(bodyAnswer.Text())
    }
}
```

```
200 OK
{
  "args": {},
  "data": "{\"user\": \"john\",\"email\":\"john@gmail.com\"}",
  "files": {},
  "form": {},
  "headers": {
    "Accept-Encoding": "gzip",
    "Content-Length": "41",
    "Content-Type": "application/json",
    "Host": "httpbin.org",
    "User-Agent": "Go-http-client/2.0",
    "X-Amzn-Trace-Id": "Root=1-6006b032-6cbe50a13751bc03798b9e0b"
  },
  "json": {
    "email": "john@gmail.com",
    "user": "john"
  },
  "origin": "111.111.111.111",
  "url": "https://httpbin.org/post"
}
```

The `http.Post` is generic and admits any content-type. For those post methods using `application/x-www-form-urlencoded` the `PostForm` function gets rid off the content-type specification and directly admits and encodes the body values into the `url-encoded` format.

Example 9.3 sends url-encoded data to the URL from the previous example. The approach only differs in the utilization of the `url.Values` type to define the url-encoded values. Observe that the returned response contains the sent data in the `form` field, not in the `data` field like in the previous example.

Example 9.3: POST request using `PostForm`

```go
package main

import (
    "bufio"
    "fmt"
    "net/http"
    "net/url"
)

func main() {

    target := "https://httpbin.org/post"

```

```go
14      resp, err := http.PostForm(target,
15          url.Values{"user": {"john"}, "email": {"john@gmail.com"}})
16      if err != nil {
17          panic(err)
18      }
19      defer resp.Body.Close()
20
21      fmt.Println(resp.Status)
22      bodyAnswer := bufio.NewScanner(resp.Body)
23      for bodyAnswer.Scan() {
24          fmt.Println(bodyAnswer.Text())
25      }
26  }
```

```
200 OK

{
  "args": {},
  "data": "",
  "files": {},
  "form": {
    "email": "john@gmail.com",
    "user": "john"
  },
  "headers": {
    "Accept-Encoding": "gzip",
    "Content-Length": "32",
    "Content-Type": "application/x-www-form-urlencoded",
    "Host": "httpbin.org",
    "User-Agent": "Go-http-client/2.0",
    "X-Amzn-Trace-Id": "Root=1-602ce931-3ad4aabf7cba926306f53fd2"
  },
  "json": null,
  "origin": "139.47.90.49",
  "url": "https://httpbin.org/post"
}
```

9.1.3. HEADERS, CLIENTS, AND OTHER METHODS

We have already mentioned that the most common HTTP methods are GET and POST. However, there are more methods such as DELETE, UPDATE or PATCH. Additionally, headers contain valuable fields that can be required to successfully interact with servers and their methods. All these elements contained in a `http.Request` type can be customised. However, when a request is created from scratch it has to be sent using an `http.Client`. This type defines a configurable client that permits a more controlled utilization of resources.

Example 9.4 shows how to use a client with a customised request to use a PUT method with body. This example is easily extensible to other HTTP methods. First, we create a body content and a `http.Header` with the required. A new request is filled indicating the HTTP method, URL and body content. Observe that the header is set after we have created the request (`req.Header = header`). Next we instantiate a `http.Client` with a request timeout of five seconds. We invoke the `Do` method to send our request. From here, we follow the same steps from the previous examples.

Example 9.4: Other HTTP requests.

```go
package main

import (
    "bufio"
    "bytes"
    "fmt"
    "net/http"
    "time"
)

func main() {
    bodyRequest := []byte(`{"user": "john","email":"john@gmail.com"}`)
    bufferBody := bytes.NewBuffer(bodyRequest)

    url := "https://httpbin.org/put"

    header := http.Header{}
    header.Add("Content-type", "application/json")
    header.Add("X-Custom-Header", "somevalue")
    header.Add("User-Agent", "safe-the-world-with-go")

    req, err := http.NewRequest(http.MethodPut, url, bufferBody)

    if err != nil {
        panic(err)
    }

    req.Header = header

    client := http.Client{
        Timeout: time.Second * 5,
    }

    resp, err := client.Do(req)
    if err != nil {
        panic(err)
```

```
37      }
38      defer resp.Body.Close()
39
40      fmt.Println(resp.Status)
41      bodyAnswer := bufio.NewScanner(resp.Body)
42      for bodyAnswer.Scan() {
43          fmt.Println(bodyAnswer.Text())
44      }
45 }
```

```
200 OK
{
  "args": {},
  "data": "{\"user\": \"john\",\"email\":\"john@gmail.com\"}",
  "files": {},
  "form": {},
  "headers": {
    "Accept-Encoding": "gzip",
    "Content-Length": "41",
    "Content-Type": "application/json",
    "Host": "httpbin.org",
    "User-Agent": "safe-the-world-with-go",
    "X-Amzn-Trace-Id": "Root=1-6006b2a7-37b6eb882f50162e167aa0d8",
    "X-Custom-Header": "somevalue"
  },
  "json": {
    "email": "john@gmail.com",
    "user": "john"
  },
  "origin": "111.111.111.111",
  "url": "https://httpbin.org/put"
}
```

The response contains the `X-Custom-Header` we sent with the request and returns the body. The `Client` has additional fields such as a timeout, a redirection policy or a cookie jar. Check the documentation for more details[1].

9.2. HTTP Server

The `net/http` package defines a `ServerMux` type that implements a HTTP request multiplexer. The server matches incoming URL requests with a list of configured patterns. These patterns have an associated handler that is invoked to serve the request.

---
[1]https://golang.org/pkg/net/http/#Client

Example 9.5 registers the function `info` as the handler for the `/info` URL. Any function to be registered as a handler must follow the **func**(ResponseWriter, *Request) signature. In this example, the server returns a body with a message and prints the headers by standard output. Our handler does not make any distinction between HTTP methods and will respond to any request. To serve requests, the `http.ListenAndServe` function blocks the execution flow and waits forever for incoming requests.

Example 9.5: HTTP server using `http.HandleFunc`.

```go
package main

import (
    "fmt"
    "net/http"
)

func info(w http.ResponseWriter, r *http.Request){
    for name, headers := range r.Header {
        fmt.Println(name,headers)
    }
    w.Write([]byte("Perfect!!!"))
    return
}

func main() {
    http.HandleFunc("/info", info)
    panic(http.ListenAndServe(":8090", nil))
}
```

```
>>> curl -H "Header1: Value1" :8090/info
Perfect!!!
...
User-Agent [curl/7.64.1]
Accept [*/*]
Header1 [Value1]
```

To test this code we have to run the server and then make the request from an HTTP client. We could write our own client as explained before. However, we can use an already implemented client to check that our server is compatible with the standards and works as expected. In this case, we used `curl` to send a GET request with header `Header1: Value1`[2]. Notice that we print additional headers that the `curl` client adds to our request.

---

[2]The `curl` command is displayed in the output frame `curl -H "Header1: Value1":8090/info`

The `http.HandleFunc` registers handlers and a URI. We can directly set a handler to be invoked independently of the URI. This forces the handler to be invoked in every request. However, this can be useful depending on the use-case.

Example 9.6 implements a `Handler` type with struct `MyHandler`. To implement the `Handler` interface the `ServeHTTP` function has to be defined. Any request will be sent to this handler, therefore we can do things like URI selection. In the example `/hello` and `/goodbye` return different messages.

Example 9.6: HTTP server and handler.

```go
package main

import "net/http"

type MyHandler struct {}

func (c *MyHandler) ServeHTTP(w http.ResponseWriter, r *http.Request) {
    switch r.RequestURI {
    case "/hello":
        w.WriteHeader(http.StatusOK)
        w.Write([]byte("goodbye\n"))
    case "/goodbye":
        w.WriteHeader(http.StatusOK)
        w.Write([]byte("hello\n"))
    default:
        w.WriteHeader(http.StatusBadRequest)
    }
}

func main() {
    handler := MyHandler{}
    http.ListenAndServe(":8090", &handler)
}
```

```
>>> curl :8090/goodbye
hello
>>> curl :8090/hello
goodbye
```

9.3. Cookies

The `Cookie`type[3] is a representation of the cookies you can find in a `Set-Cookie` header. They can be added to a `Request` and extracted from a `Response` type.

Example 9.7 instantiates a server that expects a cookie with a counter. The value received in the cookie is sent in the response incremented. The example is self-contained, the server is executed in a goroutine and the client sends requests to the server. After instantiating the cookie, we add it to the current request with `req.AddCookie(&c)`. Cookies are accessible in key-value pairs at both requests and responses. On the server-side, the function `r.Cookie("counter")` gets that cookie from the request if it was found. Similarly, we can set the cookie in the response using the `http.SetCookie` function. In the output, we capture the headers from the request and the response. The response contains the `Set-Cookie` header with the new value for the counter.

Example 9.7: Adding cookies to requests and responses.

```go
package main

import (
    "fmt"
    "net/http"
    "strconv"
    "time"
)

func cookieSetter(w http.ResponseWriter, r *http.Request) {
    counter, err := r.Cookie("counter")
    if err != nil {
        w.WriteHeader(http.StatusInternalServerError)
        return
    }
    value, err := strconv.Atoi(counter.Value)
    if err != nil {
        w.WriteHeader(http.StatusInternalServerError)
        return
    }
    value = value + 1
    newCookie := http.Cookie{
        Name:  "counter",
        Value: strconv.Itoa(value),
    }
    http.SetCookie(w, &newCookie)
    w.WriteHeader(http.StatusOK)
    return
```

---

[3]https://golang.org/pkg/net/http/#Cookie

```
29  }
30
31  func main() {
32      http.HandleFunc("/cookie", cookieSetter)
33      go http.ListenAndServe(":8090", nil)
34
35      url := "http://localhost:8090/cookie"
36      req, err := http.NewRequest("GET",url,nil)
37      if err != nil {
38          panic(err)
39      }
40
41      client := http.Client{}
42
43      c := http.Cookie{
44          Name:"counter", Value:"1", Domain: "127.0.0.1",
45          Path: "/", Expires: time.Now().AddDate(1,0,0)}
46      req.AddCookie(&c)
47
48      fmt.Println("-->", req.Header)
49
50      resp, err := client.Do(req)
51      if err != nil {
52          panic(err)
53      }
54
55      fmt.Println("<--",resp.Header)
56  }
```

```
--> map[Cookie:[counter=1]]
<-- map[Content-Length:[0] Date:[Tue, 19 Jan 2021 20:12:59 GMT]
Set-Cookie:[counter=2]]
```

9.3.1. COOKIEJAR

The previous example is a basic description of how to manipulate cookies. One drawback of our example is that we have to manually set the new cookie for future requests. This could be easily done considering that we only have one cookie. However, when interacting with web applications it is common to use many and it would be more efficient to have a non-supervised approach to update these cookies.

The [4] type from the package `net/http/cookiejar` implements an in-memory storage

---
[4]https://golang.org/pkg/net/http/cookiejar/

solution for cookies that follow the `CookieJar` interface from `net/http`. Example 9.8 extends Example 9.7 with a client using a `CookieJar`. The `SetCookies` method associate an array of cookies with an URL. Now every time the client operates with that URL, the `CookieJar` will update the corresponding cookies. This enhancement is only required at the client side. Finally, we iteratively send requests to the server which returns the updated cookie. Notice that without the `CookieJar` we would have to manually update the cookie for the next request.

This can be done adding the cookies to the `CookieJar` (`jar.SetCookies`) and setting the jar field in the `http.Client`. After every request cookies are automatically updated and we can check their values.

Example 9.8: Use of `CookieJar` to set cookie values.

```go
package main

import (
    "fmt"
    "net/http"
    "net/http/cookiejar"
    url2 "net/url"
    "strconv"
)

func cookieSetter(w http.ResponseWriter, r *http.Request) {
    counter, err := r.Cookie("counter")
    if err != nil {
        w.WriteHeader(http.StatusInternalServerError)
        return
    }
    value, err := strconv.Atoi(counter.Value)
    if err != nil {
        w.WriteHeader(http.StatusInternalServerError)
        return
    }
    value = value + 1
    newCookie := http.Cookie{
        Name: "counter",
        Value: strconv.Itoa(value),
    }
    http.SetCookie(w, &newCookie)
    w.WriteHeader(http.StatusOK)
}

func main() {
    http.HandleFunc("/cookie", cookieSetter)
    go http.ListenAndServe(":8090", nil)
```

```
35      jar, err := cookiejar.New(nil)
36      if err != nil {
37          panic(err)
38      }
39      cookies := []*http.Cookie{
40          &http.Cookie{Name:"counter",Value:"1"},
41      }
42
43      url := "http://localhost:8090/cookie"
44      u, _ := url2.Parse(url)
45      jar.SetCookies(u, cookies)
46
47      client := http.Client{Jar: jar}
48
49      for i:=0; i<5; i++ {
50          _, err := client.Get(url)
51          if err != nil {
52              panic(err)
53          }
54          fmt.Println("Client cookie",jar.Cookies(u))
55      }
56  }
```

```
Client cookie [counter=2]
Client cookie [counter=3]
Client cookie [counter=4]
Client cookie [counter=5]
Client cookie [counter=6]
```

9.4. Middleware

Imagine an HTTP API that requires users to be authenticated in the system. A simple approach is to implement a basic authentication header checker to determine if a request must be processed or not. Additionally, certain operations are restricted to some user roles. These operations have to be done in every request. From the point of view of the implementation, this is a repetitive task that should be implemented once and reutilized accordingly. This is a clear example of middleware.

This middleware should run before any handler is invoked to process the request. The net/http package does not provide any tool to manage middleware solutions. However, this can be easily done by implementing handlers. The idea is to concatenate specialized middleware handlers that provide additional features.

```go
func Middleware(next http.Handler) http.Handler {
    return http.HandlerFunc(func(w http.ResponseWriter, r *http.Request){
        // Do something before the next handler is invoked
        next.ServeHTTP(w, r)
        // Do something when the next handler has finished
    })
}
// ...
http.ListenAndServe(":8090",Middleware(Middleware(Handler)))
```

The code above summarizes the definition of a middleware handler. This handler receives another handler that has to be invoked with the same `Request` and `ResposeWriter`. This handler can modify both elements depending on its logic before and after the next handler is invoked. To apply the middleware to every request, we concatenate it with other handlers. Because the middleware returns a `Handler` we can concatenate other middlewares until finally invoke the target handler with the expected logic.

Example 9.9 implements a basic authorization mechanism for a server. Basic authorization is based on a header like `Authorization:Basic credential` where credentials is a string encoded in base64. The `AuthMiddleware` function checks if this header exists, decodes the credential and authorizes the request if it matches Open Sesame. If any of the steps fails, the middleware sets the request as non authorized (error 401) and returns.

Example 9.9: Basic authorization middleware handler.

```go
package main

import (
    "encoding/base64"
    "net/http"
    "strings"
    "fmt"
)

type MyHandler struct{}

func (mh *MyHandler) ServeHTTP(w http.ResponseWriter, r *http.Request){
    w.WriteHeader(http.StatusOK)
    w.Write([]byte("Perfect!!!"))
    return
}

func AuthMiddleware(next http.Handler) http.Handler {
    return http.HandlerFunc(func(w http.ResponseWriter, r *http.Request){
        header := r.Header.Get("Authorization")
        if header == "" {
```

```
22                w.WriteHeader(http.StatusUnauthorized)
23                return
24            }
25
26            authType := strings.Split(header," ")
27            fmt.Println(authType)
28            if len(authType) != 2 || authType[0] != "Basic" {
29                w.WriteHeader(http.StatusUnauthorized)
30                return
31            }
32            credentials,err := base64.StdEncoding.DecodeString(authType[1])
33            if err != nil {
34                w.WriteHeader(http.StatusUnauthorized)
35                return
36            }
37            if string(credentials) == "Open Sesame" {
38                next.ServeHTTP(w, r)
39            }
40        })
41 }
42
43 func main() {
44     targetHandler := MyHandler{}
45     panic(http.ListenAndServe(":8090",AuthMiddleware(&targetHandler)))
46 }
```

```
>>> auth=$(echo -n "Open Sesame" | base64);
>>> echo $auth
T3BlbiBTZXNhbWU=
>>> curl :8090 -w "%{http_code}"
401
>>> curl :8090 -w "%{http_code}" -H "Authorization: Basic Hello"
401
>>> curl :8090 -w "%{http_code}" -H "Authorization: Basic $auth"
Perfect!!!200
```

Now requests will be unauthorized until the authorization middleware finds the correct authorization header. To obtain the base64 encoding you can use any online encoder or the commands shown below if you use a Unix-like environment.

Now that we have seen how we can define a middleware handler a practical question is how to easily concatenate all the middleware. And this is an interesting question because we can expect applications to deal with several handlers and sophisticated configurations. The main idea is to replace `AuthMiddleware(&targetHandler)` for something that can be programmatically executed.

Example 9.10 defines a type `Middleware` and the `ApplyMiddleware` function to help the concatenation of multiple handlers. The idea is that `ApplyMiddleware` returns a handler that results from applying a collection of middlewares to the handler passed by argument. When registering handlers for our server, we simply invoke the function with the final handler and the middleware items. In our case, we register `/three` and `/one` URIs that apply three and one times the `SimpleMiddleware`. This middleware checks the simple header and adds a tick. The number of ticks in the response header will the same of these middlewares executed when serving the request.

Example 9.10: Concatenation of several middleware handlers.

```go
package main

import "net/http"

type MyHandler struct{}

func (mh *MyHandler) ServeHTTP(w http.ResponseWriter, r *http.Request){
    w.WriteHeader(http.StatusOK)
    w.Write([]byte("Perfect!!!"))
    return
}

type Middleware func(http.Handler) http.Handler

func ApplyMiddleware(h http.Handler, middleware ... Middleware) http.Handler {
    for _, next := range middleware {
        h = next(h)
    }
    return h
}

func SimpleMiddleware(next http.Handler) http.Handler {
    return http.HandlerFunc(func(w http.ResponseWriter, r *http.Request){
        value := w.Header().Get("simple")
        if value == "" {
            value = "X"
        } else {
            value = value + "X"
        }
        w.Header().Set("simple", value)
        next.ServeHTTP(w,r)
    })
}

func main() {

    h := &MyHandler{}

```

```
39      http.Handle("/three", ApplyMiddleware(
40          h, SimpleMiddleware, SimpleMiddleware, SimpleMiddleware))
41      http.Handle("/one", ApplyMiddleware(
42          h, SimpleMiddleware))
43
44      panic(http.ListenAndServe(":8090", nil))
45  }
```

Using `curl` we can see how `/three` returns the header `Simple: XXX` while `/one` returns `Simple: X`. Obviously these middleware function only has demonstration purposes. However, applying other more realistic or sophisticated solutions can use exactly the same ideas.

```
>>> curl :8090/three  -i
HTTP/1.1 200 OK
Simple: XXX
Date: Wed, 17 Feb 2021 20:49:55 GMT
Content-Length: 10
Content-Type: text/plain; charset=utf-8

Perfect!!!%
>>> curl :8090/one  -i
HTTP/1.1 200 OK
Simple: X
Date: Wed, 17 Feb 2021 16:50:01 GMT
Content-Length: 10
Content-Type: text/plain; charset=utf-8

Perfect!!!%
```

9.5. Summary

HTTP is widely used and offers many possibilities not only to retrieve web content but also to access remote APIs. This Chapter exposes how Go works with the main elements of HTTP including requests, responses, headers, and cookies. Extra material is explained regarding middleware and how easy it can be to define sophisticated pipelines to process HTTP requests.

10. TEMPLATES

While you read these lines, there are thousands of millions of reports, web pages and other structured and non-structured data collections being generated. Many of them share a common template that is filled with information extracted from users and processed accordingly to a pre-defined logic. For example, the email sent to your account to reset your forgotten password is always the same, except for small chunks containing data you should be aware of.

From a practical perspective, these templates should be easy to change and modify without necessarily requiring to modify any source code. Go provides data-driven templates for generating textual output. These templates are executed by applying data structures that contain the data to be represented in the `template` package. This Chapter explores how to use these templates with some examples using the `text/template` and `html/template` packages for text and HTML output respectively.

10.1. FILLING TEMPLATES WITH STRUCTS

The `text/template`[1] package defines the syntax to generate textual templates. Our goal is to fill the gaps of a template with incoming data. Let's consider the string below.

```
Dear {{.Name}},
You were registered with id {{.UserId}}
and e-mail {{.Email}}.
```

---

[1] https://golang.org/pkg/text/template/

This string defines a template that is expected to be filled with a `struct` with fields `Name`, `UserId`, and `Email`. Example 10.1 uses this template in conjunction with a `User` type to generate personalized messages.

Example 10.1: Fill template with a `struct`.

```go
package main

import (
    "text/template"
    "os"
)

type User struct{
    Name string
    UserId string
    Email string
}

const Msg = `Dear {{.Name}},
You were registered with id {{.UserId}}
and e-mail {{.Email}}.
`

func main() {
    u := User{"John", "John33", "john@gmail.com"}

    t := template.Must(template.New("msg").Parse(Msg))
    err := t.Execute(os.Stdout, u)
    if err != nil {
        panic(err)
    }
}
```

```
Dear John,
You were registered
with id John33
and e-mail john@gmail.
com.
```

Templates are allocated with the `New` function which receives a name for the template. The `Parse` method analyzes a template string definition. This method can return an error if the template parsing was not possible. The `template.Must` is a function wrapper that helps the template definition as shown in line 22. Finally, the method `Execute` applies a template to an `interface{}` type and writes the resulting output to an `io.Writer`. The resulting output is our template filled with the initialized `u` variable.

10.2. ACTIONS

Templates permit the definition of certain logic depending on the data value. Example 10.2 changes the output according to the user's gender. The statement `{{if .Woman}}Mrs.{{- else}}Mr.{{- end}}` prints two different messages depending on the boolean field `Female`.

Example 10.2: Template `if/else`.

```go
package main

import (
    "text/template"
    "os"
)

type User struct{
    Name string
    Female bool
}

const Msg = `
{{if .Female}}Mrs.{{- else}}Mr.{{- end}} {{.Name}},
Your package is ready.
Thanks,
`
func main() {
    u1 := User{"John", false}
    u2 := User{"Mary", true}

    t := template.Must(template.New("msg").Parse(Msg))
    err := t.Execute(os.Stdout, u1)
    if err != nil {
        panic(err)
    }
    err = t.Execute(os.Stdout, u2)
    if err != nil {
        panic(err)
    }
}
```

```
Mr. John,
Your package is ready.
Thanks,

Mrs. Mary,
Your package is ready.
Thanks,
```

For binary variable comparisons templates use a different syntax than the one used in Go. Check Table 10.1 for a list of equivalences.

Example 10.3 defines personalized messages depending on the score of every user.

Go	Templates
<	lt
>	gt
<=	le
>=	ge
==	eq
!=	ne

Table 10.1: Comparison operators in Go and templates.

Example 10.3: Template `if/else` binary variable comparisons.

```go
package main

import (
    "text/template"
    "os"
)

type User struct{
    Name string
    Score uint32
}

const Msg = `
{{.Name}} your score is {{.Score}}
your level is:
{{if le .Score 50}}Amateur
{{else if le .Score 80}}Professional
{{else}}Expert
{{end}}
`

func main() {
    u1 := User{"John", 30}
    u2 := User{"Mary", 80}

    t := template.Must(template.New("msg").Parse(Msg))
    err := t.Execute(os.Stdout, u1)
    if err != nil {
        panic(err)
    }
    err = t.Execute(os.Stdout, u2)
    if err != nil {
        panic(err)
    }
}
```

```
John your score is 30
your level is:
Amateur

Mary your score is 80
your level is:
Professional
```

Another common use case is the iteration through a collection of items. We can call a **range** iterator as we would do in a Go loop. The statement `{{range .}}{{print .}} {{end}}` iterates through a collection and prints every item. Example 10.4 uses this action to print the content of a string array containing the name of the musketeers.

Example 10.4: Template **range** iteration.

```go
package main

import (
    "text/template"
    "os"
)

const msg = `
The musketeers are:
{{range .}}{{print .}} {{end}}
`

func main() {
    musketeers := []string{"Athos", "Porthos", "Aramis","D'Artagnan"}

    t := template.Must(template.New("msg").Parse(msg))
    err := t.Execute(os.Stdout, musketeers)
    if err != nil {
        panic(err)
    }
}
```

```
The musketeers are:
Athos Porthos Aramis D'
Artagnan
```

10.3. Functions

Functions can be defined inside the template or in the global function map. The templates specification sets a variety of already available functions. Many of them are similar to functions already available in Go. However, we recommend you to take a look at the reference[2] for further details. Example 10.5 uses the function `{{slice . 3}}` which is equivalent to `x[3]` to get the item with index 3 from a slice.

Example 10.5: Template **slice** function.

---

[2]https://golang.org/pkg/text/template/#hdr-Functions

```go
package main

import (
    "text/template"
    "os"
)

const Msg = `
The fourth musketeer is:
{{slice . 3}}
`

func main() {
    musketeers := []string{"Athos", "Porthos", "Aramis","D'Artagnan"}

    t := template.Must(template.New("msg").Parse(Msg))

    err := t.Execute(os.Stdout, musketeers)
    if err != nil {
        panic(err)
    }
}
```

```
The fourth musketeer is:
[D'Artagnan]
```

In other situations, we may need other functions not available at the current specification. In these situations, we can use the `FuncMap` type to define a map of available functions. Afterwards, we have to add this map of functions to our template to be callable. Example 10.6 declares a functions map where `"join"` maps the `strings.Join` function. Now we can call this new function from our template using `{{join . ", "}}`.

Example 10.6: Use of `FuncMap`.

```go
package main

import (
    "strings"
    "text/template"
    "os"
)

const Msg = `
The musketeers are:
{{join . ", "}}
`

func main() {
    musketeers := []string{"Athos", "Porthos", "Aramis","D'Artagnan"}

```

```
The musketeers are:
Athos, Porthos, Aramis, D'
Artagnan
```

```go
17      funcs := template.FuncMap{"join": strings.Join}
18
19      t, err := template.New("msg").Funcs(funcs).Parse(Msg)
20      if err != nil {
21          panic(err)
22      }
23      err = t.Execute(os.Stdout, musketeers)
24      if err != nil {
25          panic(err)
26      }
27  }
```

It is possible to execute templates inside other templates using the `{{block "name" .}}{{end}}` and `{{define "name"}}{{end}}` actions. In Example 10.7, we define two template strings in `Header` and `Welcome`. The idea is that our `Welcome` template prints a collection of items after printing a header. The `{{define "hello"}}` statement looks for the template `"hello"` and executes it. Notice that we parse both templates independently. However, the second one uses the `helloMsg` instead of creating a new one. Finally, we have to execute both templates in the order the are expected to appear.

Example 10.7: Rendering templates inside other templates.

```go
1  package main
2
3  import (
4      "os"
5      "text/template"
6  )
7
8  const Header = `
9  {{block "hello" .}}Hello and welcome{{end}}`
10
11 const Welcome = `
12 {{define "hello"}}
13 {{range .}}{{print .}} {{end}}
14 {{end}}
15 `
16
17 func main() {
18     musketeers := []string{"Athos", "Porthos", "Aramis","D'Artagnan"}
19
20     helloMsg, err := template.New("start").Parse(Header)
21     if err != nil {
22         panic(err)
23     }
24
25     welcomeMsg, err := template.Must(helloMsg.Clone()).Parse(Welcome)
```

```
Hello and welcome

Athos Porthos Aramis D'Artagnan
```

```go
26      if err != nil {
27          panic(err)
28      }
29
30      if err := helloMsg.Execute(os.Stdout, musketeers); err != nil {
31          panic(err)
32      }
33      if err := welcomeMsg.Execute(os.Stdout, musketeers); err != nil {
34          panic(err)
35      }
36  }
```

10.4. HTML

Templates are particularly useful to serve HTML content. However, due to safety reasons and potential code injection attacks, Go provides a specific package for HTML templates in `html/template`. The different functions and methods from this package are fairly similar to those already explained for `text/template`.

In Example 10.8 we populate a web page with a collection of items. As you can see, we generate the output in the same way we did for text templates. Notice that the output follows the HTML specification automatically escaping characters when needed.

Example 10.8: HTML list with a template.

```go
1  package main
2
3  import (
4      "html/template"
5      "os"
6  )
7
8  const Page = `
9  <html>
10 <head>
11     <title>{{.Name}}'s Languages</title>
12 </head>
13 <body>
14     <ul>
15     {{range .Languages}}<li>{{print .}}</li>{{end}}
16     </ul>
17 </body>
18 </html>
19 `
20
```

```go
21  type UserExperience struct {
22      Name string
23      Languages []string
24  }
25
26  func main() {
27      languages := []string{"Go","C++","C#"}
28      u := UserExperience{"John", languages}
29
30      t:= template.Must(template.New("web").Parse(Page))
31
32      err := t.Execute(os.Stdout, u)
33      if err != nil {
34          panic(err)
35      }
36  }
```

```
<html>
<head>
    <title>John's Languages</title>
</head>
<body>
    <ul>
    <li>Go</li><li>C&#43;&#43;</li><li>C#</li>
    </ul>
</body>
</html>
```

10.5. Summary

This Chapter explains how Go provides a language to define templates that can be filled on run-time. The examples from this Chapter demonstrate how to create templates and how to define template variations depending on incoming data.

11. TESTING

Testing is one of the most important tasks to develop a successful project. Unfortunately, testing is usually postponed or not seriously taken into consideration by developers. Testing can be repetitive and sometimes even convoluted. Fortunately, Go defines tests in a simple manner that reduces tests adoption and help developers to focus more on the test and less on language constructions. This Chapter explores testing, benchmarking and profiling.

11.1. TESTS

Go provides an integrated solution for testing. Actually, any function with signature `TestXXX(t *testing.T)` is interpreted as a testing function. Example 11.1 is a naive demonstration of how to check the correctness of a 2+2 operation. In this case, no error is going to occur. However, if any error is found, the `t` argument provides access to the `Error` function that sets this test to be failed.

Example 11.1: Single test.

```go
package example_01

import "testing"

func TestMe(t *testing.T) {
    r := 2 + 2
    if r != 4 {
        t.Error("expected 2 got", r)
    }
}
```

Tests are thought to be used in conjunction with the `go test` tool. For the example above we can run the test as follow:

```
>>> go test
PASS
ok      github.com/juanmanuel-tirado/SaveTheWorldWithGo/10_testing/testing/
    example_01 0.341s
>>> go test -v
=== RUN   TestMe
--- PASS: TestMe (0.00s)
PASS
ok      github.com/juanmanuel-tirado/SaveTheWorldWithGo/10_testing/testing/
    example_01 0.090s
```

The basic output from `go test` is the final status of the testing (`OK`) and the elapsed time. When using the verbose flag (`-v`) this information is printed for every test. Now, if we force an error we get:

```
>>> go test
--- FAIL: TestMe (0.00s)
    example01_test.go:8: expected 2 got 3
FAIL
exit status 1
FAIL    github.com/juanmanuel-tirado/SaveTheWorldWithGo/10_testing/testing/
    example_01 0.089s
```

The output shows that the final status is `FAIL` with the error message we added in case of error.

Tests are intended to improve the reliability of our code while helping us find potential errors. In Example 11.2, we test a toy function that prints a Schwarzenegger's movie quote. To test the completeness of our implementation, we call `MovieQuote` with all the movies we have. Unfortunately, we forgot to define a quote for the Predator movie[1].

Example 11.2: Function test.

```go
package example_02

import "testing"

type Quote string
type Movie string
```

---

[1] A candidate quote could be `Choppa Quote = "Get to the choppa!!!"`.

```go
const (
    Crush    Quote = "To crush your enemies..."
    T1000    Quote = "I'll be back"
    Unknown  Quote = "unknown"

    Conan       Movie = "conan"
    Terminator2 Movie = "terminator2"
    Predator    Movie = "predator"
)

func MovieQuote(movie Movie) Quote {
    switch movie {
    case Conan:
        return Crush
    case Terminator2:
        return T1000
    default:
        return Unknown
    }
}

func TestMovieQuote(t *testing.T) {
    movies := []Movie{Conan, Predator, Terminator2}
    for _, m := range movies {
        if q := MovieQuote(m); q==Unknown{
            t.Error("unknown quote for movie", m)
        }
    }
}
```

```
=== RUN
TestMovieQuote
    example02_test.go
    :33: unknown quote
    for movie predator
--- FAIL:
TestMovieQuote (0.00s)
FAIL
```

The `testing` package offers a good number of features to help test creation. In this sense, testing requirements may change depending on factors such as timing. Sometimes depending on the testing stage time restrictions may appear. Tests can be skipped using `t.Skip()`. This can be used with the `testing.Short()` function that returns **true** when the `-short` param is set in the `go test` command to avoid exhaustive testing. Example 11.3 shows how to skip a test when the duration of an iteration goes beyond a given timeout. If the `-short` flat is set, test skipping will be automatically done.

Example 11.3: Test skipping.

```go
package example_03

import (
    "fmt"
    "math"
    "testing"
```

```
 7      "time"
 8 )
 9
10 func Sum(n int64, done chan bool) {
11      var result int64 = 0
12      var i int64
13      for i = 0; i<n; i++ {
14          result = result + i
15      }
16      done <- true
17 }
18
19 func TestSum(t *testing.T) {
20      var i int64
21      done := make(chan bool)
22      for i = 1000; i<math.MaxInt64; i+=100000 {
23          go Sum(i, done)
24          timeout := time.NewTimer(time.Millisecond)
25          select {
26          case <- timeout.C:
27              t.Skip(fmt.Sprintf("%d took longer than 1 millisecond",i))
28          case <- done:
29
30          }
31      }
32 }
```

```
go test -v
=== RUN   TestSum
    example03_test.go:27: 4101000 took longer than 1 millisecond
--- SKIP: TestSum (0.02s)
PASS
ok      github.com/juanmanuel-tirado/SaveTheWorldWithGo/10_testing/testing/example_03 0.256s
```

11.1.1. SUBTESTS

Certain tests can be reutilized to test particular code properties. permit triggering tests from other tests using the t.Run() function.

```
func TestFoo(t *testing.T) {
    // ...
    t.Run("A=1", func(t *testing.T) { ... })
```

CHAPTER 11. TESTING

```go
    t.Run("A=2", func(t *testing.T) { ... })
    t.Run("B=1", func(t *testing.T) { ... })
    // ...
}
```

In the example above, `TestFoo` invokes three testing functions. Subsequently, these testing functions can invoke others. The first argument is a string that can be conveniently set to a `key=value` format. This identifies the test and permits us to isolate what tests to be run in the `go test` command.

We show how to work with subtests with a practical example. Because the code can be a bit large to be shown at once, we split it into two sections for better readability. In this example, we want to test a `User` type that can be saved in XML and JSON formats. Check Chapter 8 if you are not familiar with encodings.

Example 11.4: Subtests in practice (part I).

```go
package example_03

import (
    "encoding/json"
    "encoding/xml"
    "errors"
    "fmt"
    "io/ioutil"
    "os"
    "testing"
)

type Encoding int

const (
    XML Encoding = iota
    JSON
)

type User struct {
    UserId string `xml:"id" json:"userId"`
    Email  string `xml:"email" json:"email"`
    Score  int    `xml:"score" json:"score"`
}

var Users []User

func (u *User) Equal(v User) bool{
    if u.UserId != v.UserId ||
        u.Email != v.Email ||
        u.Score != v.Score {
```

```go
32          return false
33      }
34      return true
35  }
36
37
38  func (u *User) encode(format Encoding) ([]byte, error) {
39      var encoded []byte = nil
40      var err error
41      switch format {
42      case XML:
43          encoded, err = xml.Marshal(u)
44      case JSON:
45          encoded, err = json.Marshal(u)
46      default:
47          errors.New("unknown encoding format")
48      }
49      return encoded, err
50  }
51
52  func (u *User) fromEncoded(format Encoding, encoded []byte) error {
53      recovered := User{}
54      var err error
55      switch format {
56      case XML:
57          err = xml.Unmarshal(encoded, &recovered)
58      case JSON:
59          err = json.Unmarshal(encoded, &recovered)
60      default:
61          err = errors.New("unknown encoding format")
62      }
63
64      if err == nil {
65          *u = recovered
66      }
67      return err
68  }
69
70  func (u *User) write(encoded []byte, path string) error {
71      err := ioutil.WriteFile(path, encoded, os.ModePerm)
72      return err
73  }
74
75  func (u *User) read(path string) ([]byte, error) {
76      encoded, err := ioutil.ReadFile(path)
77      return encoded, err
78  }
79
80  func (u *User) ToEncodedFile(format Encoding, filePath string) error {
81      encoded,err := u.encode(format)
```

```go
 82      if err != nil {
 83          return err
 84      }
 85      err = u.write(encoded, filePath)
 86      return err
 87  }
 88
 89  func (u *User) FromEncodedFile(format Encoding, filePath string) error {
 90      encoded, err := u.read(filePath)
 91      if err != nil {
 92          return err
 93      }
 94      err = u.fromEncoded(format, encoded)
 95      return err
 96  }
```

Example 11.4 shows the code to be tested. The `User` type can be written to a file and recovered from a file with `ToEncodedFile` and `FromEncodedFile` methods respectively. The `Encoding` type is an enum to indicate the format we are using.

For the same type we have various features: we can work with XML and JSON formats and we can write and read both formats. We can use subtests to obtain finer granularity and better control. Example 11.5 continues Example 11.4 with all the corresponding tests. The entry point for testing is `TestMain` where we can set up code to be later used during the testing process. Afterwards, we invoke `m.Run()` to start the tests as usual.

Example 11.5: Subtests in practice (part II).

```go
 98  func testWriteXML(t *testing.T) {
 99      tmpDir := os.TempDir()
100      for _, u := range Users {
101          f := tmpDir+u.UserId+".xml"
102          err := u.ToEncodedFile(XML, f)
103          if err != nil {
104              t.Error(err)
105          }
106      }
107  }
108
109  func testWriteJSON(t *testing.T) {
110      tmpDir := os.TempDir()
111      for _, u := range Users {
112          f := tmpDir+u.UserId+".json"
113          err := u.ToEncodedFile(JSON, f)
114          if err != nil {
115              t.Error(err)
116          }
117      }
```

```go
118  }
119
120
121  func testReadXML(t *testing.T) {
122      tmpDir := os.TempDir()
123      for _, u := range Users {
124          f := tmpDir+"/"+u.UserId+".xml"
125          newUser := User{}
126          err := newUser.FromEncodedFile(XML, f)
127          if err != nil {
128              t.Error(err)
129          }
130          if !newUser.Equal(u) {
131              t.Error(fmt.Sprintf("found %v, expected %v",newUser, u))
132          }
133      }
134  }
135
136  func testReadJSON(t *testing.T) {
137      tmpDir := os.TempDir()
138      for _, u := range Users {
139          f := tmpDir+"/"+u.UserId+".json"
140          newUser := User{}
141          err := newUser.FromEncodedFile(JSON, f)
142          if err != nil {
143              t.Error(err)
144          }
145          if !newUser.Equal(u) {
146              t.Error(fmt.Sprintf("found %v, expected %v",newUser, u))
147          }
148      }
149  }
150
151  func testXML(t *testing.T) {
152      t.Run("Action=Write", testWriteXML)
153      t.Run("Action=Read", testReadXML)
154
155      tmpDir := os.TempDir()
156      for _, u := range Users {
157          f := tmpDir + "/" + u.UserId + ".xml"
158          _ = os.Remove(f)
159      }
160  }
161
162  func testJSON(t *testing.T) {
163      t.Run("Action=Write", testWriteJSON)
164      t.Run("Action=Read", testReadJSON)
165
166      tmpDir := os.TempDir()
167      for _, u := range Users {
```

CHAPTER 11. TESTING

```
168            f := tmpDir + "/" + u.UserId + ".json"
169            _ = os.Remove(f)
170        }
171 }
172
173 func TestEncoding(t *testing.T) {
174     t.Run("Encoding=XML", testXML)
175     t.Run("Encoding=JSON", testJSON)
176 }
177
178 func TestMain(m *testing.M) {
179     UserA := User{"UserA","usera@email.org",42}
180     UserB := User{"UserB", "userb@email.org", 333}
181     Users = []User{UserA, UserB}
182
183     os.Exit(m.Run())
184 }
```

Notice that only `TestEncoding` is a valid testing function because it is named with an uppercase letter. The other functions (`testJSON`, `testXML`, `testReadJSON`, etc.) are not test functions and will not be executed alone when running `go test`. This is done in this way to permit a testing route using subsets starting at `TestEncoding`. The main idea is to test encodings (XML and JSON) separately as well as their write and read operations.

```
>>> go test -v
=== RUN    TestEncoding
=== RUN    TestEncoding/Encoding=XML
=== RUN    TestEncoding/Encoding=XML/Action=Write
=== RUN    TestEncoding/Encoding=XML/Action=Read
=== RUN    TestEncoding/Encoding=JSON
=== RUN    TestEncoding/Encoding=JSON/Action=Write
=== RUN    TestEncoding/Encoding=JSON/Action=Read
--- PASS: TestEncoding (0.00s)
    --- PASS: TestEncoding/Encoding=XML (0.00s)
        --- PASS: TestEncoding/Encoding=XML/Action=Write (0.00s)
        --- PASS: TestEncoding/Encoding=XML/Action=Read (0.00s)
    --- PASS: TestEncoding/Encoding=JSON (0.00s)
        --- PASS: TestEncoding/Encoding=JSON/Action=Write (0.00s)
        --- PASS: TestEncoding/Encoding=JSON/Action=Read (0.00s)
PASS
ok    github.com/juanmanuel-tirado/SaveTheWorldWithGo/10_testing/testing/example_03 0.087s
```

The output shows the routes containing the labels we defined in the subtests (e.g. `TestEncoding/Encoding=XML/Action=Write`). Now we can filter what tests to be run. For example, we can test JSON operations only by using the `-run` flag with a regular expression matching the labels we created for the subtests (`Encoding=JSON`).

```
go test -v -run /Encoding=JSON
=== RUN   TestEncoding
=== RUN   TestEncoding/Encoding=JSON
=== RUN   TestEncoding/Encoding=JSON/Action=Write
=== RUN   TestEncoding/Encoding=JSON/Action=Read
--- PASS: TestEncoding (0.00s)
    --- PASS: TestEncoding/Encoding=JSON (0.00s)
        --- PASS: TestEncoding/Encoding=JSON/Action=Write (0.00s)
        --- PASS: TestEncoding/Encoding=JSON/Action=Read (0.00s)
PASS
ok      github.com/juanmanuel-tirado/SaveTheWorldWithGo/10_testing/testing/example_03 0.087s
```

Or we can run every write operation with the regular expression `/./Action=Write` that matches any encoding.

```
go test -v -run /./Action=Write
=== RUN   TestEncoding
=== RUN   TestEncoding/Encoding=XML
=== RUN   TestEncoding/Encoding=XML/Action=Write
=== RUN   TestEncoding/Encoding=JSON
=== RUN   TestEncoding/Encoding=JSON/Action=Write
--- PASS: TestEncoding (0.00s)
    --- PASS: TestEncoding/Encoding=XML (0.00s)
        --- PASS: TestEncoding/Encoding=XML/Action=Write (0.00s)
    --- PASS: TestEncoding/Encoding=JSON (0.00s)
        --- PASS: TestEncoding/Encoding=JSON/Action=Write (0.00s)
PASS
ok      github.com/juanmanuel-tirado/SaveTheWorldWithGo/10_testing/testing/example_03 0.083s
```

Observe that only testing the read operation will fail because this operation expects a file previously written by the writing tests. Modifying the code to permit running `go test -v -run /./Action=Read` remains as an exercise for the reader.

11.2. EXAMPLES

In the same way, tests are defined in Go with functions starting with `Test`, examples can be defined with functions starting with . An interesting feature of examples is that the standard output they generate can be checked during testing. This is an important feature to ensure code coherence. Additionally, examples are included in Go generated documentation as described in Chapter 12.2.

Examples follow the naming convention described below.

```
func Example(...) // for the package
func ExampleF(...) // F for functions
func ExampleT(...) // T for types
func ExampleT_M(...) // M method of type T
func ExampleT_M_suffix(...) // with a suffix if more than one
```

To check the output correctness, every example must define the expected output to be generated. This is indicated using the `Output` comment as shown below. Where the last line must match the expected output. In those cases the output order is not guaranteed, we can use `Unordered output:` instead of `Output:`.

```
func ExampleX() {
    ...
    // Output:
    // Expected output
}
```

Example 11.6 defines the `User` type and its methods. Notice that the notation for the different examples follows the above guidelines. Examples are run like tests.

Example 11.6: Definition of examples.

```go
package example_01

import (
    "fmt"
    "strings"
)

type User struct {
    UserId string
    Friends []User
}

func (u *User) GetUserId() string {
    return strings.ToUpper(u.UserId)
}

func (u *User) CountFriends() int {
    return len(u.Friends)
}
```

```go
20
21  func CommonFriend(a *User, b *User) *User {
22      for _, af := range a.Friends {
23          for _, bf := range b.Friends {
24              if af.UserId == bf.UserId {
25                  return &af
26              }
27          }
28      }
29      return nil
30  }
31
32  func ExampleUser() {
33      j := User{"John", nil}
34      m := User{"Mary", []User{j}}
35      fmt.Println(m)
36      // Output:
37      // {Mary [{John []}]}
38  }
39
40  func ExampleCommonFriend() {
41      a := User{"a", nil}
42      b := User{"b", []User{a}}
43      c := User{"c", []User{a,b}}
44
45      fmt.Println(CommonFriend(&b,&c))
46      // Output:
47      // &{a []}
48  }
49
50  func ExampleUser_GetUserId() {
51      u := User{"John",nil}
52      fmt.Println(u.GetUserId())
53      // Output:
54      // JOHN
55  }
56
57  func ExampleUser_CountFriends() {
58      u := User{"John", nil}
59      fmt.Println(u.CountFriends())
60      // Output:
61      // 0
62  }
```

```
>>> go test -v
=== RUN    ExampleUser
--- PASS: ExampleUser
(0.00s)
=== RUN
ExampleCommonFriend
--- PASS:
ExampleCommonFriend
(0.00s)
=== RUN
ExampleGetUserId_User
--- PASS:
ExampleGetUserId_User
(0.00s)
=== RUN
ExampleCountFriends_User

--- PASS:
ExampleCountFriends_User
 (0.00s)
PASS
```

11.3. BENCHMARKING

Go provides benchmarking for those functions starting with the `Benchmark` prefix. Benchmarks are executed with the `go test` command when the `-bench` flag is present. They use the `testing.B` type instead of `testing.T` like normal tests.

A basic benchmarking is shown in Example 11.7 for a loop computing a sum of numbers. The value of `b.N` contains the number of repetitions of the operation in which performance is being measured. As can be confirmed from the benchmark output, the benchmark is run three times with different `b.N` values. This is done to ensure the reliability of the benchmark. Benchmarks are highly configurable using the available `go test` flags[2]. The benchmark output indicates the benchmark with the number of available goroutines (`BenchmarkSum-16`), the number of executed iterations (3817), and the nanoseconds elapsed per iteration (265858).

Example 11.7: Function benchmarking.

```go
package example_01

import (
    "fmt"
    "testing"
)

func Sum(n int64) int64 {
    var result int64 = 0
    var i int64
    for i = 0; i<n; i++ {
        result = result + i
    }
    return result
}

func BenchmarkSum(b *testing.B) {
    fmt.Println("b.N:",b.N)
    for i:=0;i<b.N;i++ {
        Sum(1000000)
    }
}
```

```
>>> go test -v -bench .
goos: darwin
```

---

[2]Check `go help testflag` for more information.

```
goarch: amd64
pkg: github.com/juanmanuel-tirado/SaveTheWorldWithGo/10_testing/benchmarking/
example_01
BenchmarkSum
b.N: 1
b.N: 100
b.N: 3817
BenchmarkSum-16            3817        265858 ns/op
PASS
ok      github.com/juanmanuel-tirado/SaveTheWorldWithGo/10_testing/benchmarking/
example_01   1.243s
```

By default, benchmark iterations are executed sequentially. In certain scenarios, particularly in those with shared resources, executing these iterations in parallel may be more valuable. The `RunParallel` method executes a function in parallel using the available testing goroutines. The number of available goroutines can be set with the `-cpu` flag in `go test`. The `Next()` function indicates if more iterations have to be executed.

```go
func BenchmarkSumParallel(b *testing.B) {
    b.RunParallel(func(pb *testing.PB){
        for pb.Next() {
            // Do something
        }
    })
}
```

Example 11.8 executes the same iterative addition from the previous example using parallel benchmarking. We vary the number of available goroutines to demonstrate how we can increase the number of operations per time. See how the suffix added to the benchmark function name reflects the current number of goroutines.

Example 11.8: Function parallel benchmarking.

```go
package example_02

import "testing"

func Sum(n int64) int64 {
    var result int64 = 0
    var i int64
    for i = 0; i<n; i++ {
        result = result + i
    }
    return result
}
```

```
13
14 func BenchmarkSumParallel(b *testing.B) {
15     b.RunParallel(func(pb *testing.PB){
16         for pb.Next() {
17             Sum(1000000)
18         }
19     })
20 }
```

```
>>> go test -v -bench . -cpu 1,2,4,8,16,32
goos: darwin
goarch: amd64
pkg: github.com/juanmanuel-tirado/SaveTheWorldWithGo/10_testing/benchmarking/example_02
BenchmarkSumParallel
BenchmarkSumParallel                 4324      249886 ns/op
BenchmarkSumParallel-2               9462      127147 ns/op
BenchmarkSumParallel-4              18202       66514 ns/op
BenchmarkSumParallel-8              31191       33927 ns/op
BenchmarkSumParallel-16             36373       32871 ns/op
BenchmarkSumParallel-32             36981       34199 ns/op
PASS
ok      github.com/juanmanuel-tirado/SaveTheWorldWithGo/10_testing/benchmarking/example_02    8.874s
```

11.4. Coverage

Test coverage aims at measuring what percentage of the code has been tested. Any Go test can be executed with the -cover flag to activate coverage metrics.

To run coverage tests we have to write tests and the code to be tested in different files. We measure the coverage of Example 11.9 with Example 11.10. We can expect poor coverage because we only explore one of the branches in the **switch** statement. We only get 22.2% of coverage.

Example 11.9: File to be tested.

```go
package example_01

func Periods(year int) string {
    switch {
    case year < -3000:
        return "Copper Age"
    case year < -2000:
        return "Bronze Age"
    case year < -1000:
        return "Iron Age"
    case year < 0:
        return "Classic Age"
    case year < 476:
        return "Roman Age"
    case year < 1492:
        return "Middle Age"
    case year < 1800:
        return "Modern Age"
    default:
        return "unknown"
    }
}
```

Example 11.10: Tests to show coverage.

```go
package example_01

import "testing"

func TestOptions(t *testing.T) {
    Periods(333)
}
```

```
>>> go test -v -cover .
=== RUN   TestOptions
--- PASS: TestOptions (0.00s)
PASS
coverage: 22.2% of statements
ok      github.com/juanmanuel-tirado/savetheworldwithgo/10_testing/coverage/
example_01   0.541s   coverage: 22.2% of statements
```

Go provides tools to get deeper insights into coverage tests. The output from the coverage test can be exported to an intermediate file using the `-coverprofile=filepath` flag. The information dumped to the chosen file can be used to print additional information using `go tool cover`. For example, `go tool cover -func=filepath` prints the coverage of every function. A more visual analysis can be done with `go tool cover -html=filepath`. This option opens up a browser and shows the coverage for code regions as shown in Figure 11.1 where it is clear that only one branch was tested.

This coverage visualization cannot be especially useful because it does not detail how many times each statement was run. This can be changed with the `-covermode` flag to one of the three available modes: `set` boolean indicating if the statement was run or not,

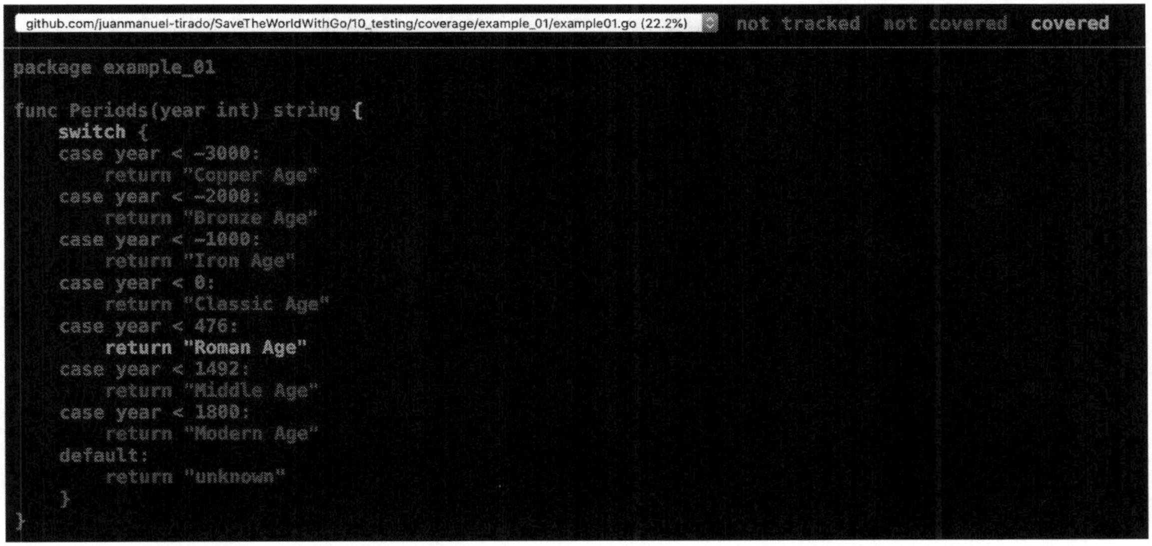

Figure 11.1: HTML detail for test coverage in Example 11.10.

`count` counting how many times it was run, and `atomic` similar to `count` but safe for multithreaded executions.

11.5. Profiling

Getting high performance and finding potential optimizations in your code is not an easy task. Profiling is a complex task that requires a deep understanding of code and the underlying language. Go provides the `runtime/pprof`[3] package with functions to define profiling entities. Fortunately, profiling functions are ready-to-use with benchmarks which facilitates the exploration of CPU and memory consumption in our code.

Profiling can be generated by launching benchmarks like described in this chapter. To force profiling, the `-cpuprofile filepath` and `-memprofile filepath` flags must be set for CPU and memory profiling respectively during `go test`. For both profiles, a file is created. These files can be interpreted by `pprof`[4] to generate and visualize useful reports. Thi tool is already integrated into the `go tool pprof` command.

To illustrate how to use the profiling, we take the benchmark from Example 11.11. The `BuildGraph` function returns a directed graph with edges connecting randomly selected vertices. The graph may not have sense, but it will help us understand how to approach a case of performance profiling.

---
[3] https://golang.org/pkg/runtime/pprof/
[4] https://github.com/google/pprof

Example 11.11: Profiling of a graph generation program.

```go
package example_01

import (
    "math/rand"
    "testing"
    "time"
)

func BuildGraph(vertices int, edges int) [][]int {
    graph := make([][]int, vertices)
    for i:=0;i<len(graph);i++{
        graph[i] = make([]int,0,1)
    }
    for i:=0;i<edges;i++{
        from := rand.Intn(vertices)
        to := rand.Intn(vertices)
        graph[from]=append(graph[from],to)
    }

    return graph
}

func BenchmarkGraph(b *testing.B) {
    rand.Seed(time.Now().UnixNano())
    for i:=0;i<b.N;i++ {
        BuildGraph(100,20000)
    }
}
```

First, we run the benchmarks dumping profiling information for memory and CPU using `go test`.

```
>>> go test -bench=. -benchmem -memprofile mem.out -cpuprofile cpu.out
goos: darwin
goarch: amd64
pkg: github.com/juanmanuel-tirado/SaveTheWorldWithGo/10_testing/profiling/example_01
BenchmarkGraph-16    1365    827536 ns/op    411520 B/op    901 allocs/op
PASS
ok   github.com/juanmanuel-tirado/SaveTheWorldWithGo/10_testing/profiling/example_01  1.759s
```

Now `mem.out` and `cpu.out` files can be used to generate the corresponding reports. First, we generate visual reports to have a superficial understanding of what is going on. In our case, we generate a PDF output for both, memory and CPU profiles.

```
>>> go tool pprof -pdf -output cpu.pdf cpu.out
Generating report in cpu.pdf
>>> go tool pprof -pdf -output mem.pdf mem.out
Generating report in mem.pdf
```

Now `cpu.pdf` and `mem.pdf` are visualizations of CPU and memory profiles. Check out the `go tool` help section for further available output formats [5]. From the visual report of the memory utilization shown in Figure 11.2 we can observe that `BuildGraph` is basically consuming all the available memory.

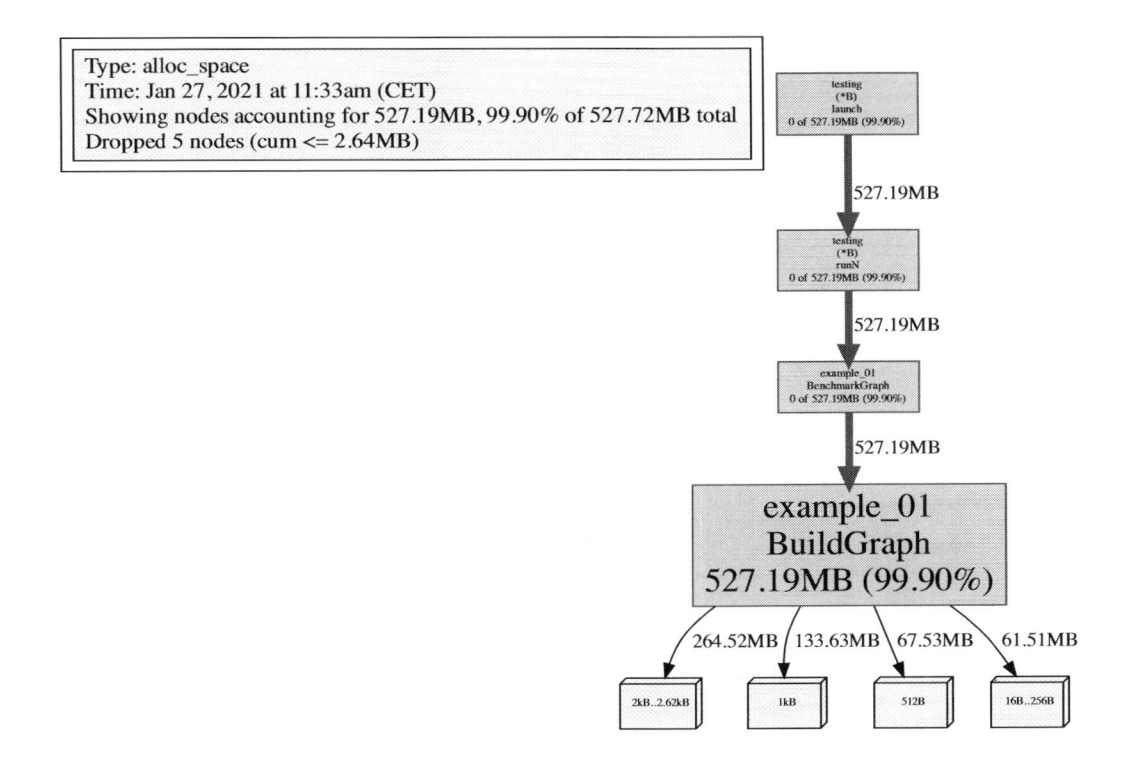

Figure 11.2: Memory profile visualization of Example 11.11.

The CPU visualization from the excerpt in Figure 11.3 looks more complex as it includes all the internal calls of the program. However, we can see that there is a bottleneck in the utilization of the random generation numbers. The largest the node size in the

---

[5] `go tool pprof --help`

report, the longer time was spent there.

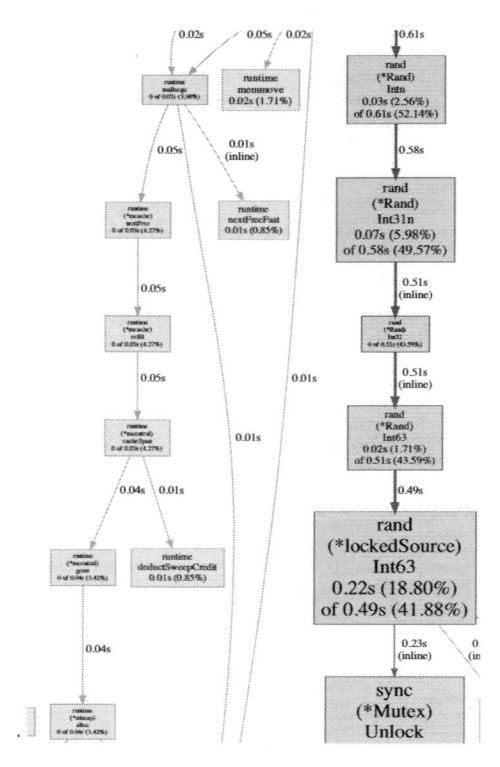

Figure 11.3: Excerpt of the CPU profile visualization from Example 11.11.

We can go for a more detailed analysis using the online mode. This mode comes with plenty of options that will help us find what is going on line by line. Entering the `go tool pprof` we can explore the profiling output we have previously generated. The command `top` prints in decreasing order the functions where the program spent more time. The column `%flat` displays the percentage of time the program spent in the function. Column `%sum` is the total percentage spent after we leave that function. For example, `math/rand.(*Rand).Intn` only uses 5% of the execution time (`%flat`). However, 74.17% of the program time has already been spent when we reach that function.

```
>>> go tool pprof cpu.out
Type: cpu
Time: Jan 27, 2021 at 12:06pm (CET)
Duration: 1.30s, Total samples = 1.20s (92.08%)
Entering interactive mode (type "help" for commands, "o" for options)
(pprof) top
Showing nodes accounting for 1010ms, 84.17% of 1200ms total
Showing top 10 nodes out of 82
```

CHAPTER 11. TESTING

```
      flat  flat%    sum%        cum    cum%
     250ms 20.83%  20.83%      250ms  20.83%   sync.(*Mutex).Unlock (inline)
     220ms 18.33%  39.17%      530ms  44.17%   math/rand.(*lockedSource).Int63
     210ms 17.50%  56.67%      210ms  17.50%   runtime.kevent
     150ms 12.50%  69.17%      690ms  57.50%   math/rand.(*Rand).Int31n
      60ms  5.00%  74.17%      750ms  62.50%   math/rand.(*Rand).Intn
      40ms  3.33%  77.50%       60ms   5.00%   math/rand.(*rngSource).Int63 (
     inline)
      20ms  1.67%  79.17%      870ms  72.50%   github.com/juanmanuel-tirado/
     SaveTheWorldWithGo/10_testing/profiling/example_01.BuildGraph
      20ms  1.67%  80.83%       20ms   1.67%   math/rand.(*rngSource).Uint64
      20ms  1.67%  82.50%       20ms   1.67%   runtime.madvise
      20ms  1.67%  84.17%       20ms   1.67%   runtime.memclrNoHeapPointers
```

We can continue exploring our program with a more detailed view of the elapsed time per line of code. We list how `BuildGraph` consumes CPU with the command `list BuildGraph`. Now it becomes clear that the generation of random numbers is the main CPU bottleneck in our program. With this information, we can try to replace these functions for other functions with better performance, or think about a different approach to our solution.

```
(pprof) list BuildGraph
Total: 1.20s
ROUTINE ======================== github.com/juanmanuel-tirado/
SaveTheWorldWithGo/10_testing/profiling/example_01.BuildGraph in /github.com/
juanmanuel-tirado/SaveTheWorldWithGo/10_testing/profiling/example_01/
example01_test.go
      20ms    870ms (flat, cum) 72.50% of Total
         .        .      5:      "testing"
         .        .      6:      "time"
         .        .      7:)
         .        .      8:
         .        .      9:func BuildGraph(vertices int, edges int) [][]int {
         .     20ms     10:      graph := make([][]int, vertices)
         .        .     11:      for i:=0;i<len(graph);i++{
         .     10ms     12:          graph[i] = make([]int,0,1)
         .        .     13:      }
         .        .     14:      for i:=0;i<edges;i++{
         .    390ms     15:          from := rand.Intn(vertices)
         .    370ms     16:          to := rand.Intn(vertices)
      20ms     80ms     17:          graph[from]=append(graph[from],to)
         .        .     18:      }
         .        .     19:
         .        .     20:      return graph
         .        .     21:}
         .        .     22:
```

11.6. SUMMARY

This Chapter presents the tools for testing available in Go. We explain how tests are carried out and organized with practical examples that may serve as a basis for any real project testing. We explore how the `testing` package also offers benchmarking tools that can take advantage of parallel execution. Finally, we show how code coverage and profiling can be done to achieve a better understanding of our code.

12. MODULES AND DOCUMENTATION

Nowadays is very difficult to find programming projects to be designed as isolated pieces of code. Projects use code developed by other developers. Other projects are designed to be incorporated into other projects. These dependencies between projects require tools to facilitate the definition of what external code a project requires. And even more important, a systematic way to document our code so it can be shared with others. This Chapter explains how Go incorporates code into our projects using modules and how we can document our programs.

12.1. MODULES

Dealing with dependencies is always key to ensure code compatibility and reproducibility. As it was explained in Chapter 2.1.1 and showed throughout this book, the most basic tool to make code accessible to our programs is `go get`. However, this is a very basic solution that does not solve issues such as code versioning. Nowadays projects require several third-party projects to run. For some years various solutions were proposed to manage code dependencies in Go, until Go modules became the official solution.

> ⑦ Go 1.16 was released while this Chapter was being written in version v0.1.0. One of the most important changes in this release is the use of go modules by default. For compatibility purposes, and to facilitate migrations the environment variable `GO111MODULE` can be set to false. However, this variable will be ignored in Go 1.17. This means, that every project will be expected to use Go modules.

Go modules facilitates the management of dependencies and makes it easier to share project requirements among developers. The idea is simple, to store the requirements of a project in a common format that can be used to acquire all the necessary code for a successful compilation. Go modules are governed by the `go.mod` file that contains information about what projects in what versions are required. Assume we start with the code from Example 12.1. This code uses a third-party logger to print a message. In the most basic approach, we would download the code using `go get`. However, with modules, we can simplify this process.

Example 12.1: Program using modules.

```go
1 package main
2
3 import "github.com/rs/zerolog/log"
4
5 func main() {
6     log.Info().Msg("Save the world with Go!!!")
7 }
```

In the folder containing our code we run `go mod init`. This creates a go.mod file which looks like:

```
module github.com/juanmanuel-tirado/SaveTheWorldWithGo/11_modules/modules/
    example_01

go 1.15
```

It contains the module name and the Go version we are running. The `go.mod` file is only generated in the root folder of the package. Now we can add a dependency. Dependencies are declared one by line using the `require package "version"` syntax. Fortunately, Go modules does this automatically for us. Every action executed with the `go` command that requires modules to be loaded (`build`, `run`, `test`, etc.) triggers the analysis of the required modules.

```
>>> go build main.go
go: finding module for package github.com/rs/zerolog/log
go: found github.com/rs/zerolog/log in github.com/rs/zerolog v1.20.0
```

Now if we check our `go.mod` file we can find a new line with the `zerolog` package and its current version. The `// indirect` comment indicates that this package has indirect dependencies. This means that additional modules were downloaded to satisfy the requirements of other modules. Actually, the zerolog package has its own `go.mod` file with its own dependencies to be satisfied.

```
module github.com/juanmanuel-tirado/SaveTheWorldWithGo/11_modules/modules/
    example_01

go 1.15

require github.com/rs/zerolog v1.20.0 // indirect
```

The required modules are downloaded into the `GOPATH` folder as usual. However, we may need to store them in a vendor folder. This is not the recommended way, but if we still need to do it running `go mod vendor` stores the required modules into the vendor folder.

> ⚠ When sharing our modules with others privately or in a public platform such as Github, be sure that you do not use a vendor folder. If so, you will ruin all the benefits of using Go modules. Furthermore, you will replicate large pieces of code that are intended to be maintained by others.

> ⚠ Go modules is the default dependencies manager in Go since version 1.16. You may find projects and modules using other solutions such as `go dep`. Be careful when importing these modules to your code, and be sure they are compatible with your Go modules.

12.1.1. Working with versions

We assume the reader to be familiar with versions, in particular semantic versioning [14]. If so, you must understand that it usually occurs that for the same project, different versions may lead to incompatibilities and undesired behaviours. By default, Go modules check for the latest available version of a module. However, our code may not use that version or there could be incompatibilities with indirect dependencies.

Go uses an algorithm called Minimal Versions Selection (MVS) to select the module versions to be used when building a module [13]. This algorithm builds a dependency graph which is explored to find the list of most recent versions that satisfies all modules' requirements. This algorithm is used by `go mod` to fulfil the `go.mod` file. However, this automatic process may not return the correct versions for your solution. In certain scenarios, it may be required to downgrade or to keep using older versions for different reasons. Go modules has a list of directives that may help you to manage these situations.

- `require`

As mentioned above, the `require` directive declares a module dependency with a given version. If not version is set, the latest one is taken. The *//indirect* comment is automatically added for transitive dependencies found during the analysis.

```
require golang.org/x/net v1.2.3
require (
    github.com/rs/zerolog v1.20.0 //indirect
)
```

- `exclude`

This directive prevents a module version from being loaded.

```
exclude golang.org/x/net v1.2.3

exclude (
    github.com/rs/zerolog v1.20.0
)
```

- `replace`

Using this directive the contents of a module can be changed by a different one. If the replacement is an absolute or relative path (./ or ../), this is interpreted to be a local file. This is a good solution when we need to use modules not exposed through the Internet.

```
replace golang.org/x/net v1.2.3 => something.com/x/net v1.2.3
replace (
    github.com/rs/zerolog v1.20.0 => example.com/rs/zerolog v1.20.0
    google.golang.org/grpc v1.35.0 => ./grpc v1.35.0
)
```

- `retract`

This directive indicates a version or versions of this module that must not be used in any `go.mod`. This may occur for example if a version has been prematurely released or if it contains some security issues.

```
retract (
    v1.2.3
    v1.0.0
```

```
)
```

This example indicates that versions v1.2.3 and v1.0.0 must not be used. In this case, if a module requires v1.0.0 the MVS algorithm will return the previously released version, perhaps v0.98.0. Something similar may occur if v1.2.3 is requested.

12.2. Documentation

Documenting code is one of those tasks developers always postpone, although we know it is a big mistake. A successful project must have good, up-to-date, and accessible documentation. Not only to ensure others understand the code but to make code maintainable. Go follows a minimalist approach to code documentation that can be summarized with the following rules:

- Comments before `package` declaration are considered to be a package comment.

- Every package *should* have a comment. For packages with multiple files, the package comment only needs to be present in one file.

- Every exported name *should* have a comment.

- Every commented item begins with the name of the item it describes.

Example 12.2 documents a piece of code following the mentioned conventions. It is important to notice that every comment starts with the name of the commented item. For large explanations, in particular, those containing code the /**/ comment marks can be used.

Example 12.2: Program documentation.

```go
// Package example_01 contains a documentation example.
package example_01

import "fmt"

// Msg represents a message.
type Msg struct{
    // Note is the note to be sent with the message.
    Note string
}

// Send a message to a target destination.
func (m *Msg) Send(target string) {
```

```
14        fmt.Printf("Send %s to %s\n", m.Note, target)
15 }
16
17 // Receive a message from a certain origin.
18 func (m *Msg) Receive(origin string) {
19        fmt.Printf("Received %s from %s\n", m.Note, origin)
20 }
```

Documented code can be processed with the `go doc` tool executing `go doc -all` in the project folder.

```
>>> go doc -all
package example_01 // import "github.com/juanmanuel-tirado/SaveTheWorldWithGo
    /11_modules/godoc/example_01"

Package example_01 contains a documentation example.

TYPES

type Msg struct {
   // Note is the note to be sent with the message.
   Note string
}
    Msg represents a message.

func (m *Msg) Receive(origin string)
    Receive a message from a certain origin.

func (m *Msg) Send(target string)
    Send a message to a target destination.
```

The `go doc` tool can actually display the documentation of any package available in the `GOPATH`. Apart from the flags and options [1] arguments are intended to follow the Go syntax. For example, `go doc fmt` prints the help for the `fmt` package, while `go doc json.decode` prints the documentation of the `Decode` method from the `json` package.

For a more interactive solution for documentation, Go provides the `godoc` server. Executing `godoc -http=:8080` serves incoming requests at port 8080 of your localhost. An interesting feature of `godoc` is the addition of runnable examples. The server interprets examples following the notation convention explained in Section 11.2. These examples must be allocated into a separated package to be interpreted. Normally, this is the same package with the `_test` suffix. In Example 12.3, we have written examples to be displayed with our documentation.

---

[1] `go help doc` for more details.

CHAPTER 12. MODULES AND DOCUMENTATION

Example 12.3: Documented examples for Example 12.2.

```go
package example_01_test

import "github.com/juanmanuel-tirado/savetheworldwithgo/11_modules/godoc/example_01"

func ExampleMsg_Send() {
    m := example_01.Msg{"Hello"}
    m.Send("John")
    // Output:
    // Send Hello to John
}

func ExampleMsg_Receive() {
    m := example_01.Msg{"Hello"}
    m.Receive("John")
    // Output:
    // Received Hello from John
}
```

To make examples more accessible, it is possible to run the server in an interactive mode that permits examples to be executed in a runtime box. The command `godoc -http =:8080 -play` activates these boxes as shown in Figure 12.1.

12.3. SUMMARY

This Chapter shows how to manage dependencies in Go using Go modules to facilitate the adoption and exchange of projects. It also introduced the pragmatic approach to code documentation in Go and how this can be queried using the Go doc server.

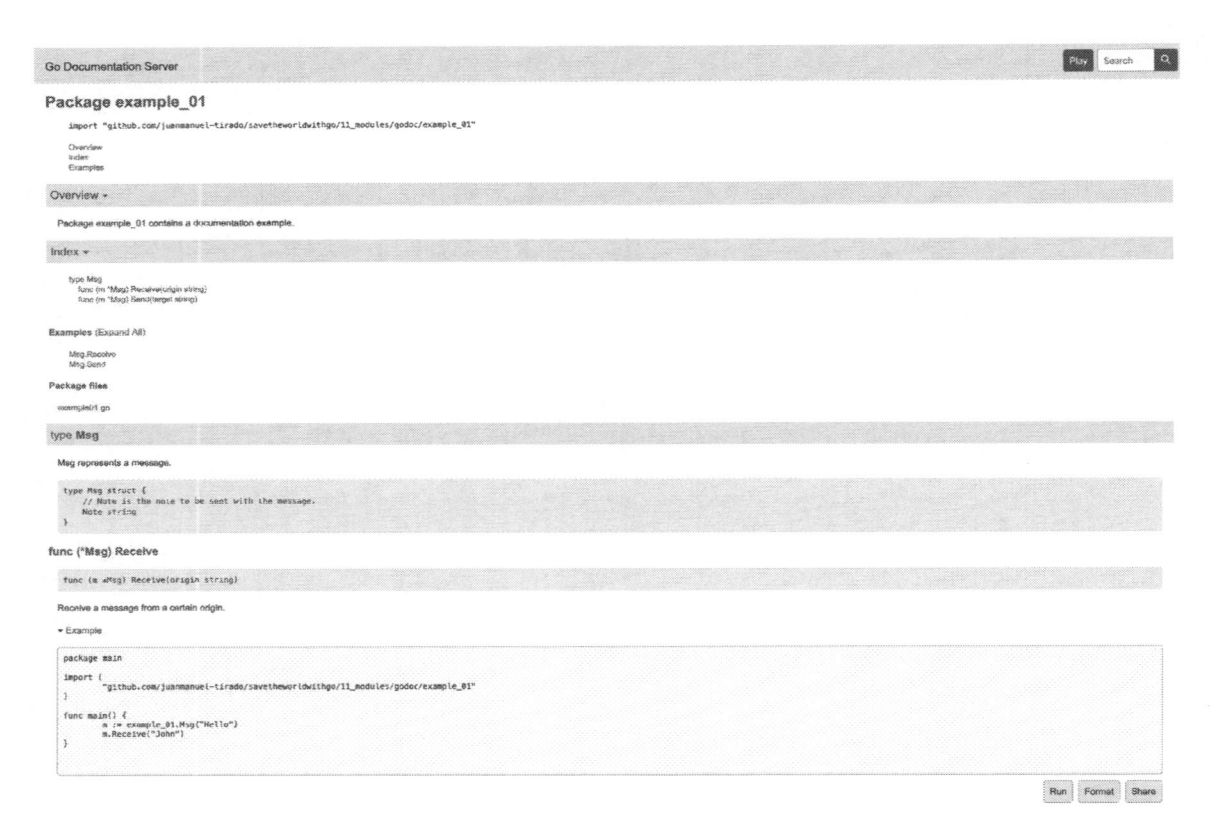

Figure 12.1: Excerpt of `godoc` Example 12.2 documentation.

13. CGO

One of the foundations of software development is code reuse. If a piece of software does the job, the wisest decision is to reuse it. Unfortunately, this is not always possible. It is common to find that the software we are looking for is written in a different programming language, or simply there is no way we can use it without over-engineering. With Cgo, we can interact with code written in C. This enables Go programs to access a large number of existing solutions. In this Chapter, we explore how to use Cgo to interact with C programs and libraries.

13.1. USE C CODE FROM GO

Using Cgo we can call code written in C from Go. More precisely, Go can use functions and structs defined in C. This can be done with the pseudopackage c that combines both programming sources into the same Go package. For example, let's assume that we have to execute the following `func_in_c` function written in C.

```
#include <stdio.h>
void func_in_c() {
   printf("printed with C code\n");
}
```

We can integrate this C code into our Go code like shown in Example 13.1. Observe that the code is added inside a commented region before the **import** `"C"` statement. This informs the Go compiler that there is C code to be linked. Alternatively, the /**/ comment delimiters can be used like shown in Example 13.2. This permits to include comments inside the C preamble.

Example 13.1: C function called from Go.

```go
package main

// #include <stdio.h>
// void func_in_c() {
//   printf("printed with C code\n");
// }
import "C"
import "fmt"

func main() {
    C.func_in_c()
    fmt.Println("printed with Go code")
}
```

```
printed with C code
printed with Go code
```

Example 13.2: C function called from Go with comments.

```go
package main

/*
#include <stdio.h>
// This is a comment
void func_in_c() {
  printf("printed with C code\n");
}
*/
import "C"
import "fmt"

func main() {
    C.func_in_c()
    fmt.Println("printed with Go code")
}
```

```
printed with C code
printed with Go code
```

The pseudopackage C makes accessible all the functions, structs, and variables from linked C code. To invoke our function we only have to invoke it like `C.func_in_c()`.

> You may find it interesting that there are other Go compilers apart from the one maintained by Google. For example, gccgo [5] is maintained by GNU under a General Public License and GopherJS [7] compiles Go code into pure Javascript.

13.2. EXCHANGING VARIABLES

When exchanging variables between Go and C, we must be aware that data types may not be defined in the same way. For example, the Go `int` type can be 32 or 64 bits depending on the architecture. However, C `int` typed variables are 16 or 32 bits long. Obviously, types must match between both languages to work correctly. Fortunately, the c pseudopackage offers functions to deal with these situations.

Example 13.3 defines a C function that sums two integers passed by argument. If the function is called using native Go integers as parameters, the compilation will fail with a message like `cannot use a (type int) as type _Ctype_int in argument to _Cfunc_sum`. Using `c.int` we can convert from Go native `int` to C following the signature of the target function.

Example 13.3: C function with arguments called from Go.

```go
package main

/*
 int sum(int a, int b) {
   return a + b;
 }
*/
import "C"
import "fmt"

func main() {
    a := 1
    b := 1
    c := C.sum(C.int(a), C.int(b))
    fmt.Printf("%d + %d = %d\n", a, b, c)
}
```

```
1 + 1 = 2
```

Some native data types offered by C have no similar types in Go, and the other way around. For example, Go has no `short` type but the `int16` type can be considered to be similar. Other types like `signed char` are not available in Go although, the `byte` type has the same size and range.

Example 13.4 shows some examples of type conversions and how they are used in C. Notice that the printed output depends on the used string formatter character from the `printf`.

Example 13.4: Casting types between Go and C.

```
1  package main
2
3  /*
4  #include<stdio.h>
5  void f_char(char in) {
6      printf("char %c\n", in);
7  }
8  void f_schar(signed char in) {
9      printf("signed char %X\n", in);
10 }
11 void f_uchar(unsigned char in) {
12     printf("unsigned char %c\n", in);
13 }
14 void f_short(short in) {
15     printf("short %d\n", in);
16 }
17 void f_ushort(unsigned short in) {
18     printf("unsigned short %u\n", in);
19 }
20 void f_int(int in) {
21     printf("int %d\n", in);
22 }
23 void f_uint(unsigned int in) {
24     printf("unsigned int %u\n", in);
25 }
26 void f_long(long in) {
27     printf("long %X\n", in);
28 }
29 void f_ulong(unsigned long in) {
30     printf("unsigned long %X\n", in);
31 }
32 void f_longlong(long long in) {
33     printf("long long %X\n", in);
34 }
35 void f_ulonglong(unsigned long long in) {
36     printf("unsigned long long %X\n", in);
37 }
38 void f_float(float in) {
39     printf("float %e\n", in);
40 }
41 void f_double(double in) {
42     printf("float %e\n", in);
43 }
44 */
45 import "C"
46 import "math"
47
48 func main() {
49     C.f_char(C.char(42))
50     C.f_schar(C.schar(-42))
```

```
char *
signed char FFFFFFD6
unsigned char *
short -42
unsigned short 42
int -42
unsigned int 2147483647
long FFFFFFD6
unsigned long FFFFFFFF
long long FFFFFFFF
unsigned long long FFFFFFFF
float 3.402823e+38
float 1.797693e+308
```

CHAPTER 13. CGO

```
51    C.f_uchar(C.uchar(42))
52
53    C.f_short(C.short(-42))
54    C.f_ushort(C.ushort(42))
55
56    C.f_int(C.int(-42))
57    C.f_uint(C.uint(math.MaxInt32))
58
59    C.f_long(C.long(-42))
60    C.f_ulong(C.ulong(math.MaxUint64))
61
62    C.f_longlong(C.longlong(math.MaxInt64))
63    C.f_ulonglong(C.ulonglong(math.MaxUint64))
64
65    C.f_float(C.float(math.MaxFloat32))
66    C.f_double(C.double(math.MaxFloat64))
67 }
```

A special case to be considered is strings manipulation. Strings in C are usually represented by an array of chars terminated with the end of string character (zero). The pseudopackage C offers three functions to manipulate strings between C and Go.

`C.CString(str)`	Returns the pointer to the first character from `str`
`C.GoString(c_str)`	Transforms a `char*` into a Go string.
`C.GoStringN(c_str,n)`	Like `C.GoString`, but it only returns the first `n` characters.

Table 13.1: Functions to manipulate strings in Cgo.

How to use these functions is shown in Example 13.5. When using the `C.CString` function, the generated string is allocated outside the control of the garbage collector. To release the allocated memory, the `free` function from C has to be called.

Example 13.5: Strings manipulation between Go and C.

```
1  package main
2
3  /*
4  #include <stdlib.h>
5  #include <stdio.h>
6  void func_c_print(char* input) {
7      printf("C prints: %s\n",input);
8  }
9  char* func_c_str() {
10     char* str = "this is a C string";
11     return str;
12 }
```

```
C prints: this is a Go string
Go prints: this is a C string
Go prints: this is a
```

```
13  */
14  import "C"
15  import (
16      "fmt"
17      "unsafe"
18  )
19
20  func main() {
21      str := "this is a Go string"
22      goToC := C.CString(str)
23      C.func_c_print(goToC)
24      defer C.free(unsafe.Pointer(goToC))
25
26      cStr := C.func_c_str()
27      cToGo := C.GoString(cStr)
28      fmt.Printf("Go prints: %s\n", cToGo)
29
30      nCToGo := C.GoStringN(cStr, 10)
31      fmt.Printf("Go prints: %s\n", nCToGo)
32  }
```

> ⚠ Remember that Go uses a garbage collector that controls memory allocation. Pointers and structs allocated by a C program escape from its control. To release a C pointer use the `free` function defined in the `stdio.h` header. From Go you can call this function with `C.free` passing a pointer by argument with `unsafe.Pointer`. Be careful. Although Go is a memory-safe language, releasing memory in this way may compromise your code.

13.3. EXCHANGING ARRAYS AND STRUCTS

We have seen how native data types and strings can be exchanged between Go and C. Other more complex data types like arrays and structs can also be shared between both languages.

For arrays using native data types, we have to provide C with a pointer to the first element. Example 13.6 uses a C function to compute the sum of an array of integers. The variable `first` is the pointer to be passed to `sum_array`. Notice that `&a[0]` is the pointer to the first integer in the slice. The casting (`*C.int`) returns the C compatible pointer required by the function.

Example 13.6: Passing arrays from Go to C.

CHAPTER 13. CGO

```
1  package main
2
3  /*
4  #include<stdio.h>
5  int sum_array(int a[], int length)  {
6      int i,result = 0;
7      for (i = 0; i < length; i++) {
8          result += a[i];
9      }
10     return result;
11 }
12 */
13 import "C"
14 import "fmt"
15
16 func main() {
17     a := []int32{0, 1, 2, 3, 4}
18     first := (*C.int)(&a[0])
19     res := C.sum_array(first, C.int(len(a)))
20     fmt.Printf("The result is: %d\n", res)
21 }
```

```
The result is: 10
```

Passing arrays from C to Go is fairly similar. Example 13.7 defines a C function that fills an array with consecutive numbers. Because this array was allocated by C, we have to release it (C.free). When printing the received value from C, we get a pointer (28297184). Using the unsafe.Pointer and the corresponding casting we can recover the slice. Notice that the conversion is done with (*[5]int32). First, the original data type was int which is similar to int32 in Go. For type safety, we have to indicate the integer size with int32. Remember, that the Go int type size may vary depending on your architecture. Next, we must indicate the size of the slice, because Go cannot determine the size of the array. Observe, that we are working with pointers that do not specify the total number of elements in the collection.

Example 13.7: Passing arrays from C to Go.

```
1  package main
2
3  /*
4  #include <stdlib.h>
5  int* create_array(int n) {
6    int* result;
7    result = (int*)malloc(sizeof(int)*n);
8    for( int i = 0; i < n; i++){
9        result[i] = i;
10   }
11   return result;
```

```
C returns a pointer: 28297184
We extract the content: &[0 1 2 3 4]
->0
->1
->2
->3
->4
```

```go
12  }
13  */
14  import "C"
15  import (
16      "fmt"
17      "unsafe"
18  )
19
20  func main() {
21      array := C.create_array(5)
22      defer C.free(unsafe.Pointer(array))
23      fmt.Printf("C returns a pointer: %d\n", array)
24      aux := (*[5]int32)(unsafe.Pointer(array))
25      fmt.Printf("We extract the content: %d\n", aux)
26      for _, i := range aux {
27          fmt.Printf("->%d\n", i)
28      }
29  }
```

The approach to exchange struct types between Go and C is very similar to what we have explored in terms of passing arrays. Structs declared in C are available in Go. This means that we can instantiate C structs. Unfortunately, we cannot manage in C structs only declared in Go. In this case, a simple solution is to declare in C structs similar to those we have in Go.

In Example 13.8, we want to process in C a struct declared in Go. To do so, the User struct has equivalent declarations in both Go and C. Observe that in Go we set the fields type size with `int32` to ensure that type sizes match between both languages. The function `print_user` receives a pointer to the struct. In Go, we cast u to pointer *C.User. Notice that we have access to the definition of the User struct declared in C. Finally, C can print the content from our Go instantiated struct.

Example 13.8: Passing structs from Go to C.

```go
1  package main
2
3  /*
4  #include <stdio.h>
5  typedef struct {
6      int id;
7      int age;
8  } User;
9
10 void print_user(User *u) {
11     printf("Id: %d\n", u->id);
12     printf("Age: %d\n", u->age);
13 }
```

```
Id: 1234
Age: 33
```

```go
14  */
15  import "C"
16  import "unsafe"
17  
18  type User struct {
19      Id  int32
20      Age int32
21  }
22  
23  func main() {
24      u := User{1234, 33}
25      userToC := (*C.User)(unsafe.Pointer(&u))
26      C.print_user(userToC)
27  }
```

The previous example was a bit artificial because from Go we have access to those structs defined in C. However, it still applies in those scenarios where our code cannot fully rely on C definitions.

In Example 13.9, Go code accesses the fields of a struct instantiated in C. Observe that these fields can be accessed as usual (`u.id`), although certain castings may be done like in the case of strings (`u.name`). As already mentioned, this allocated struct must be released. In this case, this is done from Go although it could be done in C.

Example 13.9: Passing structs from C to Go.

```go
1   package main
2   
3   /*
4   #include <stdlib.h>
5   typedef struct {
6     char* name;
7     int id;
8   } User;
9   
10  User* create_user(char* name) {
11     User* u;
12     u = (User*)malloc(sizeof(User*));
13     u -> name = name;
14     u -> id = 1234;
15     return u;
16  }
17  */
18  import "C"
19  import (
20      "fmt"
21      "unsafe"
22  )
```

```
User name: John
User id: 1234
```

```go
23
24 func main() {
25     name := C.CString("John")
26     u := C.create_user(name)
27     defer C.free(unsafe.Pointer(u))
28     fmt.Printf("User name: %s\n", C.GoString(u.name))
29     fmt.Printf("User id: %d\n", u.id)
30 }
```

Finally, Example 13.10 shows how to instantiate a C struct from Go. This is done like a regular Go struct. The only consideration is to use compatible data types. In this case, we have to declare a C string and convert the integer to a C compatible format. One question that may arise is whether the x variable should be released or not. This is a simple exercise for the reader to be tested. The answer depends on whether this struct is under the control of the garbage collector or not.

Example 13.10: Instantiating C structs in Go.

```go
1  package main
2
3  /*
4  #include <stdlib.h>
5  typedef struct {
6    char* name;
7    int id;
8  } User;
9  */
10 import "C"
11 import (
12    "fmt"
13    "unsafe"
14 )
15
16 func main() {
17    name := C.CString("John")
18    defer C.free(unsafe.Pointer(name))
19    x := C.User{name: name, id: C.int(1234)}
20    fmt.Println(C.GoString(x.name), x.id)
21    // Should we release x?
22    //C.free(unsafe.Pointer(&x))
23 }
```

```
John 1234
```

13.4. Linking libraries

Accessing external libraries is one of the most powerful features of Cgo. This makes it possible to use a large variety of already existing solutions. The Cgo preamble admits pseudo `#cgo` directives to indicate to the compiler what libraries and headers to use.

The preamble below is an example of what instructions can be given to the compiler. Refer to the documentation for a complete list of available directives[1]. If you are familiar with C compilation directives, you have probably recognized the flags to link libraries (`-lpng`) or other compilation flags (`-DPNG_DEBUG=1`).

```
/*
#cgo LDFLAGS: -L/libfolder -lpng
#cgo CFLAGS: -I/headersfolder -DPNG_DEBUG=1
#cgo amd64 386 CFLAGS: -DX86=1
*/
import "C"
```

An interesting example of what we can get with these directives is the utilization of functions implemented in other libraries. In Example 13.10, we use some mathematical functions implemented in C. We link the standard maths library using `#cgo LDFLAGS: -lm`. Remember that following the compiler notation, the library to be linked by `-lm` is `libm.so`. If no alternative library path is given with `-L`, the default path is assumed. The `math.h` headers file exposes the signature of all the functions and constants from the library. Finally, we can call any function defined in the `math.h` header. In the example, we compute logarithms, sines, and cosines just to show some of the available options.

Example 13.11: Go executing functions from the C math library.

```
package main

/*
#cgo LDFLAGS: -lm
#include <math.h>
*/
import "C"
import "fmt"

func main() {
    fmt.Printf("Log10 10: %f\n", C.log10(C.double(10)))
    fmt.Printf("Sine Pi: %f\n", C.sin(C.M_PI/2))
    fmt.Printf("Cosine Pi: %f\n", C.cos(C.M_PI))
```

```
Log10 10: 1.000000
Sine Pi: 1.000000
Cosine Pi: -1.000000
```

[1] https://golang.org/cmd/cgo/#hdr-Using_cgo_with_the_go_command

13.5. Calling Go functions from C

We have explored how to pass arguments between Go and C. From the previous examples, we can conclude that Go can easily execute C functions. One remaining question is how can Go functions be called from C. This situation differs from calling C functions from Go. Check the following example.

Example 13.12: Incorrect definition of Go function to be called from C.

```
/*
#include <stdio.h>
void cFunction() {
    printf("cFunction will call goFunction\n");
    goFunction();
}
*/
import "C"
import "fmt"

func main() {
    C.cFunction()
}

func goFunction() {
    fmt.Println("goFunction was called")
}
```

This code will not work because `goFunction` is not exposed to C. This can be fixed with the reserved word `export` followed by the function name just before the function. This makes the compiler copy the function definition to the `_cgo_export.h` header. Unfortunately, there is a restriction that forces us to not include any function definition in the C preamble[2]. Functions must be defined in a separated file or using certain function modifiers as we will see. This occurs because functions defined in the preamble are also copied to C headers and this results in the same function defined twice which triggers a linking error.

Considering these restrictions we can set our code to correctly expose Go functions to be called from C. We differentiate three cases based on the arguments of the Go function to be called.

---

[2] https://golang.org/cmd/cgo/#hdr-C_references_to_Go

13.5.1. GO FUNCTIONS WITHOUT ARGUMENTS

Example 13.13 shows a working solution for the previous example. First, in the C preamble we define the `goFunction()` as an extern function to make it fully visible. The implementation of this function is available in our Go program. The compiler will link this C function with the Go implementation because we have declared the *//export goFunction* statement.

Example 13.13: Go function without arguments called from C.

```
 1  package main
 2
 3  /*
 4  #include <stdio.h>
 5  extern void goFunction();
 6
 7  static inline void cFunction() {
 8      printf("cFunction will call goFunction\n");
 9      goFunction();
10  }
11  */
12  import "C"
13  import "fmt"
14
15  // call function no parameters
16  func main() {
17      C.cFunction()
18  }
19
20  //export goFunction
21  func goFunction() {
22      fmt.Println("goFunction was called")
23  }
```

```
cFunction will call goFunction
goFunction was called
```

We mentioned that one restriction of using the `export` statement in Go is that no functions can be implemented in the C preamble. However, we have implemented `cFunction` how is that possible? This can be done because the `static inline` embeds the given code and does not require additional function definitions. If this modifier is not used then, the function must be defined in an external C file. When the program runs, we get the message from the C function followed by the message from Go.

> ⓘ A `static inline` function permits the compiler to embed the content of the function. This is different from executing a call to the function itself. This technique is particularly useful to improve the performance of repetitive chunks of

> code.

> ⑦ The `extern` modifier in C sets a function or variable to be visible from all the files. Its counterpart is `static` which makes a function or variable only visible to the current file. Some people consider the definition of `extern` in C to be a flaw of the language because by default functions and variables are globally visible if not stated otherwise.

13.5.2. GO FUNCTIONS WITH ARGUMENTS

Now that we have defined the mechanics to call Go functions from C, we can extend our solution to something more sophisticated. It is possible to pass arguments to a Go function from C. However, not all the types can be mapped. Check Table 13.2 for some examples.

Go type	C type
`int32`	`int`
`int`	Lengths may not match. Use `C.int` instead.
`structs`	Not supported. Use C structs.
`arrays`	Not supported. Use C pointer.

Table 13.2: Type conversions when calling Go functions from C.

In Example 13.14, we call a Go function that expects an integer value. The type of argument in Go is **int32**. We cannot use **int** because there is no automatic conversion type for Go **int** from C to Go. Remember, that type sizes may not match because in Go the size of the **int** type is platform dependant. Another plausible solution is to use `C.int` instead.

Example 13.14: Go functions with arguments called from C.

```
 1  package main
 2
 3  /*
 4  #include <stdio.h>
 5  extern int goFunction(int number);
 6
 7  static inline void cFunction(int number) {
 8      printf("cFunction will call goFunction with %d\n", number);
 9      int x = goFunction(number);
10      printf("goFunction returned %d\n", x);
11  }
```

```
cFunction will call goFunction with 42
goFunction was called with 42
goFunction returned 84
```

CHAPTER 13. CGO

```
12  */
13  import "C"
14  import "fmt"
15
16  // call function with parameters
17  func main() {
18      C.cFunction(42)
19  }
20
21  //export goFunction
22  func goFunction(number int32) int32 {
23      fmt.Println("goFunction was called with", number)
24      return number * 2
25  }
```

13.5.3. FUNCTIONS WITH FUNCTIONS AS ARGUMENTS

For the previous cases, there is not too much engineering to be done. We must be sure to expose the Go function and to set data types correctly. Things are different when the arguments of the function to be called are pointers to functions. This is common when defining callback functions. When a Go function is exposed to C, Cgo generates a stub for this function. This is a problem because Go pointers to functions may vary and are not directly visible to C. A gateway function must be provided.

We show how this can be done through an example. To better understand the data flow and involved components see Figure 13.1.

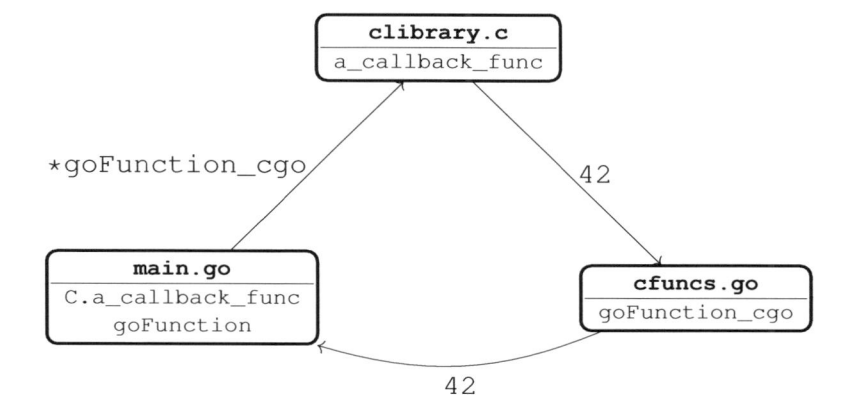

Figure 13.1: Arguments and functions used to call a function with functions as arguments from C.

In our example, we have a pure C program implemented in `clibrary.c`. It has a function called `a_callback_func` that receives a pointer to a function. By default, it will call the passed function with parameter 42. Notice that the function to be called is not a Go function. Actually, it is a gateway function implemented in the C preamble of the file `cfuncs.go`. The gateway function, `goFunction_cgo`, which was initially passed by parameter to our pure C program, has access to the target `goFunction` fully implemented in Go.

For our example, we initially define a pure C program with a function that expects a pointer to a function with an integer as argument. As it is usually is done in C, we define the header and the corresponding implementation in files `clibrary.h` and `clibrary.c` like shown in Examples 13.15 and 13.16 respectively. By default `a_callback_func` will call the provided function with argument 42.

Example 13.15: Cgo function pointers (clibrary.h)

```
1  #ifndef CLIBRARY_H
2  #define CLIBRARY_H
3  typedef void (*callback_f) (int);
4  void a_callback_func(callback_f);
5  #endif
```

Example 13.16: Cgo function pointers (clibrary.c)

```
1  #include "clibrary.h"
2
3  #include <stdio.h>
4
5  void a_callback_func(callback_f f) {
6      printf("C a_callback_func calls a Go gateway function\n");
7      printf("      with argument 42\n");
8      f(42);
9  }
```

As shown in this Chapter, if we compile our C program into a library this can be linked into a C preamble. Example 13.17, contains the code for the `main.go` file. Observe that the C preamble uses the `#cgo` directives to link the `clibrary` from the compilation of our C program. Additionally, the preamble defines the `goFunction_cgo` which is our gateway function.

The `C` pseudopackage has access to `a_callback_func` because we have already included the corresponding C header file. When calling this function from Go, we use a pointer to the gateway function `goFunction_cgo` to explicitly cast to the expected C type `callback_f`. In this way, our C library can find a target function. Now, we only have to

CHAPTER 13. CGO

implement our gateway function.

Example 13.17: Cgo function pointers (main.go)

```go
package main

import (
    "fmt"
    "unsafe"
)

/*
#cgo CFLAGS: -I .
#cgo LDFLAGS: -L . -lclibrary

#include "clibrary.h"

void goFunction_cgo(int number);
*/
import "C"

func main() {
    fmt.Println("Go main() calls a_callback_func")
    C.a_callback_func((C.callback_f)(unsafe.Pointer(C.goFunction_cgo)))
}

//export goFunction
func goFunction(number int) {
    fmt.Println("Go goFunction was finally called with", number)
}
```

The gateway function is implemented in the `cfuncs.go` file like shown in Example 13.18. We simply call `goFunction` from the C preamble. Remember that this function is available because it uses the `export` statement.

Example 13.18: Cgo function pointers (cfuncs.go)

```go
package main

/*
#include <stdio.h>
void goFunction_cgo(int number) {
    printf("go_Function_cgo with number %d\n",number);
    void goFunction(int);
    goFunction(number);
}
*/
```

```
11   import "C"
```

The following lines, compile the C code into a library and build the corresponding executable file.

```
gcc -c clibrary.c
ar cr libclibrary.a clibrary.o
go build *.go
```

After these commands finish, the executable file `cfuncs` will run the program. The printed messages give an idea of the followed execution workflow.

```
Go main() calls a_callback_func
C a_callback_func calls a Go gateway function
      with argument 42
go_Function_cgo with number 42
Go goFunction was finally called with 42
```

13.6. Summary

This Chapter discusses how Go programs can interact with C. We have covered how to call functions, exchange structs, and how to manage data types between both languages. Additionally, we have explored the potential issues that may arise when mixing the Go memory model with C pointers. Using Cgo unveils a large potential in terms of the number of existing libraries your Go program can use.

Part II

Building systems

Image by Egon Elbre (@egonelbre)

14
PROTOCOL BUFFERS

Nowadays systems are mainly distributed. The distribution comes with major advantages such as redundancy, resiliency, or scalability. However, the components of any system are not isolated and have to talk to each other. This communication is usually carried out with messages, understanding by message a piece of information exchanged between two speakers with some purpose.

Messages must be platform and language agnostic so they can be used by the largest number of solutions. Formats such as XML, JSON or YAML (see Chapter 8) are commonly used to exchange information because they are easy to parse and human friendly. However, they are not efficient solutions in terms of message size and serialization costs. To mitigate these problems, Google developed protocol buffers[1] as a language-neutral and platform-neutral serialization mechanism. Protocol buffers is available for various languages including Go.

This Chapter introduces protocol buffers, explains what they are, how they are built, and how they help us to define a common exchanging framework between applications and systems.

14.1. THE PROTO FILE

The definition of messages in protocol buffers (PB from now on) is independent of the programming language. The proto file manages the definition of exchangeable entities in PB. This file is interpreted by the `protoc` tool which generates the code required to marshal and unmarshal (see Chapter 8) these entities. A single proto file can be used to generate the corresponding code for every supported language. This is an abstraction

---
[1] https://developers.google.com/protocol-buffers

```
package user;
// ...
type User struct {
    // ...
    UserId string `protobuf:"bytes,1,...
    Email  string `protobuf:"bytes,2,...
}
// ...
```

```
syntax = "proto3";
package user;

option go_package="user";
message User {
   string user_id = 1;
   string email = 2;
}
// ...
```

```
// ...
import "user"
// ...
u := user.User {
      Email:"john@gmail.com",
      UserId: "John"
   }
// ...
```

Figure 14.1: Steps to define and use protocol buffer.

mechanism that releases the developer from the complexities of defining low level data transfer mechanisms.

Figure 14.1 depicts the steps carried out to define and use entities defined with PB. This is represented as an iterative cycle where changes in the definition of PB entities require recompilations of the serialization mechanisms, but may not require changes in the final code using these entities. This detaches serialization mechanisms from the logic of the program.

The following examples show how to define a basic PB message entity and use it in a Go program using PB version 3. Before starting, be sure to install the PB environment following the corresponding instructions for your platform[2]. The basic tool is the `protoc` command that transforms the messages defined in the protos file into Go code.

Imagine we plan to build a system with a User entity. This entity will be exchanged between different applications that may not be written in the same programming language. Additionally, we expect the message definition to evolve over time. PB seems to be a reasonable solution for our system. We start defining a User message like shown in Example 14.1.

Example 14.1: Proto file user.proto defining a User message.

---

[2] https://developers.google.com/protocol-buffers/docs/downloads

CHAPTER 14. PROTOCOL BUFFERS

```
1  syntax = "proto3";
2  package user;
3
4  option go_package="github.com/juanmanuel-tirado/savetheworldwithgo/12
       _protocolbuffers/pb/example_01/user";
5
6  message User {
7      string user_id = 1;
8      string email = 2;
9  }
```

PB permits defining messages with their fields and corresponding types. This definition is done in a file with the .proto suffix. The PB version is set with the `syntax` statement. PB entities are organized into packages that can be imported from other proto files. In our example, we work with package user. PB permits the definition of various options that may help the generation of code for certain languages. The go_package option indicates the path of the package where the generated Go code will be saved. This package must be accessible to be imported into our code.

Any message is composed of fields and every field has a type, a name, and a field tag. Field types resemble those used in Go **int32**, **uint32**, **string**, **bool** although there are some additional types like **float**, **double**, **sint64** among others. The equivalent type in every PB supported language is described in the official documentation[3]. The field tag indicates the position of the field after marshaling. In this case, user_id will be the first marshalled field followed by the email.

Once we have defined our message, we can create the corresponding Go implementation. To do so, we have to run the protoc command. For this example, protoc --go_out= $GOPATH/src user.proto. The --go_out parameter indicates where to write the generated Go files. Remember that these files must be accessible from your final code and must match the go_package statement. The generated output is contained into the user.pb.go file. This file contains all the code that defines the type User and the functions to encode it following the PB protocol specification.

Finally, we can import the types defined in our user.pb.go file from any package. Example 14.2 creates a User and uses the PB code to marshal it and then, unmarshal it. Remember that once the type is marshalled, it can be sent through the network and unmarshalled by any other recipient independently of the programming language and platform.

Example 14.2: Using protos from Example 14.1.

```
1  package main
2
```

---

[3]https://developers.google.com/protocol-buffers/docs/proto3#scalar

```go
 3  import (
 4      "fmt"
 5      "github.com/juanmanuel-tirado/savetheworldwithgo/12_protocolbuffers/pb/
            example_01/user"
 6      "google.golang.org/protobuf/proto"
 7  )
 8
 9  func main() {
10      u := user.User{Email:"john@gmail.com", UserId: "John"}
11
12      fmt.Println("To encode:", u.String())
13      encoded, err := proto.Marshal(&u)
14      if err != nil {
15          panic(err)
16      }
17
18      v := user.User{}
19      err = proto.Unmarshal(encoded, &v)
20      if err != nil {
21          panic(err)
22      }
23      fmt.Println("Recovered:", v.String())
24  }
```

```
To encode: user_id:"John" email:"john@gmail.com"
Recovered: user_id:"John" email:"john@gmail.com"
```

There are some considerations before you run this code. In Example 14.2 we import the package `google.golang.org/protobuf/proto` that contains the `Marshal` and `Unmarshal` functions. It is a third-party package and it is not available in the basic Go installation. The package can be installed using `go get` (see Section 2.1.1). However, we recommend to use `go mod` to make it more flexible. To revisit how `go mod` works visit Chapter 12. As a brief reminder, initialize the modules file with `go mod init`. Then you can build the code with `go build main.go` and the `go.mod` file will have all the required dependencies.

> ⚠ There is another proto package defined in `github.com/golang/protobuf`. This package is also valid and can be used. However, it has been superseded by `google.golang.org/protobuf/proto` and it is not recommended to be used.

14.2. COMPLEX MESSAGES

PB facilitates the definition of complex message structures with sophisticated types. We extend our `User` message example to demonstrate how to use other types such as enumerations and repeated fields.

Example 14.3 defines a message that represents a group of users. Every group has an id, a category, a certain score, and a list of users that belong to the group. Notice that the user category is an enumerated value. Enumerated values are defined with the reserved word **enum**. For every item of the enumeration, we need the name and the associated value. Do not confuse this value with the field tag. The `category` field in `Group` is defined as type `Category`. For the list of users, we indicate that a field can appear several times with the reserved word `repeated`. This list of users has no limit size and can be empty.

Example 14.3: Definition of complex messages.

```
1  syntax = "proto3";
2  package user;
3
4  option go_package="github.com/juanmanuel-tirado/savetheworldwithgo/12
       _protocolbuffers/pb/example_02/user";
5
6  message User {
7      string user_id = 1;
8      string email = 2;
9  }
10
11 enum Category {
12     DEVELOPER = 0;
13     OPERATOR = 1;
14 }
15
16 message Group {
17     int32 id = 1;
18     Category category = 2;
19     float score = 3;
20     repeated User users = 4;
21 }
```

The new `Group` type is used in Example 14.4. When defining enumerations, for every item PB creates a variable named with the concatenation of the enumeration and the name of the item. The enumeration of categories generates `Category_DEVELOPER` and `Category_OPERATOR` constants. The list of users is translated into a slice of `User` type. Observe that actually, this slice uses pointers to the `User` type.

Example 14.4: Utilization of messages from Example 14.3.

```go
package main

import (
    "github.com/juanmanuel-tirado/savetheworldwithgo/12_protocolbuffers/pb/example_02/user"
    "google.golang.org/protobuf/proto"
    "fmt"
)

func main() {
    userA := user.User{UserId: "John", Email: "john@gmail.com"}
    userB := user.User{UserId: "Mary", Email:"mary@gmail.com"}

    g := user.Group{Id: 1,
        Score: 42.0,
        Category: user.Category_DEVELOPER,
        Users: []*user.User{&userA,&userB},
    }
    fmt.Println("To encode:", g.String())

    encoded, err := proto.Marshal(&g)
    if err != nil {
        panic(err)
    }
    recovered := user.Group{}
    err = proto.Unmarshal(encoded, &recovered)
    fmt.Println("Recovered:", recovered.String())
}
```

```
To encode: id:1 score:42 users:{user_id:"John" email:"john@gmail.com"} users:{user_id:"Mary" email:"mary@gmail.com"}
Recovered: id:1 score:42 users:{user_id:"John" email:"john@gmail.com"} users:{user_id:"Mary" email:"mary@gmail.com"}
```

14.3. IMPORTING OTHER PROTO DEFINITIONS

Protocol buffer definitions can be imported into other proto files. This facilitates the reuse of messages and enables the creation of complex solutions. Continuing with the previous example where we defined users and groups of users, we decided to separate both types into separate packages. Now there will be a user package and a group package. For this case, we have to define two separated proto files. However, the `Group` message uses the

CHAPTER 14. PROTOCOL BUFFERS

definition of a `User` message. Examples 14.5 and 14.6 show the definition of `User` and `Group` messages respectively.

Example 14.5: User proto definition.

```
1  syntax = "proto3";
2  package user;
3
4  option go_package="user";
5
6  message User {
7      string user_id = 1;
8      string email = 2;
9  }
```

Example 14.6: Group proto importing Users proto.

```
1  syntax = "proto3";
2  package group;
3
4  option go_package="group";
5
6  import "user.proto";
7
8  enum Category {
9      DEVELOPER = 0;
10     OPERATOR = 1;
11 }
12
13 message Group {
14     int32 id = 1;
15     Category category = 2;
16     float score = 3;
17     repeated user.User users = 4;
18 }
```

The `import "user.proto"` statement makes accessible the messages defined at the `user.proto` file to `group.proto`. The `users` field in the `Group` message has to be taken from its corresponding package with `user.User`. Additionally, the target Go packages are different[4].

In order to replicate the logic from Example 14.3 now we have to import `group` and `user` after running `protoc`. Check how this is done in Example 14.6 and compare it with the previous version using only one package.

Example 14.7: Utilization of protos from Examples 14.5 and 14.6.

```
1  package main
2
3  import (
4      "github.com/juanmanuel-tirado/savetheworldwithgo/12_protocolbuffers/pb/
           example_03/group"
5      "github.com/juanmanuel-tirado/savetheworldwithgo/12_protocolbuffers/pb/
           example_03/user"
6      "google.golang.org/protobuf/proto"
7      "fmt"
```

---

[4]In the example package paths have been trimmed for clarity purposes.

```go
 8 )
 9
10 func main() {
11     userA := user.User{UserId: "John", Email: "john@gmail.com"}
12     userB := user.User{UserId: "Mary", Email:"mary@gmail.com"}
13
14     g := group.Group{Id: 1,
15         Score: 42.0,
16         Category: group.Category_DEVELOPER,
17         Users: []*user.User{&userA,&userB},
18     }
19     fmt.Println("To encode:", g.String())
20
21     encoded, err := proto.Marshal(&g)
22     if err != nil {
23         panic(err)
24     }
25     recovered := group.Group{}
26     err = proto.Unmarshal(encoded, &recovered)
27     fmt.Println("Recovered:", recovered.String())
28 }
```

14.4. Nested types

Certain messages may only make sense when found within other messages. PB permits the definition of nested types that are only accessible through other types. Our `Group` message can be rewritten using the `User` message as an embedded field as shown in Example 14.8. Now the `User` type is defined in the context of `Group`. The `Winner` message represents a user who won in a given category. Observe, that the `user` field has to be referred to as `Group.User`.

Example 14.8: Group definition with nested User type.

```protobuf
 1 syntax = "proto3";
 2 package group;
 3
 4 option go_package="github.com/juanmanuel-tirado/savetheworldwithgo/12
       _protocolbuffers/pb/example_04/group";
 5
 6 enum Category {
 7     DEVELOPER = 0;
 8     OPERATOR = 1;
 9 }
10
```

```
11  message Group {
12      int32 id = 1;
13      Category category = 2;
14      float score = 3;
15      message User {
16          string user_id = 1;
17          string email = 2;
18      }
19      repeated User users = 4;
20  }
21
22  message Winner {
23      Group.User user = 1;
24      Category category = 2;
25  }
```

PB renames these nested types in Go code by adding suffixes as shown in Example 14.9. The `User` message is renamed `Group_User`.

Example 14.9: Utilization of messages from Example 14.8.

```go
1  package main
2
3  import (
4      "github.com/juanmanuel-tirado/savetheworldwithgo/12_protocolbuffers/pb/example_04/group"
5      "google.golang.org/protobuf/proto"
6      "fmt"
7  )
8
9  func main() {
10     userA := group.Group_User{UserId: "John", Email: "john@gmail.com"}
11     userB := group.Group_User{UserId: "Mary", Email:"mary@gmail.com"}
12
13     g := group.Group{Id: 1,
14         Score: 42.0,
15         Category: group.Category_DEVELOPER,
16         Users: []*group.Group_User{&userA, &userB},
17     }
18     fmt.Println("To encode:", g.String())
19
20     encoded, err := proto.Marshal(&g)
21     if err != nil {
22         panic(err)
23     }
24     recovered := group.Group{}
25     err = proto.Unmarshal(encoded, &recovered)
26     fmt.Println("Recovered:", recovered.String())
```

```
27 }
```

```
To encode: id:1 score:42 users:{user_id:"John" email:"john@gmail.com"} users:{
user_id:"Mary" email:"mary@gmail.com"}
Recovered: id:1 score:42 users:{user_id:"John" email:"john@gmail.com"} users:{
user_id:"Mary" email:"mary@gmail.com"}
```

14.5. Type Any

Messages are allowed to have fields with no defined type. This may occur when at the time of defining a field type the content of this field is not clear yet. The type Any is a byte serialization of any size with a URL that works as a unique identifier for the type contained in the field.

The proto file in Example 14.10 uses Any to define the info field to allocate any available data. This type is not available by default, and it has to be imported from the any.proto definition.

Example 14.10: Utilization of type Any.
```
1  syntax = "proto3";
2  package user;
3
4  option go_package="github.com/juanmanuel-tirado/savetheworldwithgo/12
       _protocolbuffers/pb/example_05/user";
5
6  import "google/protobuf/any.proto";
7
8  message User {
9      string user_id = 1;
10     string email = 2;
11     repeated google.protobuf.Any info = 3;
12 }
```

When translated into Go (Example 14.11), the type Any can be initialized with any array of bytes and a string as the URL. Notice that the anypb package has to be imported to have the Go definition of the Any type.

Example 14.11: Utilization of messages from Example 14.10.

```go
1  package main
2
3  import (
4      "fmt"
5      "google.golang.org/protobuf/proto"
6      "google.golang.org/protobuf/types/known/anypb"
7      "github.com/juanmanuel-tirado/savetheworldwithgo/12_protocolbuffers/pb/
           example_05/user"
8  )
9
10 func main() {
11     info := anypb.Any{Value: []byte(`John rules`), TypeUrl: "urltype"}
12     userA := user.User{UserId: "John", Email: "john@gmail.com", Info: []*anypb.
           Any{&info}}
13
14     fmt.Println("To encode:", userA.String())
15
16     encoded, err := proto.Marshal(&userA)
17     if err != nil {
18         panic(err)
19     }
20     recovered := user.User{}
21     err = proto.Unmarshal(encoded, &recovered)
22     fmt.Println("Recovered:", recovered.String())
23 }
```

```
To encode: user_id:"John" email:"john@gmail.com" info:{type_url:"urltype" value
:"John rules"}
Recovered: user_id:"John" email:"john@gmail.com" info:{type_url:"urltype" value
:"John rules"}
```

14.6. Type Oneof

If a message with many fields can only have one field when is sent, there is no point in sending all the fields. The type `oneof` forces messages to only include one field from a given collection.

Example 14.12 extends the User message with a field indicating which type of user we have. A user can only be a developer or an operator. Additionally, developers have information about the language they use, while operators have information about the platform they administrate.

Example 14.12: Utilization of type `OneOf`.

```
1  syntax = "proto3";
2  package user;
3
4  option go_package="github.com/juanmanuel-tirado/savetheworldwithgo/12
       _protocolbuffers/pb/example_06/user";
5
6  message Developer {
7      string language = 1;
8  }
9  message Operator {
10     string platform = 1;
11 }
12
13 message User {
14     string user_id = 1;
15     string email = 2;
16     oneof type {
17         Developer developer = 3;
18         Operator operator = 4;
19     }
20 }
```

When using `oneof`, PB defines nested types in the `User` message. In our case, types `User_Developer` and `User_Operator` must contain a `Developer` or `Operator` type respectively. This forces the message to only contain one of those types as shown in Example 14.13.

Example 14.13: Utilization of messages from Example 14.12.

```
1  package main
2
3  import (
4      "fmt"
5      "google.golang.org/protobuf/proto"
6      "github.com/juanmanuel-tirado/savetheworldwithgo/12_protocolbuffers/pb/
           example_06/user"
7  )
8
9  func main() {
10     goDeveloper := user.Developer{Language: "go"}
11     userA := user.User{UserId: "John", Email: "john@gmail.com",
12         Type: &user.User_Developer{&goDeveloper}}
13     aksOperator := user.Operator{Platform: "aks"}
14     userB := user.User{UserId: "Mary", Email: "mary@gmail.com",
15         Type: &user.User_Operator{&aksOperator}}
16
```

```go
17      encodedA, err := proto.Marshal(&userA)
18      if err != nil {
19          panic(err)
20      }
21      encodedB, err := proto.Marshal(&userB)
22      if err != nil {
23          panic(err)
24      }
25
26      recoveredA, recoveredB := user.User{}, user.User{}
27      _ = proto.Unmarshal(encodedA, &recoveredA)
28      _ = proto.Unmarshal(encodedB, &recoveredB)
29      fmt.Println("RecoveredA:", recoveredA.String())
30      fmt.Println("RecoveredB:", recoveredB.String())
31  }
```

```
RecoveredA: user_id:"John"  email:"john@gmail.com"  developer:{language:"go"}
RecoveredB: user_id:"Mary"  email:"mary@gmail.com"  operator:{platform:"aks"}
```

14.7. Maps

Messages can contain maps with key/value pairs. Example 14.14 defines the `Teams` message containing a field with a map of string keys and a `UserList` message as value. Additionally, the `UserList` is a collection of users defined in the same `.proto` file.

Example 14.14: Utilization of maps.

```
1  syntax = "proto3";
2  package user;
3
4  option go_package="github.com/juanmanuel-tirado/savetheworldwithgo/12
       _protocolbuffers/pb/example_07/user";
5
6  message User {
7      string user_id = 1;
8      string email = 2;
9  }
10
11 message UserList {
12     repeated User users = 1;
13 }
14
```

```
15  message Teams {
16      map<string, UserList> teams = 1;
17  }
```

A map field is treated in Go like a regular **map** type. See in Example 14.13 how a `map[string]*User.UserList` is enough to populate the corresponding `Teams` type.

Example 14.15: Utilization of messages from Example 14.14.

```
1  package main
2
3  import (
4      "fmt"
5      "google.golang.org/protobuf/proto"
6      "github.com/juanmanuel-tirado/savetheworldwithgo/12_protocolbuffers/pb/
           example_07/user"
7  )
8
9  func main() {
10     userA := user.User{UserId: "John", Email: "john@gmail.com"}
11     userB := user.User{UserId: "Mary", Email: "mary@gmail.com"}
12
13     teams := map[string]*user.UserList {
14         "teamA": &user.UserList{Users:[]*user.User{&userA,&userB}},
15         "teamB": nil,
16     }
17
18     teamsPB := user.Teams{Teams: teams}
19
20     fmt.Println("To encode:", teamsPB.String())
21
22     encoded, err := proto.Marshal(&teamsPB)
23     if err != nil {
24         panic(err)
25     }
26     recovered := user.Teams{}
27     err = proto.Unmarshal(encoded, &recovered)
28     if err != nil {
29         panic(err)
30     }
31     fmt.Println("Recovered:", recovered.String())
32  }
```

```
To encode: teams:{key:"teamA" value:{users:{user_id:"John" email:"john@gmail.
com"} users:{user_id:"Mary" email:"mary@gmail.com"}}} teams:{key:"teamB" value
```

:{}}
Recovered: teams:{key:"teamA" value:{users:{user_id:"John" email:"john@gmail.com"} users:{user_id:"Mary" email:"mary@gmail.com"}}} teams:{key:"teamB" value:{}}

14.8. JSON

PB encodings are JSON compatible extending the number of systems that can use a `.proto` file. If you check any PB generated `*.pb.go` file you can see that the structs representing message types have JSON encoding tags (see Section 8.2), therefore they can be represented in a JSON format.

Example 14.16 uses the `encodings/json` package to marshal and unmarshal the message types defined in Example 14.14. The applicability of JSON encoding is straight forward and does not require additional code. For a low-level detail explanation of JSON mappings in PB check the official documentation[5].

Example 14.16: Encoding PB messages from Example 14.14 into JSON.

```go
package main

import (
    "encoding/json"
    "fmt"
    "github.com/juanmanuel-tirado/savetheworldwithgo/12_protocolbuffers/pb/example_08/user"
)

func main() {
    userA := user.User{UserId: "John", Email: "john@gmail.com"}
    userB := user.User{UserId: "Mary", Email: "mary@gmail.com"}

    teams := map[string]*user.UserList {
        "teamA": &user.UserList{Users: []*user.User{&userA,&userB}},
        "teamB": nil,
    }

    teamsPB := user.Teams{Teams: teams}

    encoded, err := json.Marshal(&teamsPB)
    if err != nil {
        panic(err)
    }
```

---

[5]https://developers.google.com/protocol-buffers/docs/proto3#json

```
24      recovered := user.Teams{}
25      err = json.Unmarshal(encoded, &recovered)
26      if err != nil {
27          panic(err)
28      }
29      fmt.Println("Recovered:", recovered.String())
30  }
```

```
Recovered: teams:{key:"teamA" value:{users:{user_id:"John" email:"john@gmail.
com"} users:{user_id:"Mary" email:"mary@gmail.com"}}} teams:{key:"teamB" value
:{}}
```

14.9. Summary

This Chapter summarizes how to use protocol buffers to define Go serializable types that can be exchanged among different solutions independently of the platform and language. The examples from this Chapter cover the definition of protocol buffer messages, the syntax, and how to use these messages in Go. An understanding of these concepts is required before exploring Chapter 15.

15
GRPC

gRPC[1] is a language and platform agnostic remote procedure call (RPC) framework. With gRPC, we can write a common definition of services and their signatures and then, create the corresponding clients and servers. This abstraction reduces development overhead and helps to maintain a healthy and evolving ecosystem of APIs available for several platforms. In this Chapter, we explore how to define services with gRPC and how to use the generated stubs with Go, how to use streaming, transcoding solutions, and interceptors.

15.1. BASIC CONCEPTS

Figure 15.1 illustrates the components of a gRPC deployment. There are two basic pieces to be defined in every deployment: messages and services. In gRPC, messages are defined using protocol buffers (see Chapter 14) setting a common serialization framework to send information between clients and servers. The services are collections of `rpc` methods that can receive messages as arguments and/or return messages.

Like shown in the Figure 15.1, the `protoc` program translates the services definition into a collection of stubs for one of the supported languages (C/C++, Java, Python, Go, etc.). These stubs implement all the logic to ensure the correctness of messages and services. Hence developers only have to define the behaviour of every exposed method following its signature.

Observe in the Figure that clients implemented in different languages (Go and Python) can call `rpc` functions running in any server independently of the employed language (C++ in the example) as long as they share the same definition of messages and services.

gRPC differentiates between synchronous and asynchronous methods. A synchronous

---
[1] https://grpc.io

```
message User {
    string user_id = 1;
    string email = 2;
}
service UserService {
    rpc GetUser (UserRequest) returns (User);
}
```

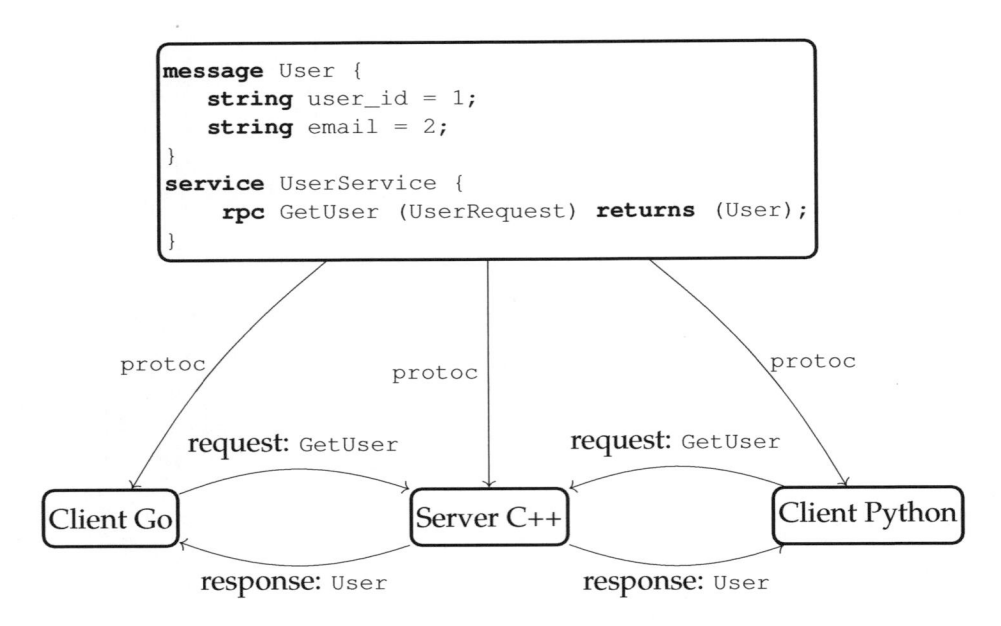

Figure 15.1: Summary of elements in a gRPC deployment.

method blocks the execution until a response or an error is received. On the other hand, an asynchronous method immediately returns the execution without blocking the current thread.

A second category of methods are unary and streaming. A unary method simply sends a message and waits (or not if it is asynchronous) for a response. gRPC is built on top of HTTP/2 which enables it to work with long-lived connection and full-duplex communication. This permits gRPC to define streaming methods in the client side, server side, or both.

> ⚠ Although gRPC defines synchronous and asynchronous methods, the last ones are not available for Go. This must be taken into consideration when implementing APIs using these kind of methods. For this reason, asynchronous methods are not detailed in this Chapter.

15.2. Definition of Services

A Remote Procedure Call (RPC) can be seen as an extension of the available functions we can invoke in a local machine. These functions are defined by an IDL (Interface Definition Language) that is used to generate stubs following the instructions from the IDL. In this case, we define messages and services in a `.proto` file as we did in Chapter 14 for protocol

CHAPTER 15. GRPC

buffers.

In gRPC, a **service** is composed of one or several RPCs. We can think of services as a mechanism to group RPCs that operate with similar entities. For example, a user management service can have several operations: get a user, register a new user, remove a user, etc. Example 15.1 shows the `.proto` file for a service to manage users. The service only has one RPC called `GetUser` which receives a `UserRequest` and returns a `User` message. We have only included one RPC call to the `UserService` for the sake of simplification, although services can have as many RPCs as needed.

Example 15.1: Service definition using gRPC.

```
1  syntax = "proto3";
2  package user;
3
4  option go_package="github.com/juanmanuel-tirado/savetheworldwithgo/13_grpc/
       example_01/user";
5
6  message User {
7      string user_id = 1;
8      string email = 2;
9  }
10
11 message UserRequest {
12     string user_id = 1;
13 }
14
15 service UserService {
16     rpc GetUser (UserRequest) returns (User);
17 }
```

We already have defined our messages and services. Now we have to create the corresponding stubs to use the services and messages in our Go code. For this task, we need the `protoc` command-line tool with the gRPC plugin. Be sure, you have already installed the `protoc` tool (see Section 14.1). The gRPC plugin works with the `protoc` tool to generate the corresponding clients and servers using the specifications from the `.proto` file. You can get the gRPC plugin running[2]:

```
>>> export GO11MODULE=on   # Enable module mode
>>> go get google.golang.org/protobuf/cmd/protoc-gen-go \
          google.golang.org/grpc/cmd/protoc-gen-go-grpc
```

---

[2] Check the documentation for more details https://grpc.io/docs/languages/go/quickstart/#prerequisites

Make sure that `protoc` can find the plugins:

```
>>> export PATH="$PATH:$(go env GOPATH)/bin"
```

If the environment is correctly set, now we can execute `protoc` and generate the gRPC stubs.

```
>>> protoc -I=. --go_out=$GOPATH/src --go-grpc_out=$GOPATH/src *.proto
```

The `--go-grpc_out` argument indicates the path for the Go stubs. Remember that the generated code must be accessible to your code and match the value set in the `go_package`. After a successful execution we have two files: `user.pb.go` and `user_grpc.pb.go`. The first one contains the definition of the messages as described in Chapter 14. The second one contains all the code generated to support servers and clients that derive from our gRPC definitions in the `.proto` file.

Example 15.2: Excerpt of a gRPC stub.

```go
type UserServiceClient interface {
    GetUser(ctx context.Context, in *UserRequest, opts ...grpc.CallOption) (*User, error)
}

type userServiceClient struct {
    cc grpc.ClientConnInterface
}

func NewUserServiceClient(cc grpc.ClientConnInterface) UserServiceClient {
    return &userServiceClient{cc}
}

func (c *userServiceClient) GetUser(ctx context.Context, in *UserRequest, opts ...grpc.CallOption) (*User, error) {
    // ...
}

type UserServiceServer interface {
    GetUser(context.Context, *UserRequest) (*User, error)
    mustEmbedUnimplementedUserServiceServer()
}
```

Example 15.2 contains an excerpt of the `user_grpc.pb.go`. We can see that `protoc` has automatically generated a set of Go types that represent the specified service. This code

15.3. Creating a server

Once the gRPC stub is generated, we can import the corresponding package into our code. This code provides us with the skeleton of the Go functions we have to implement to have the server defined in our `.proto` file. Notice that right now we have only defined the signature of the remote functions, not the logic itself. This has to be done on a server. We can consider three steps prior to have a server up and running: the server implementation, the service registration, and the server waiting for incoming requests.

Example 15.3: User service server.

```go
package main

import (
    "context"
    "fmt"
    pb "github.com/juanmanuel-tirado/savetheworldwithgo/13_grpc/grpc/example_01/user"
    "google.golang.org/grpc"
    "net"
)

type UserServer struct{
    pb.UnimplementedUserServiceServer
}

func (u *UserServer) GetUser(ctx context.Context, req *pb.UserRequest) (*pb.User, error) {
    fmt.Println("Server received:", req.String())
    return &pb.User{UserId: "John", Email: "john@gmail.com"}, nil
}

func main() {
    lis, err := net.Listen("tcp", "localhost:50051")
    if err != nil {
        panic(err)
    }
    s := grpc.NewServer()
    pb.RegisterUserServiceServer(s, &UserServer{})

    if err := s.Serve(lis); err != nil {
        panic(err)
    }
}
```

1. Example 15.3 is a minimalist server implementation of `UserService`. The `UserServer` type must implement the `UserServiceServer` interface defined in the stub. You can find the interface definition in Example 15.2. Every RPC defined in the `.proto` file inside the `UserService` must have its corresponding method implemented by the server. Only if all the methods are implemented, the server type will be a valid server.

    Unary **rpc** methods have similarly structured signatures:

    ```
    func RPCName(ctx context.Context, req *Request) (*Response, error)
    ```

    We have a context for the request (see Section 6.6) and an incoming request. The method returns a response and an error. In our example, we simply print the incoming request and return a manually populated `User` type.

2. The complexity of a server varies depending on the task and the number of RPCs to be implemented. However, once the server is defined we have to expose it in such a way that requests can be correctly served by our code. The gRPC stub generates the function `RegisterUserServiceServer` that links a type implementing the `UserServiceServer` with any incoming request to this service. This must be done with a gRPC server type (lines 25–26).

3. Finally, we can run the GRPC server in an endless loop waiting for incoming requests. The `s.Serve` method blocks the execution until the program is stopped or **panic** occurs.

The server code can be compared with the implementation of HTTP functions seen in Chapter 9. Notice that this code requires third-party components that may not be available on your platform. You can use `go mod` to ensure you have the required code (See Chapter 12).

15.4. Creating clients

Creating a gRPC client requires fewer steps than running a server. We have to define the address of the target server as shown in Example 15.4. The `UserServiceClient` type provides methods to call the **rpc** methods defined in the `.proto`. A `UserServiceClient` instance can be obtained with the `NewUserServiceClient` and a connection to the server. We can create a connection with the `grpc.Dial` function. This function receives the server address and none or several `DialOption` values. The `DialOption` type setups the connection with the server. In the example, we use `WithInsecure` to indicate that there is no encryption and `WithBlock` to block the execution flow until the connection with the server is up. Further details about how to use `DialOption` are given in Section 15.7 when explaining interceptors.

Example 15.4: User service client.

```go
package main

import (
    "context"
    "fmt"
    pb "github.com/juanmanuel-tirado/savetheworldwithgo/13_grpc/grpc/example_01/user"
    "google.golang.org/grpc"
    "time"
)

func main() {
    conn, err := grpc.Dial("localhost:50051", grpc.WithInsecure(), grpc.WithBlock())
    if err != nil {
        panic(err)
    }
    defer conn.Close()

    c := pb.NewUserServiceClient(conn)

    ctx, cancel := context.WithTimeout(context.Background(), time.Second)
    defer cancel()

    r, err := c.GetUser(ctx, &pb.UserRequest{UserId: "John"})
    if err != nil {
        panic(err)
    }
    fmt.Println("Client received:", r.String())
}
```

Running the server and then the client code you should get the outputs below. Remember, that the server must be running before the client is executed. The server will keep running until the program is killed.

```
Client received: user_id:"John"          Server received: user_id:"John"
email:"john@gmail.com"
```

15.5. STREAMING

HTTP/2 permits full-duplex communication between client and server. This makes it possible to establish a streaming channel between both ends. The channel can be reused reducing the overhead and latency of involved networking operations in the channel negotiation process. gRPC leverages this HTTP/2 feature to offer procedures that receive or return data inside streams. Next, we explain how to work with streaming for servers and clients in one direction or bidirectional flavours.

15.5.1. SERVER STREAMING

Consider the .proto file from Example 15.5. The Rnd remote procedure receives a request to receive n random numbers in the range between from and to values. These numbers are not returned in a single batch, instead they are returned using a stream. This can be particularly useful in scenarios where n is very large.

Example 15.5: Definition of a server streaming method.

```proto
syntax = "proto3";
package numbers;

option go_package="github.com/juanmanuel-tirado/savetheworldwithgo/13_grpc/
    streaming/example_01/numbers";

message NumRequest {
    int64 from = 1;
    int64 to = 2;
    int64 n = 3;
}

message NumResponse {
    int64 i = 1;
    int64 remaining = 2;
}

service NumService {
    rpc Rnd (NumRequest) returns (stream NumResponse);
}
```

CHAPTER 15. GRPC

The data flow for this scenario is depicted in Figure 15.2. The client starts the communication with a request (NumRequest in this example). Afterwards, the server sends responses to the client using the same channel until the server closes the channel sending an EOF.

```
client                                              server
    |  NumRequest n:5, from:0, to:100  |
    |--------------------------------->|
    |  NumResponse i:33, remaining:99  |
    |<---------------------------------|
    |  NumResponse i:42, remaining:98  |
    |<---------------------------------|
    |               ...                |
    |<---------------------------------|
    |  NumResponse i:66, remaining:0   |
    |<---------------------------------|
    |               EOF                |
    |<---------------------------------|
```

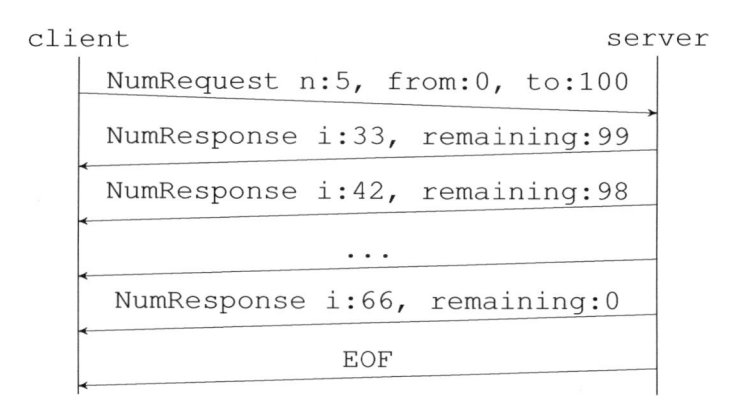

Figure 15.2: Client-server communication in a server streaming scenario.

The server implementation in Example 15.6 generates n random numbers for the given range. Notice that the signature function to be implemented differs from unary **rpc** methods. The server implements the remote procedure Rnd which receives a request and a type that encapsulates a stream type. This stream type is the communication channel the client opened when invoking this procedure. Our server uses the method stream.Send to send new responses to the client. When we are finished, returning **nil** is enough to close the channel and send an EOF (End Of File) informing the client that the communication is finished.

Example 15.6: Implementation of streaming method on the server side.

```go
package main

import (
    "errors"
    "fmt"
    pb "github.com/juanmanuel-tirado/savetheworldwithgo/13_grpc/streaming/example_01/numbers"
    "google.golang.org/grpc"
    "math/rand"
    "net"
    "time"
)

type NumServer struct{
```

```
14      pb.UnimplementedNumServiceServer
15  }
16
17  func (n *NumServer) Rnd(req *pb.NumRequest, stream pb.NumService_RndServer)
        error {
18      fmt.Println(req.String())
19      if req.N <= 0 {
20          return errors.New("N must be greater than zero")
21      }
22      if req.To <= req.From {
23          return errors.New("to must be greater or equal than from")
24      }
25      done := make(chan bool)
26      go func() {
27          for counter:=0;counter<int(req.N);counter++{
28              i := rand.Intn(int(req.To) - int(req.From) +1) + int(req.To)
29              resp := pb.NumResponse{I:int64(i), Remaining:req.N-int64(counter)}
30              stream.Send(&resp)
31              time.Sleep(time.Second)
32          }
33          done <- true
34      }()
35      <- done
36      return nil
37  }
38
39  func main() {
40      lis, err := net.Listen("tcp", "localhost:50051")
41      if err != nil {
42          panic(err)
43      }
44      s := grpc.NewServer()
45
46      pb.RegisterNumServiceServer(s, &NumServer{})
47
48      if err := s.Serve(lis); err != nil {
49          panic(err)
50      }
51  }
```

On the other side, the client listens to new incoming responses from the server after sending the initial request. When invoking the remote method from the client-side, a streaming client with a Recv function is returned. Example 15.7 shows how to consume data from this function until an EOF is found. An important aspect to be considered is the utilization of contexts. The context declared when invoking the remote method (ctx in line 21) lives during all the stream. This means that in the case of using a context with timelines if this context expires the stream will be closed. For the current example, the channel will be closed after 10 seconds. It remains as an exercise for the reader to extend

the length of the requested range to check how the expiration of the context terminates
the stream.

> **Example 15.7:** Implementation of a client consuming responses from a streaming server.

```go
package main

import (
    "context"
    "fmt"
    pb "github.com/juanmanuel-tirado/savetheworldwithgo/13_grpc/streaming/example_01/numbers"
    "google.golang.org/grpc"
    "io"
    "time"
)

func main() {
    conn, err := grpc.Dial(":50051", grpc.WithInsecure(), grpc.WithBlock())
    if err != nil {
        panic(err)
    }
    defer conn.Close()

    c := pb.NewNumServiceClient(conn)

    ctx, cancel := context.WithTimeout(context.Background(), time.Second*10)
    defer cancel()

    stream, err := c.Rnd(ctx, &pb.NumRequest{N:5, From:0, To: 100})
    if err != nil {
        panic(err)
    }

    done := make(chan bool)
    go func() {
        for {
            resp, err := stream.Recv()
            if err == io.EOF {
                done <- true
                return
            }
            if err != nil {
                panic(err)
            }
            fmt.Println("Received:", resp.String())
        }
    }()
    <- done
```

```
44        fmt.Println("Client done")
45 }
```

The asynchronous nature of these operations is a perfect use-case for timeouts and goroutines. If you do not feel familiar with these concepts, please revisit Chapter 6. The outputs for the client an server executions are shown below.

```
Received: i:165   remaining:5
Received: i:182   remaining:4
Received: i:129   remaining:3
Received: i:187   remaining:2
Received: i:148   remaining:1
Client done
```

```
to:100 n:5
```

15.5.2. Client streaming

In a client streaming scenario, the client directly opens a data stream with the server. When the client decides to stop sending data, it can close the channel or close the channel and wait for a response from the server. What regards the server, it receives all the data from the client until an EOF is found. Afterwards, depending on the procedure it can send a response back or not.

Example 15.8 defines the Sum procedure that receives a stream of requests. This procedure will compute the sum of all the numbers sent through the stream and return the result to the client. To define a streaming input, we have to add the stream modifier to the incoming message.

Example 15.8: Definition of a client streaming method.

```
1  syntax = "proto3";
2  package numbers;
3
4  option go_package="github.com/juanmanuel-tirado/savetheworldwithgo/13_grpc/
       streaming/example_02/numbers";
5
6  message NumRequest {
7      int64 x = 1;
8  }
9
10 message NumResponse {
11     int64 total = 1;
12 }
13
```

CHAPTER 15. GRPC

```
14  service NumService {
15      rpc Sum (stream NumRequest) returns (NumResponse);
16  }
```

The expected client-server communication is depicted in Figure 15.3. Observe that the client directly opens a stream sending requests and the server does not respond until the EOF is sent.

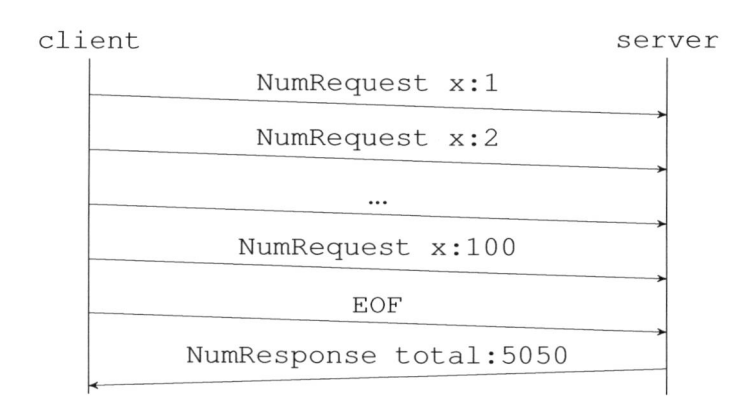

Figure 15.3: Client-server communication in a client streaming scenario.

On the client-side (Example 15.9) the Sum function does not receive any request, only a context. This function returns a streaming client that can be used to send requests to the server once the connection is established. If the stream has to be finished, then there are two options. We can close the stream if we do not expect any answer with Close, or we can close the stream and wait for a server response with CloseAndRecv. In both cases, the server is informed that the client has closed the channel. In our example, we close and wait for the server response containing the result with the sum of all the numbers it has received.

Example 15.9: Client sending data in streaming.

```go
1  package main
2
3  import (
4      "context"
5      "fmt"
6      pb "github.com/juanmanuel-tirado/savetheworldwithgo/13_grpc/streaming/
           example_02/numbers"
7      "google.golang.org/grpc"
8      "time"
9  )
```

```go
10
11  func main() {
12      conn, err := grpc.Dial(":50051", grpc.WithInsecure(), grpc.WithBlock())
13      if err != nil {
14          panic(err)
15      }
16      defer conn.Close()
17
18      c := pb.NewNumServiceClient(conn)
19
20      ctx, cancel := context.WithTimeout(context.Background(), time.Second*10)
21      defer cancel()
22
23      stream, err := c.Sum(ctx)
24      if err != nil {
25          panic(err)
26      }
27
28      from, to := 1,100
29
30      for i:=from;i<=to;i++ {
31          err = stream.Send(&pb.NumRequest{X:int64(i)})
32          if err!= nil {
33              panic(err)
34          }
35      }
36      fmt.Println("Waiting for response...")
37      result, err := stream.CloseAndRecv()
38      if err != nil {
39          panic(err)
40      }
41      fmt.Printf("The sum from %d to %d is %d\n", from,to, result.Total)
42  }
```

The server implementation from Example 15.10 is mostly contained in an endless `for` loop. When the `Sum` method is invoked in the server, this can check the input stream until the EOF or an error occurs. If no error or EOF is found, the server accumulates the incoming values (line 28) otherwise, the server invokes `SendAndClose` sending the accumulated value to the client.

Example 15.10: Server processing client stream and responding.

```go
1  package main
2
3  import (
4      "fmt"
5      pb "github.com/juanmanuel-tirado/savetheworldwithgo/13_grpc/streaming/
```

```go
            example_02/numbers"
 6      "google.golang.org/grpc"
 7      "io"
 8      "net"
 9 )
10
11 type NumServer struct{
12     pb.UnimplementedNumServiceServer
13 }
14
15 func (n *NumServer) Sum(stream pb.NumService_SumServer) error {
16     var total int64 = 0
17     var counter int = 0
18     for {
19        next, err := stream.Recv()
20        if err == io.EOF {
21            fmt.Printf("Received %d numbers sum: %d\n",counter,total)
22            stream.SendAndClose(&pb.NumResponse{Total: total})
23            return nil
24        }
25        if err != nil {
26            return err
27        }
28        total = total + next.X
29        counter++
30     }
31
32     return nil
33 }
34
35 func main() {
36     lis, err := net.Listen("tcp", "localhost:50051")
37     if err != nil {
38         panic(err)
39     }
40     s := grpc.NewServer()
41
42     pb.RegisterNumServiceServer(s, &NumServer{})
43
44     if err := s.Serve(lis); err != nil {
45         panic(err)
46     }
47 }
```

```
Waiting for response...
The sum from 1 to 100 is 5050
```

```
Received 100 numbers sum: 5050
```

15.5.3. BIDIRECTIONAL STREAMING

We have already mentioned that gRPC provides full-duplex communication using HTTP/2. This makes it possible to use bidirectional streaming between client and server. Bidirectional streaming may be particularly suitable for scenarios where data may arise on the fly or even to define your protocols on top of gRPC.

In Example 15.11, we define a chat service that sends back to the user her data consumption stats. In a chat service, client and server are expected to send data asynchronously. The client can send text messages to the server at any moment. On the other side, the server periodically sends stats to the user with some periodicity that may vary. Observe that the remote method `SendTxt` sets the argument and response to be streams.

Example 15.11: Definition of a bidirectional streaming method.

```
1  syntax = "proto3";
2  package numbers;
3
4  option go_package="github.com/juanmanuel-tirado/savetheworldwithgo/13_grpc/
       streaming/example_03/chat";
5
6  message ChatRequest {
7      int64 id = 1;
8      int64 to = 2;
9      string txt = 3;
10 }
11
12 message StatsResponse {
13     int64 total_char = 1;
14 }
15
16 service ChatService {
17     rpc SendTxt (stream ChatRequest) returns (stream StatsResponse);
18 }
```

Figure 15.4 depicts this communication scenario. The client starts the communication by establishing a new stream with the server. Both ends listen to the stream for any incoming message. Finally, both the client or server can close the connection at any moment. In our case, it is the client who finishes the communication.

The client implementation from Example 15.12 sends a chat message until the server stats informs that the number of sent characters is greater than a limit. Because the two actions are asynchronous we use two goroutines: one to send chat messages and other to monitor chat stats. The `ChatService_SendTxtClient` has methods for both sending and receiving data. The `Stats` function receives stats from the server and closes the stream (line 36).

CHAPTER 15. GRPC

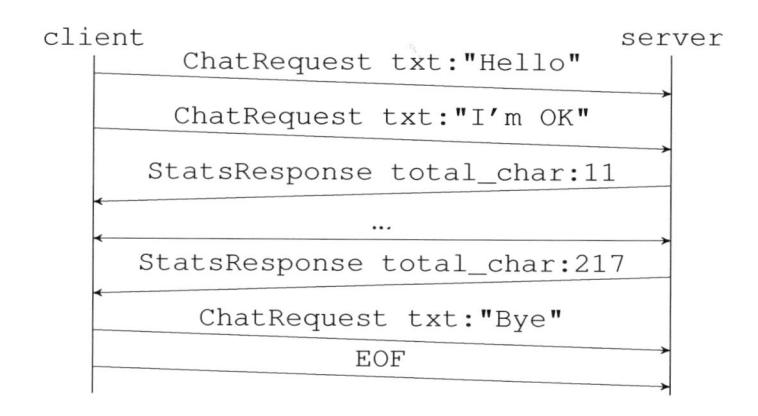

Figure 15.4: Client-server communication in a bidirectional streaming scenario.

Example 15.12: Client using bidirectional streaming.

```go
package main

import (
    "context"
    "fmt"
    pb "github.com/juanmanuel-tirado/savetheworldwithgo/13_grpc/streaming/example_03/chat"
    "google.golang.org/grpc"
    "time"
)

func Chat(stream pb.ChatService_SendTxtClient, done chan bool) {
    t := time.NewTicker(time.Millisecond*500)
    for {
        select {
        case <- done:
            return
        case <- t.C:
            err := stream.Send(&pb.ChatRequest{Txt:"Hello", Id:1, To:2})
            if err != nil {
                panic(err)
            }
        }
    }
}

func Stats(stream pb.ChatService_SendTxtClient, done chan bool) {
    for {
        stats, err := stream.Recv()
        if err != nil {
            panic(err)
```

```go
            }
            fmt.Println(stats.String())
            if stats.TotalChar > 35 {
                fmt.Println("Beyond the limit!!!")
                done <- true
                stream.CloseSend()
                return
            }
        }
}

func main() {
    conn, err := grpc.Dial(":50051", grpc.WithInsecure(), grpc.WithBlock())
    if err != nil {
        panic(err)
    }
    defer conn.Close()

    c := pb.NewChatServiceClient(conn)

    stream, err := c.SendTxt(context.Background())
    if err != nil {
        panic(err)
    }
    done := make(chan bool)
    go Stats(stream, done)
    go Chat(stream, done)

    <- done
}
```

The server implementation from Example 15.13 listens for incoming chat messages and count the number of received characters. Additionally, every two seconds it sends a message with the current value of the characters counter. Notice that sending stats is completely independent of the incoming messages and occurs at a regular pace. The server expects the client to close the connection by checking any incoming EOF.

Example 15.13: Server using bidirectional streaming.

```go
package main

import (
    "fmt"
    pb "github.com/juanmanuel-tirado/savetheworldwithgo/13_grpc/streaming/example_03/chat"
    "google.golang.org/grpc"
    "io"
```

```go
8      "net"
9      "time"
10 )
11
12 type ChatServer struct{
13     pb.UnimplementedChatServiceServer
14 }
15
16 func (c *ChatServer) SendTxt(stream pb.ChatService_SendTxtServer) error {
17     var total int64 = 0
18     go func(){
19         for {
20             t := time.NewTicker(time.Second*2)
21             select {
22             case <- t.C:
23                 stream.Send(&pb.StatsResponse{TotalChar: total})
24             }
25         }
26     }()
27     for {
28         next, err := stream.Recv()
29         if err == io.EOF {
30             fmt.Println("Client closed")
31             return nil
32         }
33         if err != nil {
34             return err
35         }
36         fmt.Println("->", next.Txt)
37         total = total + int64(len(next.Txt))
38     }
39
40     return nil
41 }
42
43 func main() {
44     lis, err := net.Listen("tcp", "localhost:50051")
45     if err != nil {
46         panic(err)
47     }
48     s := grpc.NewServer()
49
50     pb.RegisterChatServiceServer(s, &ChatServer{})
51
52     if err := s.Serve(lis); err != nil {
53         panic(err)
54     }
55 }
```

The output obtained after running the server and the client reveals how the client closes the connection when it exceeds its limit of characters and how the server detects the closed stream.

```
total_char:15
total_char:40
Beyond the limit!!!
```

```
-> Hello
-> Hello
-> Hello
-> Hello
-> Hello
-> Hello
-> Hello
-> Hello
Client closed
```

15.6. TRANSCODING

gRPC works on top of the HTTP/2 transfer protocol offering full-duplex communication, high performance, among other features. Unfortunately, HTTP/2 is not available in every scenario and sometimes can become a drawback. Many servers are behind load balancers and/or proxies that do not support HTTP/2. In other scenarios, remote clients cannot work with gRPC due to other limitations simply because they cannot easily adopt this technology.

Transcoding permits gRPC to emulate REST APIs (HTTP + JSON). This can be done using annotations in the `.proto` file. Using the grpc-gateway[3] plugin, the `protoc` program can generate reverse proxies transcoding HTTP requests to the corresponding gRPC handler. Figure 15.5 shows a schema of HTTP transcoding to gRPC where a HTTP client sends a GET request to a remote server. This request travels through the Internet and may traverse different load balancers or service providers. Finally, the request reaches the target HTTP server. The incoming request is transformed into a gRPC compatible request and sent to the corresponding gRPC server.

This transformation is obtained adding the `google.api.http` notations to the `.proto` file. Observe in the figure that the output from `protoc` includes two files like in a regular gRPC scenario, but `user_grpc.pb.go` has been replaced by `usr.pb.gw.go`. This file contains the definition of the necessary transcoding operations. Transcoding is a powerful option to enable accessing remote methods to a vast number of clients with minimal coding.

---

[3] https://github.com/grpc-ecosystem/grpc-gateway

CHAPTER 15. GRPC

```
//...
service UserService {
    rpc GetUser (UserRequest) returns (User) {
        option(google.api.http) = {
            get: "/v1/user/{user_id}"};
    }
}
```

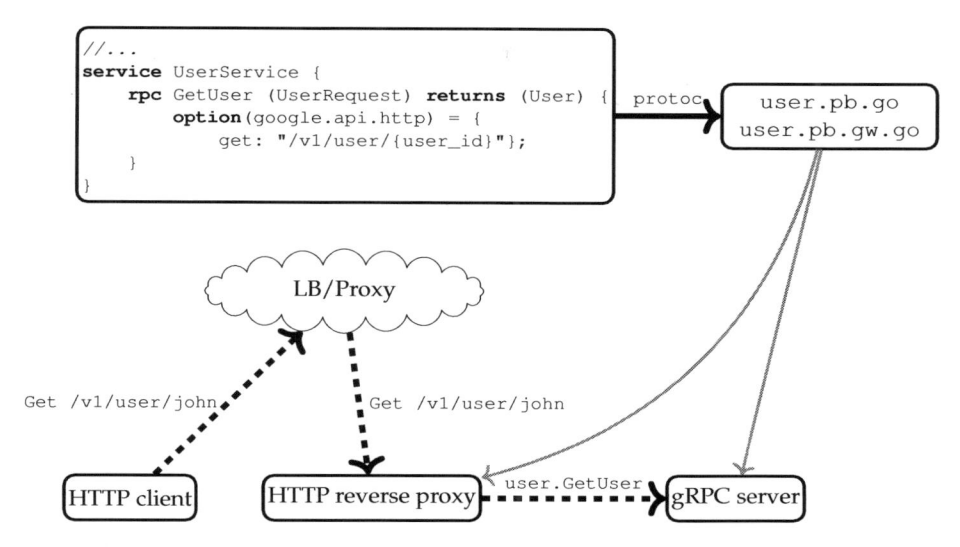

Figure 15.5: Summary of elements in a gRPC deployment.

15.6.1. GENERATION OF STUBS AND GRPC-GATEWAY

Transcoding is defined in the `.proto` file using annotations. Example 15.14, defines a user service that creates and gets users. There are two important elements we have added here. First, we have imported the `annotations.proto` file that defines the `google.api.http` option.

Example 15.14: gRPC services definition with transcoding notations.

```
1  syntax = "proto3";
2  package user;
3
4  option go_package="github.com/juanmanuel-tirado/savetheworldwithgo/13_grpc/
       transcoding/example_01/user";
5
6  import "google/api/annotations.proto";
7
8  message User {
9      string user_id = 1;
10     string email = 2;
11 }
12
13 message UserRequest {
14     string user_id = 1;
15 }
16
```

```
17  service UserService {
18      rpc Get (UserRequest) returns (User) {
19          option(google.api.http) = {
20              get: "/v1/user/{user_id}"
21          };
22      }
23      rpc Create (User) returns (User) {
24          option(google.api.http) = {
25              post: "/v1/user"
26              body: "*"
27          };
28      }
29  }
```

For every RPC method we want to expose through HTTP we must define the path and the required HTTP method. The remote method `Get` will be served at `/v1/user/{user_id}`, where `{user_id}` corresponds to the field with the same name from the corresponding input message. In this case, this will fill the unique field from the `UserRequest` message. Similarly, the `Create` remote function is a HTTP `POST` method with a `User` message to be sent into the body of the HTTP request. By setting `body: "*"`, we indicate that a `User` message will be filled with all the available data from the body. If required, single fields can be specified, for example, `body: "email"` will only expect the body to contain the `email` field.

> Remember that the URL of a remote procedure should not be changed unilaterally once this function is consumed by others. There are some good practices to be followed like indicating the API version in the URL. In other cases, you can define additional bindings for the same procedure.
>
> ```
> rpc Get (UserRequest) returns (User) {
>     option(google.api.http) = {
>         get: "/v1/user/{user_id}"
>         additional_bindings {
>             get: "/v2/user/{user_id}"
>         }
>     };
> }
> ```

Before running `protoc`, we must install the grpc-gateway plugin[4].

---

[4]For additional details check: https://github.com/grpc-ecosystem/grpc-gateway.

CHAPTER 15. GRPC

```
>>> go install \
github.com/grpc-ecosystem/grpc-gateway/v2/protoc-gen-grpc-gateway \
github.com/grpc-ecosystem/grpc-gateway/v2/protoc-gen-openapiv2 \
google.golang.org/protobuf/cmd/protoc-gen-go \
google.golang.org/grpc/cmd/protoc-gen-go-grpc
```

Now `protoc` should be able to use the additional plugins by running:

```
>>> protoc -I . \
-I $GOPATH/src/github.com/grpc-ecosystem/grpc-gateway/third_party/googleapis \
--go_out=plugins=grpc:$GOPATH/src \
--grpc-gateway_out=logtostderr=true:$GOPATH/src *.proto
```

This execution assumes you are in the same folder as the `.proto` file. Some arguments may vary depending on your environment.

15.6.2. CREATE AN HTTP SERVER

To demonstrate how transcoding works, we are going to implement the remote methods we have defined in the previous `.protoc` file and serve them using gRPC as we have already explained, then we show how this can be done using an HTTP server. For clarity, we split the code into two parts. First, in Example 15.15 contains the code with the logic of the remote procedures defined in our `.proto` file. This code is similar to the examples we have already explained. The only method you may find weird is `ServeGrpc`, which simply encapsulates the gRPC server starting logic.

Example 15.15: gRPC gateway using HTTP (part I).

```go
package main

import (
    "context"
    "fmt"
    "github.com/grpc-ecosystem/grpc-gateway/v2/runtime"
    pb "github.com/juanmanuel-tirado/savetheworldwithgo/13_grpc/transcoding/example_01/user"
    "google.golang.org/grpc"
    "net"
    "net/http"
)

type UserServer struct{
    httpAddr string
```

```go
15      grpcAddr string
16      pb.UnimplementedUserServiceServer
17  }
18
19  func (u *UserServer) Get(ctx context.Context, req *pb.UserRequest) (*pb.User,
         error) {
20      fmt.Println("Server received:", req.String())
21      return &pb.User{UserId: "John", Email: "john@gmail.com"}, nil
22  }
23
24  func (u *UserServer) Create(ctx context.Context, req *pb.User) (*pb.User, error
        ) {
25      fmt.Println("Server received:", req.String())
26      return &pb.User{UserId: req.UserId, Email: req.Email}, nil
27  }
28
29  func (u *UserServer) ServeGrpc() {
30      lis, err := net.Listen("tcp", u.grpcAddr)
31      if err != nil {
32          panic(err)
33      }
34      s := grpc.NewServer()
35      pb.RegisterUserServiceServer(s, u)
36      fmt.Println("Server listening GRCP:")
37
38      if err := s.Serve(lis); err != nil {
39          panic(err)
40      }
41  }
```

When all the elements needed to run our gRPC server are ready, we can include our HTTP transcoding. Example 15.16 contains the code to serve the remote procedures defined in the previous example using HTTP. We have to register every service xxx from the `.proto` file using the corresponding `RegisterXXXHandlerFromEndPoint` function. This function binds the gRPC server address to a `Mux` server[5]. For simplicity, the `UserServer` type has two addresses one for gRPC and the other for HTTP. Remember that the HTTP server is a gateway that forwards incoming requests to our gRPC server.

Example 15.16: gRPC gateway using HTTP (part II).

```go
1  func (u *UserServer) ServeHttp() {
2      mux := runtime.NewServeMux()
3      opts := []grpc.DialOption{grpc.WithInsecure()}
4      endpoint := u.grpcAddr
5
```

---

[5]https://golang.org/pkg/net/http/#ServeMux

```
 6      err := pb.RegisterUserServiceHandlerFromEndpoint(context.Background(), mux,
            endpoint, opts)
 7      if err != nil {
 8          panic(err)
 9      }
10
11      httpServer := &http.Server{
12          Addr: u.httpAddr,
13          Handler: mux,
14      }
15
16      fmt.Println("Server listing HTTP:")
17      if err = httpServer.ListenAndServe(); err!=nil{
18          panic(err)
19      }
20  }
21
22  func main() {
23      us := UserServer{httpAddr:":8080",grpcAddr:":50051"}
24      go us.ServeGrpc()
25      us.ServeHttp()
26  }
```

Finally, in the `main` function we start our gRPC and HTTP servers. Now gRPC clients can invoke remote procedures in port 5051 and HTTP clients can use port 8080. Now we can send HTTP requests to the indicated URLs using an HTTP client like `curl`.

```
>>> curl   http://localhost:8080/v1/user/john
{"userId":"John","email":"john@gmail.com"}
>>> curl  -d '{"user_id":"john","email":"john@gmail"}' http://localhost:8080/v1
    /user
{"userId":"john","email":"john@gmail"}
```

As you can observe, the addition of the gRPC gateway has not impacted the logic of our code. We have added a small piece of code and now our server makes available the same API using gRPC and HTTP/JSON.

15.7. Interceptors

Interceptors is the name for middleware components in gRPC. Operations such as user authentication, message tracing, request validation, etc. can be done with interceptors. Interceptors are allocated between the client and the server data flow like in Figure 15.6. When an interceptor is introduced into the data flow, this is executed for every message and has access to all the communication elements. An interceptor can manipulate message metadata, for example adding authentication headers on the client-side, or annotating additional information about IP addresses, client time zone, etc.

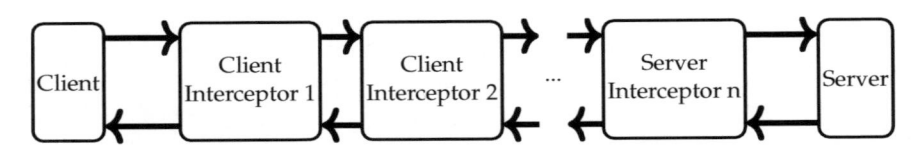

Figure 15.6: Data flow from client to server using interceptors.

Interceptors are thought to be used for common tasks and can be reused in several solutions. The gRPC-ecosystem has an available collection of interceptors to be used[6]. However, the exact interceptor required for your problem may not be available. Fortunately, gRPC facilitates the implementation of four types of interceptors depending if they are on the client or server-side and if they are designed for unary or streaming requests. In this section, we explore server and client interceptors for unary requests. Streaming versions of these interceptors are very similar and can be easily implemented starting from unary request versions.

15.7.1. SERVER INTERCEPTORS

gRPC servers are instantiated with the `grpc.NewServer` function that receives arguments of type `ServerOption`. We can build types that implement the `ServerOption` type to work as interceptors. The following lines sketch the elements required to build a server interceptor.

```go
func MyServerInterceptor(...) (interface{}, error) {
// ...
func withMyServerInterceptor() grpc.ServerOption{
    return grpc.UnaryInterceptor(MyServerInterceptor)
}
// ...
s := grpc.NewServer(withMyServerInterceptor())
```

To build a `ServerOption` we invoke the `grpc.UnaryInterceptor` function which expects a `UnaryServerInterceptor` type. This type is a function that must be implemented by our interceptor. The function signature is:

---

[6]https://github.com/grpc-ecosystem/go-grpc-middleware

```
type UnaryServerInterceptor func(ctx context.Context, req interface{},
    info *UnaryServerInfo, handler UnaryHandler) (resp interface{}, err error)
```

where,

- `ctx` is the context.

- `req` contains the actual request.

- `info` contains server information and the URI of the invoked method.

- `handler` is the handler in charge of the request.

To illustrate how to implement a server interceptor, assume the initial implementation from Example 15.3. We want to enhance this server to only permit authenticated users. Example 15.17 is an excerpt of the server implementation containing an interceptor that provides a naive authentication method.

Example 15.17: Server interceptor (excerpt).

```
23  func AuthServerInterceptor(
24      ctx context.Context,
25      req interface{},
26      info *grpc.UnaryServerInfo,
27      handler grpc.UnaryHandler) (interface{}, error) {
28      md, found := metadata.FromIncomingContext(ctx)
29      if !found {
30          return nil, status.Errorf(codes.InvalidArgument, "metadata not found")
31      }
32      password, found := md["password"]
33      if !found {
34          return nil, status.Errorf(codes.Unauthenticated, "password not found")
35      }
36
37      if password[0] != "go" {
38          return nil, status.Errorf(codes.Unauthenticated, "password not valid")
39      }
40
41      h, err := handler(ctx, req)
42      return h, err
43  }
44
45  func withAuthServerInterceptor() grpc.ServerOption {
46      return grpc.UnaryInterceptor(AuthServerInterceptor)
47  }
48
```

```
49  func main() {
50      lis, err := net.Listen("tcp", "localhost:50051")
51      if err != nil {
52          panic(err)
53      }
54      s := grpc.NewServer(withAuthServerInterceptor())
55      pb.RegisterUserServiceServer(s, &UserServer{})
56
57      if err := s.Serve(lis); err != nil {
58          panic(err)
59      }
60  }
```

The logic of our interceptor is contained into the AuthServerInterceptor function that implements the UnaryServerInterceptor type. The code looks into the gRPC request metadata for the key/value pair "password". If it is found and is equal to "go", we authenticate the user. In this case, we simply return the result of the handler with the given context and original request. We could go further by removing the password from the metadata and adding another field with the authenticated user id, role, etc.

Additional code prepares the interceptor to be converted into a ServerOption as explained above. Now every request will pass through our interceptor. However, the client must include the corresponding metadata otherwise, requests will not be authorized.

Example 15.18: Client extended metadata (excerpt).

```
12  func main() {
13      conn, err := grpc.Dial("localhost:50051", grpc.WithInsecure(), grpc.
            WithBlock())
14      if err != nil {
15          panic(err)
16      }
17      defer conn.Close()
18
19      c := pb.NewUserServiceClient(conn)
20
21      ctx, cancel := context.WithTimeout(context.Background(), time.Second)
22      ctx = metadata.AppendToOutgoingContext(ctx, "password","go")
23      defer cancel()
24
25      r, err := c.GetUser(ctx, &pb.UserRequest{UserId: "John"})
26      if err != nil {
27          panic(err)
28      }
29      fmt.Println("Client received:", r.String())
30  }
```

CHAPTER 15. GRPC

Example 15.18 shows how the client puts additional metadata into the context before sending the request (line 22). For demonstration purposes and simplicity, the user was fixed. You can check that modifying the username returns an error from the server-side. Adding this metadata could be done using an interceptor on the client-side. Check the next section to understand how to write a client interceptor.

15.7.2. CLIENT INTERCEPTORS

Client interceptors work similarly to server interceptors. The three major elements to be filled are schematically shown below.

```
func MyClientInterceptor(...) error {
// ...
func withMyClientInterceptor() grpc.DialOption{
    return grpc.WithUnaryInterceptor(MyClientInterceptor)
}
// ...
conn, err := grpc.Dial(":50051", withMyClientInterceptor())
```

Our interceptor must implement the function signature defined by the `UnaryClientInterceptor` type.

```
type UnaryClientInterceptor func(ctx context.Context, method string, req,
    reply interface{}, cc *ClientConn, invoker UnaryInvoker, opts ...
        CallOption) error
```

where,

- `ctx` is the context.
- `method` is the URI of the invoked procedure.
- `req` is the request.
- `reply` is the server response.
- `cc` is the connection.
- `invoker` the function to be called to continue the gRPC call.

Now we plan to extend Example 15.4 by adding to every request metadata information about the environment used by the client. Example 15.19 defines the function `ClientLoggerInterceptor` that adds metadata with the client operating system and timezone.

Observe that before returning, the interceptor calls the `invoker` function to continue the data workflow.

Example 15.19: Client interceptor with logging metadata (excerpt).

```go
func ClientLoggerInterceptor(
    ctx context.Context,
    method string,
    req interface{},
    reply interface{},
    cc *grpc.ClientConn,
    invoker grpc.UnaryInvoker,
    opts ...grpc.CallOption) error {

    os := runtime.GOOS
    zone, _ := time.Now().Zone()

    ctx = metadata.AppendToOutgoingContext(ctx, "os", os)
    ctx = metadata.AppendToOutgoingContext(ctx, "zone", zone)

    err := invoker(ctx, method, req, reply, cc, opts...)
    return err
}

func withUnaryClientLoggerInterceptor() grpc.DialOption {
    return grpc.WithUnaryInterceptor(ClientLoggerInterceptor)
}

func main() {
    conn, err := grpc.Dial("localhost:50051", grpc.WithInsecure(),
        grpc.WithBlock(), withUnaryClientLoggerInterceptor())
    if err != nil {
        panic(err)
    }
    defer conn.Close()

    c := pb.NewUserServiceClient(conn)

    ctx, cancel := context.WithTimeout(context.Background(), time.Second)
    defer cancel()

    r, err := c.GetUser(ctx, &pb.UserRequest{UserId: "John"})
    if err != nil {
        panic(err)
    }
    fmt.Println("Client received:", r.String())
}
```

For completeness, we have created a server interceptor that captures this metadata for logging purposes in Example 15.20. The steps to prepare this interceptor are similar to those described in the previous section.

Example 15.20: Server interceptor consuming logging metadata (excerpt).

```go
func RequestLoggerInterceptor(ctx context.Context,
    req interface{},
    info *grpc.UnaryServerInfo,
    handler grpc.UnaryHandler) (interface{}, error){
    md, found := metadata.FromIncomingContext(ctx)
    if found {
        os, _ := md["os"]
        zone, _ := md["zone"]
        fmt.Printf("Request from %s using %s\n", zone, os)
    }

    h, err := handler(ctx, req)
    return h, err
}
```

The output obtained from running the server and its client reveals how the client transparently sent the time zone and operating system to the server.

```
Client received: user_id:"John"
email:"john@gmail.com"
```

```
Request from [CET] using [darwin]
Server received: user_id:"John"
```

15.8. Summary

gRPC is a modern, powerful, and versatile RPC framework. This Chapter has shown how to harness all the powerful features of gRPC. In conjunction with protocol buffers, gRPC is a must in every data system designed to be scalable, portable, and maintainable. We have explained how to implement servers with their corresponding clients, to use streaming connections, and how to provide HTTP interfaces for our gRPC procedures with minimal code using transcoding. Finally, for advanced designs, we have shown how interceptors can be used to enhance the logic of our data communication channels.

16
Logging with Zerolog

The execution of a program generates a substantial amount of information. Part of this information is dedicated to ensuring the correctness of the program or recording what happened. Logging is therefore a basic component of any program. For any software developer, logging must be one of the first elements to be designed in any solution. Projects such as Zerolog, take advantage of Go features to offer a modern and complete logging solution. This Chapter exhaustively explores how to create logs in Go with special attention to the Zerolog project.

16.1. The log package

Go provides a basic logging solution in the `log` package[1]. This package defines three types of messages `Fatal`, `Panic`, and `Println`. The first two messages are equivalent to executing `Print` followed by `os.Exit` and `panic` functions respectively. Messages can be customized using prefixes and flags as shown in Example 16.1.

Example 16.1: `log` package messaging.

```go
package main

import "log"

func main() {
    // Panic or fatal messages stop the execution flow
    // log.Fatal("This is a fatal message")
    // log.Panic("This is a panic message")
```

[1] https://golang.org/pkg/log

```go
9      log.Println("This is a log message")
10     log.SetPrefix("prefix -> ")
11     log.Println("This is a log message")
12     log.SetFlags(log.Lshortfile)
13 }
```

```
2021/02/08 19:30:34 This is a log message
prefix -> 2021/02/08 19:30:34 This is a log message
```

More customized loggers can be defined using the `log.New` function which receives a writer argument, a prefix, and a flag. This facilitates logs using file writers as shown in Example 16.2.

Example 16.2: `log` package messaging.

```go
 1 package main
 2
 3 import (
 4     "io/ioutil"
 5     "log"
 6     "os"
 7 )
 8
 9 func main() {
10     tmpFile, err := ioutil.TempFile(os.TempDir(),"logger.out")
11     if err != nil {
12         log.Panic(err)
13     }
14     logger := log.New(tmpFile, "prefix -> ", log.Ldate)
15     logger.Println("This is a log message")
16 }
```

16.2. Zerolog basics

The previous Section explored how to use the basic logging features provided within the `log` package. The limitations of this package in terms of customization, efficiency, and adaptability made third-party developers write their own logging solutions. A remarkable solution is Zerolog[2] which provides JSON oriented logging using zero-allocation.

---

[2] https://github.com/rs/zerolog

The simplest Zerolog message defines a logging level and a message string. The generated output is a JSON object with the level, the time, and the message. There are seven log levels as shown in Example 16.3 from panic (level 5) to trace (level -1).

Example 16.3: Logging messages in zerolog.

```go
package main

import (
    "github.com/rs/zerolog/log"
)

func main() {
    // Panic or fatal messages stop the execution flow
    // log.Panic().Msg("This is a panic message")
    // log.Fatal().Msg("This is a fatal message")
    log.Error().Msg("This is an error message")
    log.Warn().Msg("This is a warning message")
    log.Info().Msg("This is an information message")
    log.Debug().Msg("This is a debug message")
    log.Trace().Msg("This is a trace message")
}
```

```
{"level":"error","time":"2021-02-08T19:00:21+01:00","message":"This is an error
 message"}
{"level":"warn","time":"2021-02-08T19:00:21+01:00","message":"This is a warning
 message"}
{"level":"info","time":"2021-02-08T19:00:21+01:00","message":"This is an
 information message"}
{"level":"debug","time":"2021-02-08T19:00:21+01:00","message":"This is a debug
 message"}
{"level":"trace","time":"2021-02-08T19:00:21+01:00","message":"This is a trace
 message"}
```

Log levels help identifying the severity of messages and can be set on the fly using the global level variable. Example 16.4 changes the global level from `Debug` to `Info`. Notice that after setting the info level, debug messages are discarded.

Example 16.4: Set global level zerolog.

```go
package main

import (
    "github.com/rs/zerolog/log"
```

```
5       "github.com/rs/zerolog"
6   )
7
8   func main() {
9       zerolog.SetGlobalLevel(zerolog.DebugLevel)
10
11      log.Debug().Msg("Debug message is displayed")
12      log.Info().Msg("Info Message is displayed")
13
14      zerolog.SetGlobalLevel(zerolog.InfoLevel)
15      log.Debug().Msg("Debug message is no longer displayed")
16      log.Info().Msg("Info message is displayed")
17  }
```

```
{"level":"debug","time":"2021-02-08T11:12:56+01:00","message":"Debug message is
 displayed"}
{"level":"info","time":"2021-02-08T11:12:56+01:00","message":"Info Message is
 displayed"}
{"level":"info","time":"2021-02-08T11:12:56+01:00","message":"Info message is
 displayed"}
```

Zerolog provides messages within a context. This context has zero or more variables accompanying the logging message. Variables are typed and can be added on the fly to any message like shown in Example 16.5. A complete list of available types can be found at the official documentation [3].

Example 16.5: Set message context.

```
1   package main
2
3   import(
4       "github.com/rs/zerolog/log"
5   )
6
7   func main() {
8       log.Info().Str("mystr","this is a string").Msg("")
9       log.Info().Int("myint",1234).Msg("")
10      log.Info().Int("myint",1234).Str("str","some string").Msg("And a regular
            message")
11  }
```

---

[3]https://github.com/rs/zerolog#standard-types

CHAPTER 16. LOGGING WITH ZEROLOG

```
{"level":"info","mystr":"this is a string","time":"2021-02-08T11:19:55+01:00"}
{"level":"info","myint":1234,"time":"2021-02-08T11:19:55+01:00"}
{"level":"info","myint":1234,"str":"some string","time":"2021-02-08T11
:19:55+01:00","message":"And a regular message"}
```

Zerolog is specially oriented to leverage JSON encoding[4]. In this sense, using JSON tags helps to display structs consistently. Example 16.6 shows how two structs are displayed in the context of a log message when they have JSON tags or not. Both types are sent to the context like interfaces. Observe that the tagged type follows the field names given in the JSON tags. Additionally, the `RawJSON` context type permits printing JSON encoded objects.

Example 16.6: JSON tagging and encoding in message logs.

```go
package main

import (
    "encoding/json"
    "github.com/rs/zerolog/log"
)

type AStruct struct {
    FieldA string
    FieldB int
    fieldC bool
}

type AJSONStruct struct {
    FieldA string    `json:"fieldA,omitempty"`
    FieldB int       `json:"fieldB,omitempty"`
    fieldC bool
}

func main() {
    a := AStruct{"a string", 42, false}
    b := AJSONStruct{"a string", 42, false}

    log.Info().Interface("a",a).Msg("AStruct")
    log.Info().Interface("b",b).Msg("AJSONStruct")

    encoded, _ := json.Marshal(b)
    log.Info().RawJSON("encoded",encoded).Msg("Encoded JSON")
}
```

---

[4]If you are not familiar with JSON encodings check Section 8.2

```
{"level":"info","a":{"FieldA":"a string","FieldB":42},"time":"2021-02-08T19
:20:59+01:00","message":"AStruct"}
{"level":"info","b":{"fieldA":"a string","fieldB":42},"time":"2021-02-08T19
:20:59+01:00","message":"AJSONStruct"}
{"level":"info","encoded":{"fieldA":"a string","fieldB":42},"time":"2021-02-08
T19:20:59+01:00","message":"Encoded JSON"}
```

Errors are very important in logs. Understanding where errors occur in a program runtime is a crucial task for any developer. The `error` type is available as a context type like shown in Example 16.7.

Example 16.7: Single error logging.

```go
package main

import (
    "errors"
    "github.com/rs/zerolog/log"
)

func main() {
    err := errors.New("there is an error")

    log.Error().Err(err).Msg("this is the way to log errors")
}
```

```
{"level":"error","error":"there is an error","time":"2021-02-08T19:38:35+01:00"
,"message":"this is the way to log errors"}
```

Printing the point in the code where an error occurred may not always be enough. Errors can be triggered by the propagation of previous mistakes. In these cases, the full stack trace can be more useful to detect where errors come from. The stack trace can be obtained as shown in Example 16.8. Setting the `ErrorStackMarshaler` to the implementation offered at `pkgerrors` permits the context `Stack()` to get the complete execution stack. The log output contains the list of invoked functions until the error was found.

Example 16.8: Stack trace logging.

```go
package main

import (
```

CHAPTER 16. LOGGING WITH ZEROLOG

```
 4      "github.com/pkg/errors"
 5      "github.com/rs/zerolog/log"
 6      "github.com/rs/zerolog"
 7      "github.com/rs/zerolog/pkgerrors"
 8  )
 9
10  func failA() error {
11      return failB()
12  }
13
14  func failB() error {
15      return failC()
16  }
17
18  func failC() error {
19      return errors.New("C failed")
20  }
21
22  func main() {
23      zerolog.ErrorStackMarshaler = pkgerrors.MarshalStack
24
25      err := failA()
26      log.Error().Stack().Err(err).Msg("")
27  }
```

```
{"level":"error","stack":[{"func":"failC","line":"19","source":"main.go"},{"
func":"failB","line":"15","source":"main.go"},{"func":"failA","line":"11","
source":"main.go"},{"func":"main","line":"25","source":"main.go"},{"func":"main
","line":"204","source":"proc.go"},{"func":"goexit","line":"1374","source":"
asm_amd64.s"}],"error":"C failed","time":"2021-02-08T19:42:22+01:00"}
```

16.3. ZEROLOG SETTINGS

Zerolog has an extensive set of configuration options. These options can modify the message output format, where is the output sent to, define subloggers, etc. In this Section, we explore some settings that a developer may find useful when defining how and what to log in a project.

16.3.1. WRITE LOGS TO A FILE

Logs in the standard output are not always the best solution, especially in unsupervised scenarios. Writing logs to a file not also permits to have a non-volatile version, it additionally facilitates forensics and can even be used to feed analytical systems. A file logger can be created using the `New` function which receives an `io.Writer`. Example 16.9 creates a logger which dumps all the messages into a temporary file.

Example 16.9: Stack trace logging.

```go
package main

import (
    "io/ioutil"
    "os"
    "fmt"
    "github.com/rs/zerolog/log"
    "github.com/rs/zerolog"
)

func main() {
    tempFile, err := ioutil.TempFile(os.TempDir(),"deleteme")
    if err != nil {
        // Can we log an error before we have our logger? :)
        log.Error().Err(err).
            Msg("there was an error creating a temporary file four our log")
    }
    defer tempFile.Close()
    fileLogger := zerolog.New(tempFile).With().Logger()
    fileLogger.Info().Msg("This is an entry from my log")
    fmt.Printf("The log file is allocated at %s\n", tempFile.Name())
}
```

```
The log file is allocated at /var/folders/6h/xffhh45j077157cb5mbk48zh0000gp/T/deleteme930052425
```

16.3.2. OUTPUT CUSTOMIZATION

We have already mentioned that Zerolog is designed to use JSON. However, JSON may not be the most user-friendly format, especially if we print logs to a console. The `Console Writer` gets rid of colons, brackets, and quotation marks from the JSON syntax and permits us to easily define our output format. Example 16.10 customizes a `ConsoleWriter` to define new formats for the level, message, field name, and field value. Every item can be redefined using a function that receives an interface and returns a string with the new value. See how in this example, the field name is surrounded by square brackets or how the log level is always fixed to a six characters string.

Example 16.10: Customized output with `ConsoleWriter`.

```go
package main

import (
    "os"
    "strings"
    "time"
    "fmt"
    "github.com/rs/zerolog"
)

func main() {
    output := zerolog.ConsoleWriter{Out: os.Stdout, TimeFormat: time.RFC3339}
    output.FormatLevel = func(i interface{}) string {
        return strings.ToUpper(fmt.Sprintf("| %-6s|", i))
    }
    output.FormatMessage = func(i interface{}) string {
        return fmt.Sprintf(">>>%s<<<", i)
    }
    output.FormatFieldName = func(i interface{}) string {
        return fmt.Sprintf("[%s]:", i)
    }
    output.FormatFieldValue = func(i interface{}) string {
        return strings.ToUpper(fmt.Sprintf("[%s]", i))
    }

    log := zerolog.New(output).With().Timestamp().Logger()

    log.Info().Str("foo", "bar").Msg("Save the world with Go!!!")
}
```

```
2021-02-08T19:16:09+01:00 | INFO  | >>>Save the world with Go!!!<<< [foo]:[BAR]
```

16.3.3. MULTI-LOGGER

It is common to separate logs depending on the log level, or the message final output (file, standard output). The `MultiLevelWriter` aggregates several loggers making it possible for a single log message to be written to different destinations with different formats. Example 16.11 defines a multi-logger that simultaneously sends every message to a file, the standard output, and a `ConsoleWriter`. The output shows the outcome from the two loggers dumping messages to the standard output and the file with the logs. Additional customizations such as setting log levels to have specialized loggers can be done. This is a common approach to separate error messages into specific log files.

Example 16.11: Simultaneously logging to several outputs with `MultiLevelWriter`.

```go
package main

import (
    "io/ioutil"
    "os"
    "fmt"
    "github.com/rs/zerolog"
    "github.com/rs/zerolog/log"
)

func main() {

    tempFile, err := ioutil.TempFile(os.TempDir(),"deleteme")
    if err != nil {
        log.Error().Err(err).
            Msg("there was an error creating a temporary file four our log")
    }
    defer tempFile.Close()
    fmt.Printf("The log file is allocated at %s\n", tempFile.Name())

    fileWriter := zerolog.New(tempFile).With().Logger()
    consoleWriter := zerolog.ConsoleWriter{Out: os.Stdout}

    multi := zerolog.MultiLevelWriter(consoleWriter, os.Stdout, fileWriter)

    logger := zerolog.New(multi).With().Timestamp().Logger()

    logger.Info().Msg("Save the world with Go!!!")
}
```

```
The log file is allocated at /var/folders/6h/xffhh45j077157cb5mbk48zh0000gp/T/
```

```
deleteme581703284
12:32PM INF Save the world with Go!!!
{"level":"info","time":"2021-02-08T12:32:18+01:00","message":"Save the world
with Go!!!"}
```

16.3.4. SUB-LOGGER

By definition, Zerolog loggers are extensible. This makes it possible to create new loggers enhancing the existing ones. These sub-loggers inherit the existing configuration and can extend the context. In Example 16.12 we create a new logger from `mainLogger` with additional context indicating the current component. Check how the output from the sub-logger maintains the same configuration from the main logger with the additional context without additional info.

Example 16.12: Extensible logging using sub-loggers.

```go
package main

import (
    "os"
    "github.com/rs/zerolog"
)

func main() {
    mainLogger := zerolog.New(os.Stdout).With().Logger()
    mainLogger.Info().Msg("This is the main logger")

    subLogger := mainLogger.With().Str("component","componentA").Logger()
    subLogger.Info().Msg("This is the sublogger")
}
```

```
{"level":"info","message":"This is the main logger"}
{"level":"info","component":"componentA","message":"This is the sublogger"}
```

16.4. ZEROLOG ADVANCED SETTINGS

This Section, extends the current overview of Zerolog features and customization by explaining examples of additional solutions for specific scenarios.

16.4.1. HOOKS

Hooks are executed every time a logger is invoked. The `Hook` interface defines the `Run` method that gives access to the arguments of a log message. The Example 16.13 uses a `Hook` to add the component name to the context of every debug message. Additionally, a second hook adds a random number to the context. Both hooks are added to the same logger modifying the final behaviour of the logger. Observe that only, the debug message contains the component string in the context.

Example 16.13: Extensible logging using sub-loggers.

```go
package main

import (
    "github.com/rs/zerolog"
    "github.com/rs/zerolog/log"
    "math/rand"
)

type ComponentHook struct {
    component string
}

func (h ComponentHook) Run(e *zerolog.Event, level zerolog.Level, msg string) {
    if level == zerolog.DebugLevel {
        e.Str("component", h.component)
    }
}

type RandomHook struct{}

func (r RandomHook) Run(e *zerolog.Event, level zerolog.Level, msg string) {
    e.Int("random",rand.Int())
}

func main() {
    logger := log.Hook(ComponentHook{"moduleA"})
    logger = logger.Hook(RandomHook{})
    logger.Info().Msg("Info message")
    logger.Debug().Msg("Debug message")
}
```

```
{"level":"info","time":"2021-02-08T13:16:37+01:00","random"
:5577006791947779410,"message":"Info message"}
{"level":"debug","time":"2021-02-08T13:16:37+01:00","component":"moduleA","
```

```
random":8674665223082153551,"message":"Debug message"}
```

16.4.2. Sampling

Logging messages can be particularly disturbing when executed inside loops. It becomes even worse for a large number of iterations. Zerolog provides sampling loggers that can be configured to adequate the number of generated log messages. The `log.Sample` function returns a Logger based on a `Sampler` type. The `Sampler` interface only contains a `Sample` method that returns true when a message has to be sampled.

The `BasicSampler` sends a message once every N calls. This is particularly useful inside loops, like in Example 16.14, where a message is printed every 200 iterations inside a loop of 1000 iterations.

Example 16.14: Logger using basic sampler.

```go
package main

import (
    "github.com/rs/zerolog"
    "github.com/rs/zerolog/log"
)

func main() {
    logger := log.Sample(&zerolog.BasicSampler{N:200})
    for i:=0;i<1000;i++{
        logger.Info().Int("i",i).Msg("")
    }
}
```

```
{"level":"info","i":0,"time":"2021-02-09T19:24:03+01:00"}
{"level":"info","i":200,"time":"2021-02-09T19:24:03+01:00"}
{"level":"info","i":400,"time":"2021-02-09T19:24:03+01:00"}
{"level":"info","i":600,"time":"2021-02-09T19:24:03+01:00"}
{"level":"info","i":800,"time":"2021-02-09T19:24:03+01:00"}
```

The `BurstSampler` permits more sophisticated policies indicating how many messages are allowed per period. Additionally, a `NextSampler` can be used to indicate what sampler has to be invoked when the burst limit is reached. In Example 16.15, the sampler defines a burst of two messages every five seconds and then one sample every 90000000 iterations. After the first two entries, the burst limit is reached. Looking at the timestamp, we see that no more consecutive messages will be printed after five seconds.

Example 16.15: Logger using burst sampler.

```go
package main

import (
    "github.com/rs/zerolog"
    "github.com/rs/zerolog/log"
    "time"
)

func main() {
    logger := log.Sample(&zerolog.BurstSampler{
        Burst: 2,
        Period: time.Second*5,
        NextSampler: &zerolog.BasicSampler{N: 90000000},
    })

    for i:=0;i<99999999;i++{
        logger.Info().Int("i",i).Msg("")
    }
}
```

```
{"level":"info","i":0,"time":"2021-02-09T19:32:08+01:00"}
{"level":"info","i":1,"time":"2021-02-09T19:32:08+01:00"}
{"level":"info","i":2,"time":"2021-02-09T19:32:08+01:00"}
{"level":"info","i":54825538,"time":"2021-02-09T19:32:13+01:00"}
{"level":"info","i":54825539,"time":"2021-02-09T19:32:13+01:00"}
{"level":"info","i":90000004,"time":"2021-02-09T19:32:17+01:00"}
```

16.4.3. INTEGRATION WITH HTTP HANDLERS

A common scenario for logging messages is HTTP handlers. Zerolog provides additional tools to integrate with `http.Handler` types[5]. The `hlog.NewHandler` returns a function that receives an `http.Handler` and returns another handler. This makes the concatenation of loggers possible and their integration with other handlers. Some logging functions are already available[6] to extend the message context adding information extracted from the requests.

---

[5] A detailed explanation of how HTTP Handlers work can be found in Chapter 9.
[6] https://github.com/rs/zerolog/blob/master/hlog/hlog.go

CHAPTER 16. LOGGING WITH ZEROLOG

In Example 16.16, we create a simple HTTP Server that returns a predefined message for every request. We extend our logger `log` with additional context extracted from HTTP requests. We add the remote IP address, the agent handler, and the request id with `RemoteAddrHandler`, `UserAgentHandler`, and `RequestIDHandler` respectively. The concatenation of the loggers with our handler creates a middleware of loggers that is available for every request. Because `hlog` works as a contextual logger, we have to invoke `hlog.FromRequest` to get a logger with the contextual information (line 17). In the final output the message from the `hlog` logger contains additional context from the incoming request without any additional intervention.

Example 16.16: Integration of contextual HTTP loggers.

```go
package main

import (
    "net/http"
    "github.com/rs/zerolog"
    "github.com/rs/zerolog/hlog"
    "os"
)

var log zerolog.Logger = zerolog.New(os.Stdout).With().
    Str("app","example_04").Logger()

type MyHandler struct {}

func(c MyHandler) ServeHTTP(w http.ResponseWriter, r *http.Request) {
    log.Info().Msg("This is not a request contextual logger")
    hlog.FromRequest(r).Info().Msg("")
    w.Write([]byte("Perfect!!!"))
    return
}

func main() {
    mine := MyHandler{}
    a := hlog.NewHandler(log)
    b := hlog.RemoteAddrHandler("ip")
    c := hlog.UserAgentHandler("user_agent")
    d := hlog.RequestIDHandler("req_id", "Request-Id")

    panic(http.ListenAndServe(":8090", a(b(c(d(mine))))))
}
```

```
{"level":"info","app":"example_04","message":"This is not a request contextual logger"}
```

```
{"level":"info","app":"example_04","ip":"::1","user_agent":"curl/7.64.1","
req_id":"c0h539p8d3b53m7iorj0"}
```

Logging HTTP requests may imply several pieces of contextual information. The way we have concatenated our loggers in Example 16.16 is valid. However, it may not be handy when the number of loggers is large or may vary frequently. In Example 16.17 the `Wrapper` type and its method `GetWrapper` extend any handler with a collection of HTTP loggers. This method invokes recursively all the layers and finally applies the received `http.Handler`. Finally, the method returns an `http.Handler` that invokes all the layers. This method simplifies the code required to start the server and makes more flexible the definition of context loggers to be used. A similar solution for HTTP middleware is shown in Example 9.10 using a sequential loop instead of recursion.

Example 16.17: Integration of several contextual HTTP loggers.

```go
package main

import (
    "net/http"
    "github.com/rs/zerolog"
    "github.com/rs/zerolog/hlog"
    "os"
)

var log zerolog.Logger = zerolog.New(os.Stdout).With().
    Str("app","example_05").Logger()

type MyHandler struct {}

func (c MyHandler) ServeHTTP(w http.ResponseWriter, r *http.Request) {
    hlog.FromRequest(r).Info().Msg("")
    w.Write([]byte("Perfect!!!"))
    return
}

type Wrapper struct {
    layers []func(http.Handler) http.Handler
}

func NewWrapper() *Wrapper {
    layers := []func(http.Handler) http.Handler {
        hlog.NewHandler(log),
        hlog.RemoteAddrHandler("ip"),
        hlog.UserAgentHandler("user_agent"),
        hlog.RequestIDHandler("req_id", "Request-Id"),
        hlog.MethodHandler("method"),
```

```
32              hlog.RequestHandler("url"),
33         }
34         return &Wrapper{layers}
35  }
36
37  func(w *Wrapper) GetWrapper(h http.Handler,i int) http.Handler {
38         if i >= len(w.layers) {
39                return h
40         }
41         return w.layers[i](w.GetWrapper(h,i+1))
42  }
43
44  func main() {
45         mine := MyHandler{}
46         wrapper := NewWrapper()
47         h := wrapper.GetWrapper(mine,0)
48
49         panic(http.ListenAndServe(":8090", h))
50  }
```

```
{"level":"info","app":"example_05","ip":"::1","user_agent":"curl/7.64.1","req_id":"c0h58jp8d3b7bcggimu0","method":"GET","url":"GET /"}
```

16.5. SUMMARY

Program logs are one of those tasks developers always postpone. However, good logs always help projects to be more comprehensive and maintainable. This Chapter demonstrates how the Zerolog library can help us to define powerful and modular logs for any Go project.

17

COMMAND LINE INTERFACE

A software developer is used to interact with command-line interfaces (CLI). Good systems not only solve problems but also are easy to use. Nowadays solutions may offer hundreds of commands with several parameters each. Defining a good command-line interface that enables users to easily execute any operation is challenging. Fortunately, the Go ecosystem offers powerful solutions that reduce the effort required to define powerful and solid CLIs. This Chapter presents how the Cobra library can help developers to define solid CLIs in an efficient and consistent way.

17.1. THE BASICS

Cobra[1] is a library that provides all the necessary items to develop CLIs in Go. This library is used by major projects such as Kubernetes, Github or Istio and has some interesting features such as intelligent suggestions, automatic help generation, documentation, shell autocompletion, it is POSIX compliant, etc.

Before explaining the basics make sure you have Cobra available in your environment. The examples from this Chapter require the library to be installed. As usual, you can use Go modules (see Chapter 12) or run the following command to download the code in your GOPATH.

```
go get github.com/spf13/cobra
```

Cobra CLIs are built around the Command type which fields define the name of the actions to be executed, their arguments, and help information. Example 17.1 contains a

---

[1] https://github.com/spf13/cobra

minimal example of a Cobra CLI for a program. This naive program is intended to be executed like `./hello` and print a message using the standard output.

Example 17.1: Basic Cobra CLI

```go
package main

import (
    "fmt"
    "github.com/spf13/cobra"
    "os"
)

var RootCmd = &cobra.Command{
    Use: "hello",
    Short: "short message",
    Long: "Long message",
    Version: "v0.1.0",
    Example: "this is an example",
    Run: func(cmd *cobra.Command, args []string) {
        fmt.Println("Save the world with Go!!!")
    },
}

func main() {
    if err := RootCmd.Execute(); err != nil {
        fmt.Fprintln(os.Stderr, err)
        os.Exit(1)
    }
}
```

Observe that the `main` function only executes the root command. In Cobra, the logic of a program is expected to be controlled, or at least triggered, by commands. In this Example, `RootCmd` is a Cobra command with some fields that are used to populate the program help displayed below. This minimal example already generates this help automatically with no additional information. The output below corresponds to the execution of the compiled program in a shell. The `>>>` indicates the shell prompt. Looking at the `Use` field in `RootCmd`, we expect the executable program to be named `hello`. If we call the program's help, we get the following.

```
>>> ./hello --help
Long message

Usage:
  hello [flags]
```

```
Examples:
this is an example

Flags:
  -h, --help       help for hello
  -v, --version    version for hello
```

We defined a long message that is displayed when the command help is invoked, an example text, and the program version that is displayed with `./hello -v`.

By convention, Cobra expects commands to be defined one per file in the `cmd` folder as shown below.

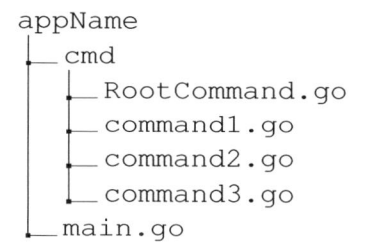

```
appName
├── cmd
│   ├── RootCommand.go
│   ├── command1.go
│   ├── command2.go
│   └── command3.go
└── main.go
```

The `main.go` file is minimal and only executes the root command. Every command file must contain the logic required to execute this command. The logic of the program, library, framework, etc. must not be coupled to these commands. Cobra commands must only be used to capture the required information to trigger actions and must not be part of the logic of your program.

As a point of clarification, the examples in this Chapter have been condensed into single files that contain all the logic. Notice that these examples are focused on demonstrating CLI concepts, not any additional logic. For demonstration purposes and better clarify, the examples contain all the commands in a single file. However, the concepts shown here can be easily adapted to the Cobra conventions.

17.2. ARGUMENTS AND FLAGS

Commands may require arguments to be executed. These arguments are passed to the `Run` field of every `Command`. In Example 17.2, the arguments received by the root command are printed.

Example 17.2: Command receiving arguments

```go
1  package main
```

```go
 2
 3 import (
 4     "fmt"
 5     "github.com/spf13/cobra"
 6     "os"
 7     "strings"
 8 )
 9
10 var RootCmd = &cobra.Command{
11     Use: "main",
12     Long: "Long message",
13     Run: func(cmd *cobra.Command, args []string) {
14         fmt.Printf("%s\n",strings.Join(args,","))
15     },
16 }
17
18 func main() {
19     if err := RootCmd.Execute(); err != nil {
20         fmt.Fprintln(os.Stderr, err)
21         os.Exit(1)
22     }
23 }
```

```
>>> ./main These are arguments
These,are,arguments
>>> ./main 1 2 three 4 five
1,2,three,4,five
```

Observe that these arguments are not typed and there is no control over the number of arguments the program expects. Using flags, Cobra parses incoming arguments that can be later used in the commands. The Example 17.3 expects a `--msg` flag with a message to be displayed with the program.

Example 17.3: Command with single string flag.

```go
 1 package main
 2
 3 import (
 4     "fmt"
 5     "github.com/spf13/cobra"
 6     "os"
 7 )
 8
 9 var RootCmd = &cobra.Command{
10     Use: "main",
```

```
11        Long: "Long message",
12        Run: func(cmd *cobra.Command, args []string) {
13            fmt.Printf("[[--%s--]]\n", *Msg)
14        },
15 }
16
17 var Msg *string
18
19 func init() {
20     Msg = RootCmd.Flags().String("msg", "Save the world with Go!!!",
21         "Message to show")
22 }
23
24 func main() {
25     if err := RootCmd.Execute(); err != nil {
26         fmt.Fprintln(os.Stderr, err)
27         os.Exit(1)
28     }
29 }
```

Flags have to be extracted in an `init`[2] function to make it accessible before `main` is invoked. Cobra parses flags only when it detects the command is expecting them. In the example, we define a flag named `msg` of type **string** with a default value, and a usage message that is displayed in the command help. The returned value is stored in the `Msg` variable which value contains the incoming argument. This flag can now be used by the command in the `Run` function.

```
>>> ./main --msg Hello
[[--Hello--]]
>>> ./main
[[--Save the world with Go!!!--]]
>>> ./main --message Hello
Error: unknown flag: --message
Usage:
  main [flags]

Flags:
  -h, --help          help for main
      --msg string    Message to show (default "Save the world with Go!!!")

unknown flag: --message
exit status 1
```

The output shows how we can set the flag to print a custom message or use the default

---

[2]For more details about init functions check Section 2.9.

value when no flag is passed. However, if the flag is unknown Cobra returns an error message and the command help.

A command can have several flags with different types like in Example 17.4. This code extends the previous example with the number of times our message will be printed.

Example 17.4: Command with several typed flags.

```go
package main

import (
    "fmt"
    "github.com/spf13/cobra"
    "os"
)

var RootCmd = &cobra.Command{
    Use: "main",
    Long: "Long message",
    Run: func(cmd *cobra.Command, args []string) {
        for i:=0;i<*Rep;i++ {
            fmt.Printf("[[--%s--]]\n", *Msg)
        }
    },
}

var Msg *string
var Rep *int

func init() {
    Msg = RootCmd.Flags().String("msg", "Save the world with Go!!!",
        "Message to show")
    Rep = RootCmd.Flags().Int("rep",1, "Number of times to show the message")
}

func main() {
    if err := RootCmd.Execute(); err != nil {
        fmt.Fprintln(os.Stderr, err)
        os.Exit(1)
    }
}
```

```
>>> ./main
[[--Save the world with Go!!!--]]
>>> ./main --msg Hello --rep 3
[[--Hello--]]
[[--Hello--]]
```

```
[[--Hello--]]
```

Flags can be marked to be required forcing the user to indicate its value. Example 17.5 extends the previous one to force users to indicate the number of repetitions. Observe that the `msg` flag can be missing but the missing `rep` flag returns a required flag error.

Example 17.5: Command with required flags.

```go
 1 package main
 2
 3 import (
 4     "fmt"
 5     "github.com/spf13/cobra"
 6     "os"
 7 )
 8
 9 var RootCmd = &cobra.Command{
10     Use: "main",
11     Long: "Long message",
12     Run: func(cmd *cobra.Command, args []string) {
13         for i:=0;i<*Rep;i++ {
14             fmt.Printf("[[--%s--]]\n", *Msg)
15         }
16     },
17 }
18
19 var Msg *string
20 var Rep *int
21
22 func init() {
23     Msg = RootCmd.Flags().String("msg", "Save the world with Go!!!",
24         "Message to show")
25     Rep = RootCmd.Flags().Int("rep",1, "Number of times to show the message")
26
27     RootCmd.MarkFlagRequired("rep")
28 }
29
30 func main() {
31     if err := RootCmd.Execute(); err != nil {
32         fmt.Fprintln(os.Stderr, err)
33         os.Exit(1)
34     }
35 }
```

```
>>> ./main
```

```
Error: required flag(s) "rep" not set
Usage:
  main [flags]

Flags:
  -h, --help          help for main
      --msg string    Message to show (default "Save the world with Go!!!")
      --rep int       Number of times to show the message (default 1)

required flag(s) "rep" not set
exit status 1
>>> ./main --rep 2
[[--Save the world with Go!!!--]]
[[--Save the world with Go!!!--]]
```

Previous examples fill the variables to be used by commands with direct assignations. A less verbose approach uses xxxVar functions with xxx the type of the flag. These functions do not return any value but expect a pointer argument to the variable to be filled with the flag value. Example 17.6 defines a `Config` type to contain all the configuration parameters passed by flags. The fields of the `cnfg` variable can be directly filled with `StringVar` and `IntVar`.

Example 17.6: Flag parsing using pointer variables.

```go
package main

import (
    "fmt"
    "github.com/spf13/cobra"
    "os"
)

var RootCmd = &cobra.Command{
    Use: "main",
    Short: "short message",
    Run: func(cmd *cobra.Command, args []string) {
        for i:=0;i<cnfg.Rep;i++ {
            fmt.Printf("[[--%s--]]\n", cnfg.Msg)
        }
    },
}

type Config struct {
    Msg string
    Rep int
}
var cnfg Config = Config{}
```

```
24
25 func init() {
26     RootCmd.Flags().StringVar(&cnfg.Msg, "msg","Save the world with Go!!!","
           Message to show")
27     RootCmd.Flags().IntVar(&cnfg.Rep,"rep",1, "Number of times to show the
           message")
28     RootCmd.MarkFlagRequired("rep")
29 }
30
31 func main() {
32     if err := RootCmd.Execute(); err != nil {
33         fmt.Fprintln(os.Stderr, err)
34         os.Exit(1)
35     }
36 }
```

17.3. Commands

A CLI may contain one or several commands, and these commands can have subcommands. Generally, the root command is not intended to run any operation. It usually displays some help and presents the actions that can be executed. A good CLI syntax should be close to natural language. The commands, subcommands, and their flags should be easy to remember and make sense if the whole command is read as a sentence.

Example 17.7 prints two different messages: hello and bye. There are several ways to implement a CLI to do this. First, we have to consider that we have two possible actions that can be translated into commands. A CLI with a syntax like `./say hello` is easy to remember and clearly identifies the requested action. It would be possible to define the final action using flags. However, it would be more difficult to remember how to operate this command (maybe `./say something --msg=hello`?). On the other hand, running `./say` clearly lacks of arguments because we expect the program to say something. In that case printing the help is the best option.

Example 17.7: CLI with several commands.

```
1 package main
2
3 import (
4     "fmt"
5     "github.com/spf13/cobra"
6     "os"
7 )
8
```

```go
 9  var RootCmd = &cobra.Command{
10      Use: "say",
11      Long: "Root command",
12  }
13
14  var HelloCmd = &cobra.Command{
15      Use: "hello",
16      Short: "Say hello",
17      Run: func(cmd *cobra.Command, args []string) {
18          fmt.Println("Hello!!!")
19      },
20  }
21
22  var ByeCmd = &cobra.Command{
23      Use: "bye",
24      Short: "Say goodbye",
25      Run: func(cmd *cobra.Command, args []string) {
26          fmt.Println("Bye!!!")
27      },
28  }
29
30  func init() {
31      RootCmd.AddCommand(HelloCmd, ByeCmd)
32  }
33
34  func main() {
35      if err := RootCmd.Execute(); err != nil {
36          fmt.Fprintln(os.Stderr, err)
37          os.Exit(1)
38      }
39  }
```

Running the root command as shown below prints the help message. Now this message includes the `bye` and `hello` commands. Commands have their specific help which shows the command definition and any subcommand if proceeds.

```
>>> ./say
Root command

Usage:
  say [command]

Available Commands:
  bye         Say goodbye
  hello       Say hello
  help        Help about any command

Flags:
```

```
    -h, --help   help for say

Use "say [command] --help" for more information about a command.
>>> ./say hello
Hello!!!
>>> ./say bye
Bye!!!
>>> ./say bye --help
Say goodbye

Usage:
  say bye [flags]

Flags:
  -h, --help   help for bye
```

17.3.1. PERSISTENT AND LOCAL FLAGS

Flags can be shared among commands or be local. Cobra differentiates between the `PersistentFlags` and `Flags` types. The first type assumes the flag to be propagated to the command's children while `Flags` are locally available only. Example 17.8 extends the previous example with the name of the person we are talking to and a custom command that sets the message to be said. In this configuration, the custom command requires an additional flag that should not be available for other commands. This is done in the code by setting the `person` flag as persistent and defining the local flag `msg` for the `CustomCmd` command.

Example 17.8: Commands using persistent and local flags.

```go
1  package main
2
3  import (
4      "fmt"
5      "github.com/spf13/cobra"
6      "os"
7  )
8
9  var RootCmd = &cobra.Command{
10     Use: "say",
11     Long: "Root command",
12 }
13
14 var HelloCmd = &cobra.Command{
15     Use: "hello",
16     Short: "Say hello",
```

```go
17      Run: func(cmd *cobra.Command, args []string) {
18          fmt.Printf("Hello %s!!!\n",person)
19      },
20  }
21
22  var ByeCmd = &cobra.Command{
23      Use: "bye",
24      Short: "Say goodbye",
25      Run: func(cmd *cobra.Command, args []string) {
26          fmt.Printf("Bye %s!!!\n",person)
27      },
28  }
29
30  var CustomCmd = &cobra.Command{
31      Use: "custom",
32      Short: "Custom greetings",
33      Run: func(cmd *cobra.Command, args []string) {
34          fmt.Printf("Say %s to %s\n",msg,person)
35      },
36  }
37
38  var msg string
39  var person string
40
41  func init() {
42      RootCmd.AddCommand(HelloCmd, ByeCmd, CustomCmd)
43
44      RootCmd.PersistentFlags().StringVar(&person, "person", "Mr X", "Receiver")
45      CustomCmd.Flags().StringVar(&msg,"msg","what's up","Custom message")
46  }
47
48  func main() {
49      if err := RootCmd.Execute(); err != nil {
50          fmt.Fprintln(os.Stderr, err)
51          os.Exit(1)
52      }
53  }
```

The custom command help indicates the person flag to be global. This means that the value is inherited and already available for the command. Anyway, we can modify it because it is defined by the root command which is the parent of the custom command.

```
>>> ./say bye --person John
Bye John!!!
>>> ./say custom --help
Custom greetings

Usage:
```

```
  say custom [flags]

Flags:
  -h, --help            help for custom
      --msg string      Custom message (default "what's up")

Global Flags:
      --person string   Receiver (default "Mr X")
>>> ./say custom --person John
Say what's up to John
```

17.3.2. HOOKS

The `Command` type offers functions that can be executed before and after the `Run` function. `PreRun` and `PostRun` are executed before and after respectively. `PersistentPreRun` and `PersistentPostRun` are inherited by children commands.

Example 17.9: Commands using hook functions.

```go
package main

import (
    "fmt"
    "github.com/spf13/cobra"
    "os"
)

var RootCmd = &cobra.Command{
    Use: "say",
    Long: "Root command",
    PersistentPreRun: func(cmd *cobra.Command, args []string) {
        fmt.Printf("Hello %s!!!\n", person)
    },
    Run: func(cmd *cobra.Command, args []string) {},
    PostRun: func(cmd *cobra.Command, args []string) {
        fmt.Printf("Bye %s!!!\n", person)
    },
}

var SomethingCmd = &cobra.Command{
    Use: "something",
    Short: "Say something",
    Run: func(cmd *cobra.Command, args []string) {
        fmt.Printf("%s\n", msg)
    },
    PostRun: func(cmd *cobra.Command, args []string) {
```

```go
28          fmt.Printf("That's all I have to say %s\n", person)
29      },
30  }
31
32  var person string
33  var msg string
34
35  func init() {
36      RootCmd.AddCommand(SomethingCmd)
37      RootCmd.Flags().StringVar(&person, "person", "Mr X", "Receiver")
38      SomethingCmd.Flags().StringVar(&msg, "msg", "", "Message to say")
39      SomethingCmd.MarkFlagRequired("msg")
40  }
41
42  func main() {
43      if err := RootCmd.Execute(); err != nil {
44          fmt.Fprintln(os.Stderr, err)
45          os.Exit(1)
46      }
47  }
```

Example 17.9 combines hooks with commands to include additional messages. Observe that simply executing the root command it prints two messages corresponding to the pre and post-run functions. Running the subcommand `something` prints the `PersistentRun` from the root command but not the `PostRun` which is replaced by the `PostRun` from the command `something`.

```
>>> ./say
Hello Mr X!!!
Bye Mr X!!!
>>> ./say something --msg "How are you?"
Hello Mr X!!!
How are you?
That's all I have to say Mr X
```

17.4. Advanced features

Cobra is a powerful and customizable library with a vast number of options. Your CLIs may require additional features beyond the definition of commands and their parameters. This Section explores some advanced features.

17.4.1. Custom help and usage

Cobra automatically generates help and usage messages for our CLI. However it is possible to define our own solutions with `SetHelpCommand`, `SetHelpFunc`, and `SetHelpTemplate` methods from the `Command` type. For the usage message, there are similar methods. Example 17.10 defines the `action` command with the flag `now`. We replace the default help and usage with functions `helper` and `usager`. By setting these functions in the root command we change the whole CLI behaviour. However, this could be changed only for specific commands.

Example 17.10: Command custom help.

```go
package main

import (
    "errors"
    "fmt"
    "github.com/spf13/cobra"
    "os"
)

var RootCmd = &cobra.Command{
    Use: "main",
    Short: "short message",
}

var ActionCmd = &cobra.Command{
    Use: "action",
    Args: cobra.MinimumNArgs(2),
    Run: func(cmd *cobra.Command, args []string) {
        fmt.Println("Do something with ",args)
    },
}

func helper (cmd *cobra.Command, args []string) {
    fmt.Printf("You entered command %s\n", cmd.Name())
    fmt.Println("And that is all the help we have right now :)")
}

func usager (cmd *cobra.Command) error {
    fmt.Printf("You entered command %s\n", cmd.Name())
    fmt.Println("And you do not know how it works :)")
    return errors.New("Something went wrong :(")
}

func main() {
    RootCmd.AddCommand(ActionCmd)
```

```
36      RootCmd.SetHelpFunc(helper)
37      RootCmd.SetUsageFunc(usager)
38
39      ActionCmd.Flags().Bool("now",false,"Do it now")
40
41      if err := RootCmd.Execute(); err != nil {
42          fmt.Fprintln(os.Stderr, err)
43          os.Exit(1)
44      }
45  }
```

Observe that the help is overwritten by the `helper` function returning a different message using the name of the requested command. If we misspelt the flag `now`, Cobra launches the usage function shown below.

```
>>> ./main  help action
You entered command action
And that is all the help we have right now :)
>>> ./main action --naw
Error: unknown flag: --naw
You entered command action
And you do not know how it works :)
Error: Something went wrong :(
exit status 1
```

17.4.2. Documented CLIs

The help entities generated by Cobra are a sort of CLI documentation. However, it cannot be considered as documentation because it requires some sort of interactive exploration. Cobra can automatically generate the documentation for a CLI using command descriptions and examples in Man pages, Markdown, Rest, or Yaml formats. The `cobra/doc` package contains functions that can explore the commands tree and generate the corresponding documentation. Example 17.11 generates the documentation for the CLI in every available format.

Example 17.11: Self-documented CLI.

```
1  package main
2
3  import (
4      "fmt"
5      "github.com/spf13/cobra"
```

```go
	"github.com/spf13/cobra/doc"
	"os"
)

var RootCmd = &cobra.Command{
	Use: "test",
	Short: "Documented test",
	Long: "How to document a command",
	Example: "./main test",
	Run: func(cmd *cobra.Command, args []string) {
		fmt.Println("Save the world with Go!!!")
	},
}

func main() {

	RootCmd.Flags().Bool("flag",true,"Some flag")

	header := &doc.GenManHeader{
		Title: "Test",
		Manual: "MyManual",
		Section: "1",
	}
	err := doc.GenManTree(RootCmd, header, ".")
	if err != nil {
		panic(err)
	}
	err = doc.GenMarkdownTree(RootCmd, ".")
	if err != nil {
		panic(err)
	}
	err = doc.GenReSTTree(RootCmd, ".")
	if err != nil {
		panic(err)
	}
	err = doc.GenYamlTree(RootCmd, ".")
	if err != nil {
		panic(err)
	}
	if err := RootCmd.Execute(); err != nil {
		fmt.Fprintln(os.Stderr, err)
		os.Exit(1)
	}
}
```

If for example we get the content from the `test.yaml` file we can see the populated fields below.

```
>>> cat test.yaml
name: test
synopsis: Documented test
description: How to document a command
usage: test [flags]
options:
- name: flag
  default_value: "true"
  usage: Some flag
- name: help
  shorthand: h
  default_value: "false"
  usage: help for test
example: ./main test
```

Additional customization can be applied to the generated output. Check the package documentation for more details [3].

17.4.3. Cobra generator

The Cobra library comes with a program for commands generation. If following Cobra conventions for commands, this generator can be helpful for filling commands with an initial template and add new ones. The following command lines initialize a project with a command named test.

```
>>> $GOPATH/bin/cobra init --pkg-name github.com/juanmanuel-tirado/
    savetheworldwithgo/15_cli/cobra/advanced/example_03
>>> $GOPATH/bin/cobra add test
```

The Cobra generator creates the folders tree below containing a license, the main file, and two templates to define the root command and the test command we added.

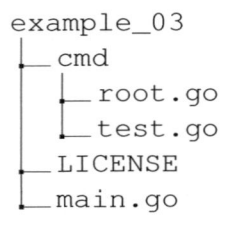

```
example_03
├── cmd
│   ├── root.go
│   └── test.go
├── LICENSE
└── main.go
```

You can run the cobra command help to check additional parameters to customize the templates for new commands, the license, or the author information.

---
[3] https://github.com/spf13/cobra/blob/master/doc/README.md

17.4.4. Shell completion

Shell completion help users to interactively find the command name, arguments and flags of a CLI. Cobra generates shell completion scripts for Bash, Zsh, Fish and PowerShell. The `Command` type offers the methods `GetXXXCompletions` to generate the corresponding completion script for the shell xxx. Normally, a `completion` command is added to the CLI to permit users to generate the corresponding completion script for their shells. When the script is loaded into the shell, pressing the key tab twice displays the valid commands and its help. Example 17.12 shows a possible implementation of a completion command using the root command [4].

Example 17.12: Shell completion command.

```go
package cmd

import (
    "os"
    "github.com/spf13/cobra"
)

var CompletionCmd = &cobra.Command{
    Use:   "completion [bash|zsh|fish|powershell]",
    Short: "Generate completion script",
    Long: "Load it into your shell for completions",
    DisableFlagsInUseLine: true,
    ValidArgs: []string{"bash", "zsh", "fish", "powershell"},
    Args: cobra.ExactValidArgs(1),
    Run: func(cmd *cobra.Command, args []string) {
        switch args[0] {
        case "bash":
            cmd.Root().GenBashCompletion(os.Stdout)
        case "zsh":
            cmd.Root().GenZshCompletion(os.Stdout)
        case "fish":
            cmd.Root().GenFishCompletion(os.Stdout, true)
        case "powershell":
            cmd.Root().GenPowerShellCompletionWithDesc(os.Stdout)
        }
    },
}
```

Assuming this command is already integrated into our CLI we can generate and load the shell completion script for Bash as follows.

---

[4] Check the documentation for additional details https://github.com/spf13/cobra/blob/master/shell_completions.md.

```
>>> ./say completion bash > /tmp/completion
>>> source /tmp/completion
```

For the CLI from Example 17.7 these are the shell completions displayed for the root command. Notice that `[tab]` represents the tab key pressed.

```
>> ./say [tab][tab]
bye          -- Say goodbye
completion   -- Generate completion script
hello        -- Say hello
help         -- Help about any command
```

Command arguments can be displayed for additional help. A list of valid arguments can be provided with the `ValidArgs` field of `Command`. Our completion command has already filled this field showing the following list of valid arguments.

```
>> ./say completion [tab][tab]
bash         fish         powershell   zsh
```

In some scenarios, the arguments of a command can only be determined at runtime. For example, assume we have an application that queries the information of a certain user in a database using her identifier. The user id is only a valid argument if it exists in the database. For these scenarios, the list of valid arguments can be defined using a function in the field `ValidArgsFunction` like in Example 17.13. This Example emulates the availability of different users with a random selector in the `UserGet` function. The `ShellCompDirective` is a binary flag used to modify the shell behaviour. Check the documentation for more information about this flag and what it does.

Example 17.13: Dynamic definition of arguments for a command.

```
 1 package main
 2
 3 import (
 4     "fmt"
 5     "github.com/juanmanuel-tirado/savetheworldwithgo/15_cli/cobra/advanced/
           example_05/cmd"
 6     "github.com/spf13/cobra"
 7     "os"
 8     "math/rand"
 9     "time"
10 )
11
```

CHAPTER 17. COMMAND LINE INTERFACE

```go
12  var RootCmd = &cobra.Command{
13      Use: "db",
14      Long: "Root command",
15  }
16
17  var GetCmd = &cobra.Command{
18      Use: "get",
19      Short: "Get user data",
20      Args: cobra.ExactValidArgs(1),
21      DisableFlagsInUseLine: false,
22      Run: func(cmd *cobra.Command, args []string) {
23          fmt.Printf("Get user %s!!!\n",args[0])
24      },
25      ValidArgsFunction: UserGet,
26  }
27
28  func UserGet (cmd *cobra.Command, args []string, toComplete string) ([]string,
         cobra.ShellCompDirective) {
29      rand.Seed(time.Now().UnixNano())
30      if rand.Int() % 2 == 0 {
31          return []string{"John", "Mary"}, cobra.ShellCompDirectiveNoFileComp
32      }
33      return []string{"Ernest", "Rick", "Mary"}, cobra.
             ShellCompDirectiveNoFileComp
34  }
35
36  func init() {
37      RootCmd.AddCommand(GetCmd, cmd.CompletionCmd)
38  }
39
40  func main() {
41      if err := RootCmd.Execute(); err != nil {
42          fmt.Fprintln(os.Stderr, err)
43          os.Exit(1)
44      }
45  }
```

After generating and loading the shell completion script, the completion dynamically suggests user ids with the `UserGet` function as shown below.

```
>>> ./db get [tab][tab]
John   Mary
>>> ./db [tab][tab]
completion  -- Generate completion script
get         -- Get user data
help        -- Help about any command
>>> ./db get [tab][tab]
Ernest  Mary   Rick
```

17.5. SUMMARY

In this Chapter, we explore how to easily define command-line interfaces using the Cobra library. This library enables developers to define complex and adaptable solutions to a wide variety of use cases. It is really difficult to show examples for every potential use case or need you may find in your developments. However, the shown examples detail the basics and some advanced features that can bring your CLI to the next level. Do not be afraid of checking the Cobra repository or how other large projects such as Kubernetes or Github implement their CLIs with this library.

18

RELATIONAL DATABASES

Databases are basic components for any data-driven system and the Structured Query Language (SQL) is the most common and accepted language for relational databases. Widely adopted solutions such as MySQL, PostgreSQL, Apache Hive, etc. use SQL to create, retrieve and manage relational data. Go offers an elegant and easy-to-use interface for SQL databases with a large variety of database drivers from different projects. This Chapter assumes the reader to have basic notions of relational databases (tables, entities, relationships, transactions, etc.). The purpose of this Chapter is not to cover all the topics of relational databases because that would require an entire book. This Chapter aims at offering the reader the foundations to understand how relational databases can be used in any Go project. With this purpose in mind, this Chapter explores how the Go standard library defines an interface for SQL databases and introduces GORM an object-relational mapping solution.

18.1. SQL IN GO

The package `database/sql`[1] defines a common interface for SQL databases. However, it does not implement any particular database driver. Specific drivers are expected to be imported from third-party projects maintaining the same interface for all of them. This permits to reuse the same code independently of the underlying database. There can be certain differences depending on the employed database, although a large portion of the code can be reused.

---

[1] https://golang.org/pkg/database/sql

18.1.1. DRIVERS AND DATABASE CONNECTIONS

The `database/sql` package is built around the `DB` type[2]. A `DB` instance can be obtained opening a database connection with the `sql.Open` or `sql.OpenDB` functions. A `DB` instance basically handles a pool of database connections.

Example 18.1 shows how to connect with a SQLite database[3]. First, we need to import a valid SQL driver for the target database. There is a large number of available drivers for many databases listed in the documentation[4]. In our examples, we use a driver for SQLite [5] if not stated otherwise to skip the installation of additional databases. Remember that SQLite can work with the local file system and does not require any database server. In any case, these examples can be applied to other databases requiring minor changes in some scenarios.

Observe that we only import the side effects of the package (line 8) defining the driver. By doing this, we register the driver and make it available for the standard library[6]. The `Open` function receives the name of the driver and the data source. For the current example, this is `"sqlite3"` and the file path of the database. For most use cases, the data source is the database hostname with the username and database name. Check the documentation of your driver to be sure you use the correct data source definition.

Example 18.1: Database connection.

```go
package main

import (
    "context"
    "database/sql"
    "fmt"
    "time"
    _ "github.com/mattn/go-sqlite3"
)

func main() {

    db, err := sql.Open("sqlite3","/tmp/example.db")

    if err != nil {
        fmt.Println(err)
        panic(err)
    }
```

Database responds

---

[2] https://golang.org/pkg/database/sql/#DB
[3] https://www.sqlite.org/
[4] https://github.com/golang/go/wiki/SQLDrivers
[5] https://github.com/mattn/go-sqlite3
[6] You can find a more detailed explanation of `init` functions in Section 2.1.1.

```
19      defer db.Close()
20      db.SetConnMaxLifetime(time.Minute * 3)
21      db.SetMaxOpenConns(10)
22      db.SetMaxIdleConns(10)
23
24      ctx := context.Background()
25      if err := db.PingContext(ctx); err == nil {
26          fmt.Println("Database responds")
27      } else {
28          fmt.Println("Database does not respond")
29          panic(err)
30      }
31  }
```

The DB instance can be configured with some parameters such as the maximum connection lifetime, the maximum number of open connections or the maximum number of idle connections. If the Open function succeeds, this does not establish any connection with the database. To ensure the connection availability, Ping or PingContext methods can be invoked. Finally, DB instances should be released using the **close** method. In this case, we use **defer** for a more proper design.

18.1.2. MODIFYING DATA STATEMENTS

The Go standard library differentiates between queries that return rows of data and queries that modify the database. When modifying the database we do not expect any row to be returned. Methods Exec and ExecContext execute queries to create, update, or insert new rows into a table. They return a Result type which contains the id of the latest inserted row if it applies, and the number of rows affected by update, insert, or delete operations. Not every database may provide these values. Check out the documentation before proceeding to operate with these values.

Example 18.2 assumes an existing DB connection and uses it to create a table and insert a new entry. The Exec and ExecContext methods receive a query in a string and none or several arguments. These arguments are used to fill the query string. Observe that the main difference between the create_table and the insert_rows functions is that the second one uses the Result value returned from the query. If we get the same value when creating the table, this will be set to zero because it does not affect any existing row.

Example 18.2: Modifying data statements (excerpt).

```
35
36  const (
37      USERS_TABLE=`CREATE TABLE users(
38      name varchar(250) PRIMARY KEY,
```

```
Database responds
Row ID: 1, Rows: 1
```

```go
39        email varchar(250)
40  )`
41      USERS_INSERT="INSERT INTO users (name, email) VALUES(?,?)"
42  )
43
44  func create_table(db *sql.DB) {
45      ctx := context.Background()
46      _, err := db.ExecContext(ctx, USERS_TABLE)
47      if err != nil {
48          panic(err)
49      }
50
51  }
52
53  func insert_rows(db *sql.DB) {
54      ctx := context.Background()
55      result, err := db.ExecContext(ctx, USERS_INSERT,
56      "John", "john@gmail.com")
57      if err != nil {
58          panic(err)
59      }
60      lastUserId, err := result.LastInsertId()
61      if err != nil {
62          panic(err)
63      }
64      numRows, err := result.RowsAffected()
65      if err != nil {
66          panic(err)
67      }
68      fmt.Printf("Row ID: %d, Rows: %d\n", lastUserId, numRows)
69  }
```

The query syntax may vary depending on the target database. For example, the insert query used in the example has to be written differently for MySQL, PostgreSQL, and Oracle.

- **MySQL:** `INSERT INTO users (name, email)VALUES(?,?)`

- **PostgreSQL:** `INSERT INTO users (name, email)VALUES($1,$2)`

- **Oracle:** `INSERT INTO users (name, email)VALUES(:val1,:val2)`

18.1.3. FETCHING DATA STATEMENTS

When executing a query that returns one or several rows, typically a SELECT, the QueryRow and Query types with their contextual variants QueryRowContext and QueryContext are used. These methods return a `*Rows` that permits to iterate through the returned rows and extract their values.

Example 18.3 selects all the rows from the table of users. To retrieve all the results from the query, we iterate until no more rows are available by checking `rows.Next`. This sets the pointer to the next available row where the `Scan` method can extract the corresponding values. In this example, we have created a `User` to be filled with the returned values. Notice that the current query is equivalent to `SELECT name, email from users` so we can populate the `Name` and `Email` fields in that order otherwise, the order must be the same.

Example 18.3: Querying data statements (excerpt).

```go
type User struct {
    Name string
    Email string
}

func get_rows(db *sql.DB) {
    ctx := context.Background()
    rows, err := db.QueryContext(ctx, "SELECT * from users")
    if err != nil {
        panic(err)
    }
    defer rows.Close()

    for rows.Next() {
        u := User{}
        rows.Scan(&u.Name, &u.Email)
        fmt.Printf("%v\n",u)
    }
}
```

```
Database responds
{John john@gmail.com}
{Mary mary@gmail.com}
```

For single-row queries the `Scan` method described above also applies.

18.1.4. Transactions

A transaction consists of a set of operations that are executed in a context and all of them must be successful otherwise, a rollback resets the database to the state before the transaction started. For Go, a transaction allocates a database connection until the transaction is finished. Transactions offer similar methods for the data modifier and data retriever scenarios we have already seen. However, these methods are provided by a `Tx` type that represents the transaction.

Example 18.4 inserts one row into the users' table inside a transactional context. Observe how the `ExecContext` method occurs inside the transaction. The `rollback` is deferred and will only be executed in case of an error occurs. The `Commit` method triggers the execution of all the queries contained within the transaction.

Example 18.4: Transaction modifying database (excerpt).

```go
35  func runTransaction(db *sql.DB) {
36      tx, err := db.BeginTx(context.Background(), nil)
37      defer tx.Rollback()
38
39      ctx := context.Background()
40      _, err = tx.ExecContext(ctx, "INSERT INTO users(name, email) VALUES(?,?)",
41          "Peter", "peter@email.com")
42      if err != nil {
43          panic(err)
44      }
45      err = tx.Commit()
46      if err != nil {
47          panic(err)
48      }
49  }
```

18.1.5. Prepared statements

Every time a query is sent to a database server this is parsed, analyzed and processed accordingly. This is an expensive operation, especially for queries that are expected to be run several times. Prepared statements permit servers to process a query in such a way that subsequent executions of the same query do not have to be parsed again.

A prepared statement `Stmt` is associated with a `DB` or `Tx` instance. Example 18.5 shows a statement to retrieve a single row matching a user name. The `Prepare` method instantiates the statement that is ready to be used if no errors were found. Observe that statements are associated with a connection and they have to be released with the `Close` method.

Example 18.5: Prepared statement (excerpt).

```go
34  type User struct {
35      Name string
36      Email string
37  }
38
39  func runStatement(db *sql.DB) {
40      stmt, err := db.Prepare("select * from users where name = ?")
41      if err != nil {
42          panic(err)
```

```
Database responds
{Peter peter@email.com}
```

```go
43      }
44      defer stmt.Close()
45      result := stmt.QueryRow("Peter")
46      u := User{}
47
48      err = result.Scan(&u.Name, &u.Email)
49      switch {
50      case err == sql.ErrNoRows:
51          panic(err)
52      case err != nil:
53          panic(err)
54      default:
55          fmt.Printf("%v\n",u)
56      }
57  }
```

18.2. GORM

GORM[7] is an Object-relational mapping (ORM) library for Go. Like any other ORM, GORM offers an abstraction layer that translates operations done with structs to SQL. It supports MySQL, PostgreSQL, SQLite, SQL Server, and Clickhouse.

18.2.1. Basics

GORM provides its own database drivers to be used. For simplicity, the examples use the SQLite driver available at package `gorm.io/driver/sqlite`. For information about other supported databases check the documentation[8]. First, we have to initialize a session to instantiate a pool of connections represented by type DB. Do not confuse this type with the one provided by the standard library described in the previous sections. In Example 18.6 we use the SQLite driver to initialize a database at path `/tmp/test.db`.

Example 18.6: Basic GORM program.

```go
1 package main
2
3 import (
4     "fmt"
```

---

[7] https://gorm.io
[8] https://gorm.io/docs/connecting_to_the_database.html

```go
5       "gorm.io/gorm"
6       "gorm.io/driver/sqlite"
7  )
8
9  type User struct {
10      ID uint
11      Name string
12      Email string
13 }
14
15 func main() {
16     db, err := gorm.Open(sqlite.Open("/tmp/test.db"), &gorm.Config{})
17     if err != nil {
18         panic("failed to connect database")
19     }
20
21     err = db.AutoMigrate(&User{})
22     if err != nil {
23         panic(err)
24     }
25
26     u := User{Name: "John", Email: "john@gmail.com"}
27     db.Create(&u)
28
29     var recovered User
30     db.First(&recovered,"name=?","John")
31     fmt.Println("Recovered", recovered)
32
33     db.Model(&recovered).Update("Email","newemail")
34     db.First(&recovered,1)
35     fmt.Println("After update", recovered)
36
37     db.Delete(&recovered, 1)
38 }
```

```
Recovered {1 John
john@gmail.com}
After update {1 John
newemail}
```

Next, we have to inform GORM about our data schema. In this case, we define the User type with a unique ID, the user name, and her email. With db.AutoMigrate GORM translates the User struct into a valid representation for our target database. Once the migration is correctly done create, read, update, and delete operations (CRUD) can be performed by GORM with none or minimal SQL code. With the current SQLite configuration the migration will create the corresponding tables. In our case a table named users with the following fields:

Notice that the name of the destination table has been automatically generated and managed by GORM. In the Example, we use the u variable to populate a new entry in the database. Next, we recover the entry from the database. Observe that when recovering the entry (db.Read) we use different approaches. The first uses SQL notation indicating the field and the value to be queried. In the second approach, we indicate the primary key

CHAPTER 18. RELATIONAL DATABASES

field	type
id	integer
name	text
email	text

number which corresponds to the ID field of type User. By default GORM sets any field named ID to be the primary key if not stated otherwise.

18.2.2. MODELLING ENTITIES

In GORM a model is a struct with basic Go types. Some conventions are applied to field names. By default, GORM assumes any field ID to be the primary key. Additionally, CreatedAt and UpdatedAt fields are used to track manipulation times. The struct below is an example with the ID as the primary key and the time tracking fields.

```
1  type User struct {
2      ID uint
3      Name string
4      Email string
5      CreatedAt time.Time
6      UpdatedAt time.Time
7  }
```

Actually, GORM defines the struct gorm.Model as follows:

```
1  type Model struct {
2      ID         uint           `gorm:"primaryKey"`
3      CreatedAt  time.Time
4      UpdatedAt  time.Time
5      DeletedAt  gorm.DeletedAt `gorm:"index"`
6  }
```

This struct can be embedded to automatically extend row metadata. Structs embedding the gorm.Model can automatically have the ID as the primary key and the corresponding time tracking fields.

In the context of database tables, embedding means that all the information from a struct has to be contained in a column value. GORM permits embedding any struct that implements the Scanner and Valuer interfaces from the database/sql package[9]. The ex-

---

[9]Check out https://pkg.go.dev/database/sql/#Scanner and https://pkg.go.dev/database/sql/driver#Valuer for more details.

ample below defines the `DevOps` struct to be a user with an associated operator. In this case, the `embedded` tag indicates the `User` field to be embedded into `Operator`.

```go
type User struct {
    Name string
    Email string
}

type Operator struct {
    ID uint
    User User `gorm:"embedded"`
    Platform string `gorm:"not null"`
}
```

Observe that we have additionally used the `"not null"` tag to indicate that the field `Platform` cannot be empty in the database. The complete list of field tags can be found in the documentation[10]. Example 18.7 shows the code that permits struct `User` to be embedded. To serialize the struct we use JSON encoding (see Section 8.2) to marshal the struct value in the `Value` method. In the `Scan` method we use the JSON unmarshal to populate the struct. Notice that the `Scan` method has the `*User` type as receiver to ensure that we modify the original value. Additional tag constraints are set in the `Dedication` field to demonstrate how they can be used. When this field is set to values lower than five the create query fails.

Example 18.7: Embedded structs in GORM.

```go
package main

import (
    "database/sql/driver"
    "encoding/json"
    "fmt"
    "gorm.io/driver/sqlite"
    "gorm.io/gorm"
)

type User struct {
    Name string
    Email string
}

func (u *User) Scan(src interface{}) error {
    input := src.([]byte)
```

```
Created {1 {John john@gmail.com} k8s 10}
Recovered {1 {John john@gmail.com} k8s 10}
```

---

[10]https://gorm.io/docs/models.html#Fields-Tags

CHAPTER 18. RELATIONAL DATABASES

```go
18        json.Unmarshal(input,u)
19        return nil
20  }
21  func(u User) Value()(driver.Value, error) {
22        enc, err := json.Marshal(u)
23        return enc,err
24  }
25
26  type Operator struct {
27        ID uint
28        User User `gorm:"embedded,embeddedPrefix:user_"`
29        Platform string `gorm:"not null"`
30        Dedication uint `gorm:"check:dedication>5"`
31  }
32
33  func main() {
34        db, err := gorm.Open(sqlite.Open("/tmp/example02.db"), &gorm.Config{})
35        if err != nil {
36              panic("failed to connect database")
37        }
38
39        err = db.AutoMigrate(&Operator{})
40        if err != nil {
41              panic(err)
42        }
43
44        op := Operator{
45              User: User{
46                    Name:  "John",
47                    Email: "john@gmail.com",
48              },
49              Platform: "k8s",Dedication:10,
50        }
51        db.Create(&op)
52        fmt.Println("Created", op)
53        var recovered Operator
54        db.First(&recovered,1)
55        fmt.Println("Recovered", recovered)
56  }
```

18.2.3. RELATIONSHIPS

GORM maps relationships between SQL entities using struct fields and some additional field tags. The schema migration generates the corresponding foreign keys and tables required to support these relationships. We explore four potential relationships.

BELONGS-TO

This relationship sets an entity to belong to another entity. This is a one-to-one relationship. For example, a user belongs to a group. In GORM we can represent this relationship indicating the foreign key and the entity. In the Example below a `User` belongs to one `Group`. This is indicated with the `GroupID` field which is the foreign key pointing to the corresponding entity group in the database, and the field `Group`.

Example 18.8: Belongs to relationship.

```
type User struct {
    ID uint
    Name string
    Email string
    GroupID uint
    Group Group
}

type Group struct {
    ID uint
    Name string
}
```

GORM analyzes field names to find relationships and set foreign key names and target entities. If the default behaviour has to be changed, this can be done using field tags.

Example 18.9: Belongs to relationship with custom foreign key.

```
type User struct {
    ID uint
    Name string
    Email string
    Ref uint
    Group Group `gorm:"foreignKey:Ref"`
}

type Group struct {
    ID uint
    Name string
}
```

The example above changes the foreign key referencing the group to be the field `Ref` instead of the default `GroupID`.

Has-one

A has-one relationship indicates that an entity has a reference to another entity. This is similar to a belongs-to relationship in the sense that both are one-to-one relationships. However, there is a semantic difference depending on the side where the relationship is observed from. In the example below, we have a user who has a laptop. In this case, the foreign key is in the laptop entity pointing to the user.

Example 18.10: Has one relationship.

```
type User struct {
    ID uint
    Name string
    Email string
    Laptop Laptop
}
type Laptop struct {
    ID uint
    SerialNumber string
    UserID uint
}
```

Has-many

A has-many relationship permits an entity to be referred to by several instances as their owner. In the example below, we declare that a user can have several laptops. Notice that to follow GORM conventions, we named a field `Laptops` to contain an array of `Laptop` type. This is translated into a table named laptops with a `user_id` column as a foreign key pointing at the corresponding user.

Example 18.11: One to many relationship.

```
type User struct {
    ID uint
    Name string
    Email string
    Laptops []Laptop
}
type Laptop struct {
    ID uint
    SerialNumber string
    UserID uint
}
```

MANY-TO-MANY

This is the most complex kind of relationship where there is no restriction in the number of entities that can be referenced to. In this example, a user can speak many languages and a language can be spoken by many users. This many-to-many relationship has to be represented using a join table. The field tag `many2many` defines the name of the join table to be used. Additionally, we have laptops shared by users. This means that a user can use many laptops and a laptop can be used by many users. In this case, `Laptops` and `Users` fields are arrays that have to be found in a many2many table. Observe, that the array items are pointers. This differs from the user speaking many languages because the language is meaningful on its own and does not belong to any user.

Example 18.12: Many to many relationship.

```go
type User struct {
    ID uint
    Name string
    Email string
    Languages []Language `gorm:"many2many:user_languages"`
    Laptops []*Laptop `gorm:"many2many:user_laptops"`
}
type Language struct {
    ID uint
    Name string
}
type Laptop struct {
    ID uint
    SerialNumber string
    Users []*User `gorm:"many2many:user_laptops"`
}
```

18.3. MANIPULATE DATA

The GORM `DB` type is the main entry to the database and the data models. It controls all the SQL statements to be generated to create, read, update, or delete instances. This Section describes how to use this type to crate, query, and manipulate database entries.

CREATE

The `db.Create` method receives any object with a migrated schema and writes a new record with the information it contains. Fields that autoincrement like GORM managed identifiers do not have to be populated. This can be seen in Example 18.13. The `Create` method returns a `*DB` that contains any error found during the operation and the number of rows affected by the operation. In the case of creating several records, the `CreateIn Batches` method optimizes the process by generating groups of SQL statements with a given number of records (5 in the Example).

Example 18.13: GORM creation of records.

```go
package main

import (
    "fmt"
    "gorm.io/driver/sqlite"
    "gorm.io/gorm"
)

type User struct {
    ID   uint
    Name string
}

func main() {
    db, err := gorm.Open(sqlite.Open("/tmp/example01.db"), &gorm.Config{})
    if err != nil {
        panic("failed to connect database")
    }

    err = db.AutoMigrate(&User{})
    if err != nil {
        panic(err)
    }

    u := User{Name: "John"}
    res := db.Create(&u)
    fmt.Printf("User ID: %d, rows: %d\n",u.ID,res.RowsAffected)

    users := []User{{Name:"Peter"},{Name:"Mary"}}
    for _,i := range users {
        db.Create(&i)
    }
    db.CreateInBatches(users,5)
}
```

```
User ID: 1, rows: 1
```

QUERY

GORM has a fully functional interface to perform SQL queries. Exploring all the available combinations is far away from the purpose of this Chapter. A complete explanation of every supported query is available at the official documentation[11]. Examples 18.14 and 18.15 are fragments of the same code showing a collection of common SQL queries.

The first Example 18.14 populates the database with some users and shows how individual users can be retrieved. First, Take, and Last return one single record depending on the primary key. First and Last return the first and last entries while Take has no associated order. Notice that between every query we set a new u value to reuse the variable. Otherwise, GORM interprets the fields in u to be the arguments of the query. If the first query returns the value where the name is John, invoking db.Last(u) will return the same record because it is the latest id with the indicated name.

Example 18.14: GORM queries (excerpt).

```go
package main

import (
    "fmt"
    "gorm.io/driver/sqlite"
    "gorm.io/gorm"
)

type User struct {
    ID   uint
    Name string
}

func main() {
    db, err := gorm.Open(sqlite.Open("/tmp/example02.db"), &gorm.Config{})
    if err != nil {
        panic("failed to connect database")
    }

    err = db.AutoMigrate(&User{})
    if err != nil {
        panic(err)
    }
    users := []User{{Name: "John"}, {Name: "Mary"}, {Name: "Peter"}, {Name: "Jeremy"}}
    db.CreateInBatches(users, 4)

    var u User
    db.First(&u)
    fmt.Println("First", u)
    u=User{}
    db.Take(&u)
    fmt.Println("Take", u)
    u=User{}
```

[11]https://gorm.io/docs/query.html

CHAPTER 18. RELATIONAL DATABASES

```
34      db.Last(&u)
35      fmt.Println("Last",u)
36      u=User{}
37      db.First(&u,2)
38      fmt.Println("First ID=2",u)
```

```
First {1 John}
Take {1 John}
Last {4 Jeremy}
First ID=2 {2 Mary}
```

Example 18.15 shows how to retrieve several records and use additional clauses. The `db.Find` method returns all the records of a table. Additional filters can be set like using primary keys (line 42). Conditional queries using `Where` plus `First` or `Find` permit to be more specific about the queried record and the number of returned entries. Observe that `Where` uses the syntax of a where SQL statement without setting the arguments. The `?` mark in the clause is replaced by the arguments. Finally, it is worth mentioning that `Where` accepts types from the schema as search arguments (line 52).

Example 18.15: GORM queries (continuation).

```
39      var retrievedUsers []User
40      db.Find(&retrievedUsers)
41      fmt.Println("Find",retrievedUsers)
42      db.Find(&retrievedUsers,[]int{2,4})
43      fmt.Println("Find ID=2,ID=4",retrievedUsers)
44      u=User{}
45      db.Where("name = ?","Jeremy").First(&u)
46      fmt.Println("Where name=Jeremy",u)
47      db.Where("name LIKE ?","%J%").Find(&retrievedUsers)
48      fmt.Println("Where name=%J%",retrievedUsers)
49      db.Where("name LIKE ?","%J%").Or("name LIKE ?","%y").Find(&retrievedUsers)
50      fmt.Println("Name with J or y",retrievedUsers)
51      u=User{}
52      db.Where(&User{Name: "Mary"}).First(&u)
53      fmt.Println("User with name Mary",u)
54      db.Order("name asc").Find(&retrievedUsers)
55      fmt.Println("All users ordered by name",retrievedUsers)
56    }
```

```
Find [{1 John} {2 Mary} {3 Peter} {4 Jeremy}]
Find ID=2,ID=4 [{2 Mary} {4 Jeremy}]
```

```
Where name=Jeremy {4 Jeremy}
Where name=%J% [{1 John} {4 Jeremy}]
Name with J or y [{1 John} {2 Mary} {4 Jeremy}]
User with name Mary {2 Mary}
All users ordered by name [{4 Jeremy} {1 John} {2 Mary} {3 Peter}]
```

EAGER LOADING

GORM offers an eager loading mode for relationships. This feature permits programmatically set queries to be executed before others. This is particularly useful to populate structs with fields that are foreign keys. In Example 18.16, we have a one-to-many relationship where a user can have several laptops. If we retrieve a user from the database using `db.First`, the returned row has no laptops. These entries are already in the database. However, these entries are referred by a foreign key and the content requires an additional query to be retrieved. Adding eager preloading with `db.Preload("Laptops")` indicates to GORM that there are laptops to be queried to populate the resulting record. When executed, the retrieved rows contain the `Laptops` field populated.

Example 18.16: GORM preload.

```
 1 package main
 2
 3 import (
 4     "fmt"
 5     "gorm.io/driver/sqlite"
 6     "gorm.io/gorm"
 7 )
 8
 9 type User struct {
10     ID uint
11     Name string
12     Email string
13     Laptops []Laptop
14 }
15
16 type Laptop struct {
17     ID uint
18     SerialNumber string
19     UserID uint
20 }
21
22 func main() {
23     // SQLite does not support foreign key constraints
24     db, err := gorm.Open(sqlite.Open("/tmp/example03.db"),
25         &gorm.Config{DisableForeignKeyConstraintWhenMigrating: true,})
```

```
Created {2 John john@gmail.com [{3 sn0000001 2}
 {4 sn0000002 2}]}
Recovered without preload {1 John john@gmail.
com []}
Recovered with preload {1 John john@gmail.com
 [{1 sn0000001 1} {2 sn0000002 1}]}
```

CHAPTER 18. RELATIONAL DATABASES

```
26
27      if err != nil {
28          panic("failed to connect database")
29      }
30
31      err = db.AutoMigrate(&User{},&Laptop{})
32      if err != nil {
33          panic(err)
34      }
35
36      laptops := []Laptop{{SerialNumber: "sn0000001"},{SerialNumber: "sn0000002"
            }}
37      u := User{
38          Name:    "John",
39          Email:   "john@gmail.com",
40          Laptops: laptops,
41      }
42      db.Create(&u)
43      fmt.Println("Created", u)
44      var recovered User
45      db.First(&recovered)
46      fmt.Println("Recovered without preload",recovered)
47      recovered = User{}
48      db.Preload("Laptops").First(&recovered)
49      fmt.Println("Recovered with preload", recovered)
50 }
```

There is something important to mention about the manner eager loading works. The number of items to be preloaded must be correctly indicated. The call `Preload("Laptops")` expects several entries. If only one entry is going to be loaded this should be `Preload("Laptop")`. Notice the subtle utilization of the plural form. The Example 18.17 defines a belongs-to relationship, where a user belongs to a group. Notice that in this case, we only expect to have one group for the user. This is mentioned in the `db.Preload("Group")` statement.

Example 18.17: GORM preload with single record.

```
1 package main
2
3 import (
4     "fmt"
5     "gorm.io/driver/sqlite"
6     "gorm.io/gorm"
7 )
8
9 type User struct {
10     ID uint
```

```
Recovered {1 John 1 {1 TheCoolOnes}}
```

```
11      Name string
12      GroupID uint
13      Group Group
14  }
15
16  type Group struct {
17      ID uint
18      Name string
19  }
20
21  func main() {
22      db, err := gorm.Open(sqlite.Open("/tmp/example04.db"), &gorm.Config{})
23      if err != nil {
24          panic("failed to connect database")
25      }
26
27      err = db.AutoMigrate(&Group{},&User{})
28      if err != nil {
29          panic(err)
30      }
31
32      g := Group{Name: "TheCoolOnes"}
33      u := User{Name: "John", Group: g}
34      db.Create(&u)
35
36      var recovered User
37      db.Preload("Group").First(&recovered,1)
38      fmt.Println("Recovered", recovered)
39  }
```

18.3.1. TRANSACTIONS

By default, GORM executes every write operation inside a transaction clause. This can be disabled as indicated in the documentation by setting the `SkipDefaultTransaction` flag[12]. This brings a relevant performance improvement. Similarly to the `database/sql` package from the standard library, GORM defines transactional environments that can rollback if something goes wrong.

The Example 18.18 uses a transaction to update the email of an existing user entry. Observe that the operations running in the transactional context are inside a function. This function receives a connection (`tx`) that can execute the operations inside the transaction. The transaction will fail on purpose when trying to recreate an already existing user. The rollback operation restores the previous state. We can check this by retrieving the user after the transaction.

---

[12]https://gorm.io/docs/transactions.html#Disable-Default-Transaction

CHAPTER 18. RELATIONAL DATABASES

Example 18.18: GORM transaction.

```go
package main

import (
    "fmt"
    "gorm.io/driver/sqlite"
    "gorm.io/gorm"
)

type User struct {
    ID    uint
    Name  string
    Email string
}
func main() {
    db, err := gorm.Open(sqlite.Open("/tmp/example01.db"), &gorm.Config{})

    if err != nil {
        panic("failed to connect database")
    }

    err = db.AutoMigrate(&User{})
    if err != nil {
        panic(err)
    }

    u := User{Name: "John", Email: "john@gmail.com"}
    db.Create(&u)

    db.Transaction(func(tx *gorm.DB) error {
        if err := tx.Model(&u).Update("Email","newemail").Error; err != nil {
            return err
        }
        var inside User
        tx.First(&inside)
        fmt.Println("Retrieved inside transaction", inside)
        if err := tx.Create(&u).Error; err != nil {
            return err
        }
        return nil
    })
    var retrieved User
    db.First(&retrieved)
    fmt.Println("Retrieved", retrieved)
}
```

```
Retrieved inside transaction {1 John newemail}
```

```
...github.com/juanmanuel-tirado/savetheworldwithgo/16_sql/gorm/transactions/
example_01/main.go:33 UNIQUE constraint failed: users.id
[0.040ms] [rows:0] INSERT INTO `users` (`name`,`email`,`id`) VALUES ("John","
newemail",1)
Retrieved {1 John john@gmail.com}
```

Transactions can be controlled manually using `Begin`, `Commit`, and `RollBack` similarly to how it is done in the standard library. Example 18.19 describes a similar situation to the one exposed in the previous Example. However, we add a savepoint to avoid losing the changes done to the user record. The savepoint is set after the record update and we rollback to that savepoint when the create operation fails. Finally, we execute the commit to finish the transaction.

Example 18.19: GORM manual transaction.

```go
package main

import (
    "fmt"
    "gorm.io/driver/sqlite"
    "gorm.io/gorm"
)

type User struct {
    ID    uint
    Name  string
    Email string
}

func RunTransaction(u *User, db *gorm.DB) error{
    tx := db.Begin()
    if tx.Error != nil {
        return tx.Error
    }
    if err := tx.Model(u).Update("Email","newemail").Error; err != nil {
        return err
    }
    tx.SavePoint("savepoint")
    if err := tx.Create(u).Error; err != nil{
        tx.RollbackTo("savepoint")
    }
    return tx.Commit().Error
}

func main() {
    db, err := gorm.Open(sqlite.Open("/tmp/example02.db"), &gorm.Config{})
```

```
33      if err != nil {
34          panic("failed to connect database")
35      }
36
37      err = db.AutoMigrate(&User{})
38      if err != nil {
39          panic(err)
40      }
41
42      u := User{Name: "John", Email: "john@gmail.com"}
43      db.Create(&u)
44
45      err = RunTransaction(&u, db)
46      if err != nil {
47          fmt.Println(err)
48      }
49      var retrieved User
50      db.First(&retrieved)
51      fmt.Println("Retrieved", retrieved)
52  }
```

```
.../github.com/juanmanuel-tirado/savetheworldwithgo/16_sql/gorm/transactions/
example_02/main.go:24 UNIQUE constraint failed: users.id
[0.040ms] [rows:0] INSERT INTO `users` (`name`,`email`,`id`) VALUES ("John","newemail",1)
Retrieved {1 John newemail}
```

18.4. Summary

This Chapter brings the reader the tools to understand how SQL databases can be used in any Go project. It offers a detailed explanation of tools provided by the Go standard library and the powerful object-relational mapping library GORM. The examples and explanations given in this Chapter bring those readers familiar with SQL concepts a strong background to be used in their SQL solutions.

19
NoSQL DATABASES

The adoption of big data solutions accelerated the exploration of new database models. This exploration exposed the limitations of classic relational databases and proposed new models beyond the Standard Query Language and the entity-relationship model. The Apache Cassandra database is one of the most widely adopted NoSQL databases. Although Go may not seem to be the most common language to develop solutions using this database, this Chapter shows that Go is a perfect candidate for any project based on Cassandra.

19.1. CASSANDRA AND GoCQL

The Apache Cassandra database[1] is a NoSQL distributed database solution. It has been adopted in scenarios demanding high performance and availability, and it has demonstrated linear scalability while ensuring fault tolerance. It is not the purpose of this Chapter to explain how Cassandra works. In case the reader is not familiar with Cassandra at all, let these lines partially illustrate the main differences between this database and classic relational databases such as MySQL or PostgreSQL.

19.1.1. A BRIEF INTRODUCTION TO CASSANDRA

In general terms, Cassandra uses terminology we can find in classic databases. However, due to its idiosyncrasy Cassandra extends this terminology with additional concepts the reader may not be used to.

---

[1] https://cassandra.apache.org/

- **Keyspaces** contain tables and define several properties such as replication policies.

- **Tables** like in SQL databases, store collections of entries. However, conceptually a table only defines the schema to be stored. This is due to the fact that a table is instantiated across several physical nodes with several partitions.

- **Primary key** like in SQL databases it is a unique field that differentiates a table entry from the other entries. However, primary keys are specially important in Cassandra because they are used to define where a table entry has to be stored. It can be composed of a partition key and a clustering key.

- **Partition key** defines the mandatory part of the primary key all rows must have.

- **Clustering key** defines how data is sorted in a node according to one or more columns.

- **Rows** like in SQL databases are a collection of columns identified by a unique primary key.

- **Column** is a typed datum that belongs to a row and is defined by the schema of a table.

Figure 19.1 illustrates how Cassandra keys are used to distribute and sort content. The example table contains historic information of warning levels per user at different times of the day. The primary key is composed of the `user_id` and the `time` columns. This makes it possible to store several rows for the same user at different times. Moreover, we define `user_id` to be the partition key for this table. Cassandra will use the values from this column to determine what physical node must store this row.

user_id	time	level
10	10:01	Normal
10	11:11	Warning
10	11:13	Normal
163	09:27	Error
400	08:00	Normal

Rows with user_id 10 → Node A; rows with user_id 163 and 400 → Node B.

Partition key: user_id
Clustering key: time
Primary key: user_id, time

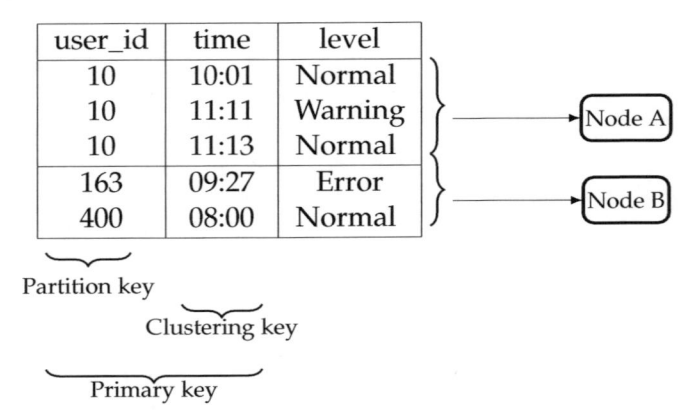

Figure 19.1: Components of a primary key in Cassandra.

In this example with two nodes (`Node A` and `Node B`), we assume entries for user 10 are stored in `Node A` while users 163 and 400 go to `Node B`. Cassandra uses the partition key to compute a hash number that indicates the target node. If a 64 bits hash is used, the range $[0, 2^{64})$ is split across the available nodes. This facilitates the read of data across the nodes. For our example, we can expect the information regarding user 10 to be found in the same physical node making read operations faster. Furthermore, using the `time` column as a clustering key indicates that stored entries must be sorted using this column. By default, entries will be returned sorted which can be particularly useful in our scenario.

Cassandra uses CQL, a language similar to SQL, to manage and query databases. The complete definition of this language is available at the official Cassandra documentation page[2]. The code below will create the table from the example.

Example 19.1: CQL statements for Figure 19.1.

```
CREATE TABLE users_warnings (
    user_id int,
    time time,
    level text,
    PRIMARY KEY (user_id, time)
) WITH CLUSTERING ORDER BY (time ASC);
```

Notice that the primary key is composed of two fields, this is called a compound key. By default, in a compound key the first field is the partition key. It is possible to define several columns to be the partition key by adding parenthesis. To define the clustering key we add the `WITH CLUSTERING ORDER BY` statement with the corresponding field names. Like in the primary key, several fields can be part of the clustering key. The `ASC` modifier indicates an ascending sorting for this key.

19.1.2. MODELLING

Data modelling in Cassandra differs from traditional relational databases. Using modelling concepts from traditional databases will probably bring bad results. The rules for data modelling in Cassandra[8] clearly state that the goals to achieve when modelling data are 1) evenly data spread around clusters and 2) minimize the number of partitions. Writes in Cassandra are cheap and disk space is not usually a problem. The main goals are more related to the current Cassandra architecture and how it can help achieve incredibly efficient and scalable queries. Data modelling must be done keeping in mind how the data is going to be processed.

This Section shows examples of how data relationships can be modelled using Cassandra. The solutions given here are a matter of discussion and only pretend to introduce the questions to be made during the data modelling phase while inviting the reader to

---
[2] https://cassandra.apache.org/doc/latest/cql/index.html

explore the particularities of Cassandra.

HAS-ONE

Imagine a users database where every user has a laptop. In a relational database, we could have two differentiated entities user and laptop and link every laptop with its user. However, in Cassandra this is not the case. The best solution depends on the final utilization of these entities. Assume we have the laptops and users tables defined as follows:

Example 19.2: Users and laptops entities.
```
CREATE TABLE users (
    user_id int PRIMARY KEY,
    name text,
    email text);
CREATE TABLE laptops (
    sn int PRIMARY KEY,
    model text,
    memory int);
```

One solution is to create an additional table that stores the relationship between a user and her laptop. The `user_laptop` table shown below sets the `user_id` as the primary key, then a user can only appear once.

Example 19.3: A user has a laptop relationship using an extra table.
```
CREATE TABLE user_laptop (
    user_id int PRIMARY KEY,
    sn int);
```

The solution above is suitable if we want to periodically get the list of users with their laptops. However, it permits a laptop to be linked with several users. Furthermore, it assumes that the laptop entity is important enough to exist on its own. However, if a laptop entry is always associated with a user we can define a laptop type and associate it with the user.

Example 19.4: A user has a laptop relationship using a laptop type.
```
CREATE TYPE laptop (
    sn int,
    model text,
    memory int);
CREATE TABLE users (
```

```
6       user_id int PRIMARY KEY,
7       name text,
8       email text,
9       laptop frozen<laptop>);
```

Now laptops are a type associated with users, not a table. The contained information is the same but it will be an attribute of a user. We use the `frozen` modifier to indicate that the individual fields of a laptop cannot be modified independently. Actually, the laptop field has to be reinserted as a whole entity. However, this solution does not guarantee a laptop to be owned by a single user. If we must guarantee this situation from a database perspective we can maintain the laptop table and include a user id.

Example 19.5: Guarantee that every laptop has a unique user.

```
1 CREATE TABLE users (
2       user_id int PRIMARY KEY,
3       name text,
4       email text);
5 CREATE TABLE laptop (
6       sn int PRIMARY KEY,
7       model text,
8       memory int,
9       user_id int);
```

Has-many

Extending our previous example with users and laptops, let's assume that now every user can have several laptops. Using the `laptop` type we can set every user to have a set of laptops.

Example 19.6: A user has many laptops using collections.

```
1 CREATE TABLE users (
2       user_id int PRIMARY KEY,
3       name text,
4       email text,
5       laptops set<frozen<laptop>>);
```

Using the set collection guarantees that the same laptop cannot appear twice in the same user and querying the laptops of every user would be straight forward. However, the same laptop can appear in two different users. To guarantee that there is only one user per laptop we can maintain the `laptop` table with the `user_id`.

Example 19.7: Guarantee that every laptop has a unique user.

```
1  CREATE TABLE laptops (
2      sn int PRIMARY KEY,
3      model text,
4      memory int,
5      user_id int);
```

Note that the primary key is used to partition the table across the nodes. If we query all the laptops of a user this query could be extended across the cluster nodes to just return a few records. However, this would be a good solution to find the user who owns a laptop.

MANY-TO-MANY

Now let's assume that laptops can be shared by many users and we have two potential queries: getting the laptops of a user and getting the users of a laptop. We can create two tables to facilitate both queries.

Example 19.8: Users and laptops in a many to many relationship.

```
1  CREATE TABLE user_laptops (
2      user_id int,
3      sn int,
4      PRIMARY KEY (user_id,sn));
5  CREATE TABLE laptops_user (
6      sn int,
7      user_id int,
8      PRIMARY KEY (sn,user_id));
```

Using a compound primary key `(user_id,sn)` partitions a table by the `user_id` and then inside the partition, the rows are ordered using the laptop serial number `sn`. Querying the laptops of a user with `SELECT * from user_laptops where user_id=?` is intended to be particularly efficient by hitting a single partition.

19.1.3. DATABASE CONNECTION

The GoCQL[3] driver provides developers with a straight forward solution to manage Cassandra databases and execute CQL statements for officially supported versions[4]. The examples shown in this Section assume an out-of-the-box Cassandra instance listening at `localhost:9042`. Most examples assume the `example` keyspace to be already available.

---

[3] https://github.com/gocql/gocql
[4] Versions 2.1.x, 2.2.x, and 3.x.x when these lines were written.

CHAPTER 19. NOSQL DATABASES

> ⚠ The GoCQL project is very dynamic and the examples may not be fully compatible with your current version of Cassandra by the time you execute them. Hopefully, the reader may find enough information in these examples to overcome possible execution errors.

Like any other database driver, GoCQL works with sessions that provide the user with the connections required to send queries and manipulate data. A `Session` can be generated by the `ClusterConfig` type through the `CreateSession` method. The `ClusterConfig` type represents the configuration to be used to instantiate new connections with a cluster.

Example 19.9 shows how to instantiate a new session for a local cluster. The `NewCluster` function returns a `ClusterConfig` type that can be customized. Check the documentation to see all the possible configurable items [5]. In the Example, we set the keyspace to be used, the consistency level, and a one minute connection timeout. Several hosts can be passed by argument and the rest of the nodes will be automatically discovered. Note that the creation of the session can fail and it has to be closed to release resources.

Example 19.9: GoCQL database connection.

```go
package main

import (
    "context"
    "github.com/gocql/gocql"
    "time"
)

const CREATE_TABLE=`CREATE TABLE example.user (
id int PRIMARY KEY,
name text,
email text
)
`

func main() {
    cluster := gocql.NewCluster("127.0.0.1:9042")
    cluster.Keyspace = "example"
    cluster.Consistency = gocql.Quorum
    cluster.Timeout = time.Minute
    session, err := cluster.CreateSession()
    if err != nil {
        panic(err)
    }
    defer session.Close()
```

---

[5] https://pkg.go.dev/github.com/gocql/gocql#ClusterConfig

```
26
27        ctx := context.Background()
28        err = session.Query(CREATE_TABLE).WithContext(ctx).Exec()
29        if err != nil {
30            panic(err)
31        }
32    }
```

For the sake of demonstration, we create a table to check that everything is OK. If we use the command line CQL shell (`cqlsh`), we will see the description of the new table.

```
cqlsh> DESCRIBE example.user ;

CREATE TABLE example.user (
    id int PRIMARY KEY,
    email text,
    name text
) WITH bloom_filter_fp_chance = 0.01
    AND caching = 'KEYS_ONLY'
    AND comment = ''
    AND compaction = {'class': 'org.apache.cassandra.db.compaction.
SizeTieredCompactionStrategy'}
    AND compression = {'sstable_compression': 'org.apache.cassandra.io.compress
.LZ4Compressor'}
    AND dclocal_read_repair_chance = 0.1
    AND default_time_to_live = 0
    AND gc_grace_seconds = 864000
    AND index_interval = 128
    AND memtable_flush_period_in_ms = 0
    AND populate_io_cache_on_flush = false
    AND read_repair_chance = 0.0
    AND replicate_on_write = true
    AND speculative_retry = '99.0PERCENTILE';
```

19.1.4. MANIPULATE DATA

Data manipulation operations create, update, insert, and delete are executed using the `Exec` method from the `Query` type. The `Query` type can be customized through different methods[6] that define the current behaviour of the query. Example 19.10 creates the users table and inserts a single row. Note that for simplicity, we can define the queries as constant strings to be reused. The CREATE TABLE query has no arguments, while the INSERT query waits for three arguments that are passed when creating the query. For additional

---
[6]https://pkg.go.dev/github.com/gocql/gocql#Query

control, we can execute the queries inside a context to, for example, limit the waiting time.

Example 19.10: GoCQL data manipulation queries.

```go
package main

import (
    "context"
    "github.com/gocql/gocql"
)

const CREATE_TABLE=`CREATE TABLE users (
id int PRIMARY KEY,
name text,
email text)`

const INSERT_QUERY=`INSERT INTO users
(id,name,email) VALUES(?,?,?)`

func main() {
    cluster := gocql.NewCluster("127.0.0.1:9042")
    cluster.Keyspace = "example"
    session, err := cluster.CreateSession()
    if err != nil {
        panic(err)
    }
    defer session.Close()

    ctx := context.Background()
    err = session.Query(CREATE_TABLE).WithContext(ctx).Exec()
    if err != nil {
        panic(err)
    }

    err = session.Query(INSERT_QUERY,1, "John", "john@gmail.com").WithContext(
        ctx).Exec()
    if err != nil {
        panic(err)
    }
}
```

CQL can execute insert, update, and delete queries in batches. Batches ensure atomicity and can improve performance. Example 19.11 uses a batch to insert a new user and modify her email. A `Batch` type is obtained from the current session with a given context using the `NewBatch` method. This batch has a collection of `BatchEntry` elements representing queries. The collection of queries is executed as a whole invoking the `ExecuteBatch` method from the current session.

Example 19.11: GoCQL data manipulation using batches.

```go
package main

import (
    "context"
    "github.com/gocql/gocql"
)

const CREATE_TABLE=`CREATE TABLE users (
id int PRIMARY KEY,
name text,
email text)`

const INSERT_QUERY=`INSERT INTO users
(id,name,email) VALUES(?,?,?)`

const UPDATE_QUERY=`UPDATE users SET email=? WHERE id=?`

func main() {
    cluster := gocql.NewCluster("127.0.0.1:9042")
    cluster.Keyspace = "example"
    session, err := cluster.CreateSession()
    if err != nil {
        panic(err)
    }
    defer session.Close()

    ctx := context.Background()
    err = session.Query(CREATE_TABLE).WithContext(ctx).Exec()
    if err != nil {
        panic(err)
    }

    b := session.NewBatch(gocql.UnloggedBatch).WithContext(ctx)
    b.Entries = append(b.Entries,
        gocql.BatchEntry {
            Stmt: INSERT_QUERY,
            Args: []interface{}{1, "John", "john@gmail.com"},
        },
        gocql.BatchEntry {
            Stmt: UPDATE_QUERY,
            Args: []interface{}{"otheremail@email.com",1},
        })
    err = session.ExecuteBatch(b)
    if err != nil {
        panic(err)
    }
}
```

CHAPTER 19. NOSQL DATABASES

> ⚠ Batch queries are particularly suitable when the target of the query is a single partition. If more than one partitions are involved in the batch, this will impact the performance. One possible reason to use batches when multiple partitions are involved could be the need to ensure the modification of two related tables. For example, changing a user email and its corresponding entry in a table using this email. Find more about good practices for batches in the CQL documentation[a].
>
> [a] https://docs.datastax.com/en/cql-oss/3.3/cql/cql_using/useBatchGoodExample.html

19.1.5. QUERIES

GoCQL differentiates between queries that return a single result or multiple results. For queries returning a single result, we can use the `Scan` method passing by argument the destination variables to be populated with the returned results. These variables must have a type compatible with the returned columns. Example 19.12 shows a query for a single entry returning the name of the user.

Example 19.12: GoCQL single result query.

```go
package main

import (
    "context"
    "fmt"
    "github.com/gocql/gocql"
)

const (
    QUERY        ="SELECT name FROM users WHERE id=1"
    CREATE_TABLE =`CREATE TABLE users (
id int PRIMARY KEY,
name text,
email text
)`
    INSERT_QUERY =`INSERT INTO users
(id,name,email) VALUES(?,?,?)`
)

func main() {
    cluster := gocql.NewCluster("127.0.0.1:9042")
    cluster.Keyspace = "example"
    session, err := cluster.CreateSession()
```

```
Retrieved name John
```

```go
24      if err != nil {
25          panic(err)
26      }
27      defer session.Close()
28
29      ctx := context.Background()
30      err = session.Query(CREATE_TABLE).WithContext(ctx).Exec()
31      if err != nil {
32          panic(err)
33      }
34
35      err = session.Query(INSERT_QUERY,1, "John", "john@gmail.com").WithContext(
            ctx).Exec()
36          if err != nil {
37          panic(err)
38      }
39      name := ""
40      err = session.Query(QUERY).WithContext(ctx).Scan(&name)
41      if err != nil {
42          panic(err)
43      }
44      fmt.Println("Retrieved name", name)
45 }
```

When a query is expected to return multiple rows like a SELECT * query, the Iter method from Query permits to iterate through the results using pagination. Pagination is controlled internally although it can be customized. Example 19.13 queries all the entries from the users table. For better navigation across the returned results, we use a Scanner type that can be easily iterated until no more results are returned. Additional examples of how Scanner works can be found at Section 7.3.

Example 19.13: GoCQL multiple results query.

```go
package main

import (
    "context"
    "fmt"
    "github.com/gocql/gocql"
)

const (
    QUERY         ="SELECT * FROM users"
    CREATE_TABLE = `CREATE TABLE users (
id int PRIMARY KEY,
name text,
email text
```

```
Found: 1 john@gmail.com John
Found: 2 mary@gmail.com Mary
```

CHAPTER 19. NOSQL DATABASES

```go
15  )`
16      INSERT_QUERY =`INSERT INTO users
17  (id,name,email) VALUES(?,?,?)`
18  )
19
20  func main() {
21      cluster := gocql.NewCluster("127.0.0.1:9042")
22      cluster.Keyspace = "example"
23      session, err := cluster.CreateSession()
24      if err != nil {
25          panic(err)
26      }
27      defer session.Close()
28
29      ctx := context.Background()
30      err = session.Query(CREATE_TABLE).WithContext(ctx).Exec()
31      if err != nil {
32          panic(err)
33      }
34
35      err = session.Query(INSERT_QUERY,2, "Mary", "mary@gmail.com").WithContext(
            ctx).Exec()
36      if err != nil {
37          panic(err)
38      }
39      err = session.Query(INSERT_QUERY,1, "John", "john@gmail.com").WithContext(
            ctx).Exec()
40      if err != nil {
41          panic(err)
42      }
43
44      scanner := session.Query(QUERY).WithContext(ctx).Iter().Scanner()
45      for scanner.Next() {
46          var id int
47          var name, email string
48          err = scanner.Scan(&id,&name,&email)
49          if err != nil {
50              panic(err)
51          }
52          fmt.Println("Found:",id,name,email)
53      }
54  }
```

As a final note, observe that we have inserted the records in the reverse order they are retrieved. This occurs because Cassandra sorts the records using the primary key.

19.1.6. USER DEFINED TYPES

User-defined types (UDTs) can be expressed using structs and tag fields. Example 19.14 defines a laptop UDT to be incorporated to the users table. The `Laptop` struct defines the field of the UDT we have created. GoCQL uses field tags like `cql:"sn"` to indicate that struct field corresponds to variable `sn` in the UDT. The `Scan` method can populate this struct without additional guidance as shown in the code.

Example 19.14: GoCQL UDT struct definition and query.

```
1  package main
2
3  import (
4      "context"
5      "fmt"
6      "github.com/gocql/gocql"
7      "time"
8  )
9
10 const LAPTOP_TYPE = `CREATE TYPE example.Laptop (
11 sn int,
12 model text,
13 memory int)`
14
15 const USERS_TABLE =`CREATE TABLE example.users (
16 user_id int PRIMARY KEY,
17 name text,
18 email text,
19 Laptop frozen<Laptop>)`
20
21 const INSERT = `INSERT INTO example.users (
22 user_id, name, email, Laptop) VALUES (?,?,?,?)`
23
24 type Laptop struct {
25     Sn int `cql:"sn"`
26     Model string `cql:"model"`
27     Memory int `cql:"memory"`
28 }
29
30 func main() {
31     cluster := gocql.NewCluster("127.0.0.1:9042")
32     cluster.Keyspace = "example"
33     cluster.Consistency = gocql.Quorum
34     cluster.Timeout = time.Minute
35     session, err := cluster.CreateSession()
36     if err != nil {
37         panic(err)
38     }
```

```
Retrieved {100 Lenovo 10}
```

```
39      defer session.Close()
40
41      ctx := context.Background()
42      err = session.Query(LAPTOP_TYPE).WithContext(ctx).Exec()
43      if err != nil {
44          panic(err)
45      }
46      err = session.Query(USERS_TABLE).WithContext(ctx).Exec()
47      if err != nil {
48          panic(err)
49      }
50
51      err = session.Query(INSERT,1,"John","john@gmail.com",&Laptop{100,"Lenovo"
            ,10}).Exec()
52      if err != nil {
53          panic(err)
54      }
55
56      var retrieved Laptop
57      err = session.Query("select laptop from users where user_id=1").Scan(&
            retrieved)
58      fmt.Println("Retrieved", retrieved)
59  }
```

19.2. Summary

This Chapter overviews the utilization of NoSQL solutions in Go. Independently of the complexity and architectural designs of the underlying technology, Go is a good solution to manage these databases. In particular, the GoCQL library permits any Go program to manipulate a Cassandra database expanding the horizon of tools that can be used in any data-driven solution.

20
KAFKA

It is common for a distributed system to have a large number of services designed to consume information in real-time. As the number of services grows, ensuring the scalability and availability of data becomes a challenge. Traditionally, the publish/subscribe pattern has been used to delegate the consumption and publication of new data to a third service in charge of ensuring this data is consumed by the corresponding subscribers as soon as possible. Apache Kafka is a widely adopted publish/subscribe event streaming distributed platform that ensures the scalability and availability of messages for large scale systems. This Chapter explores how to use Go to produce and consume data from Kafka using third-party clients and how to write our own HTTP clients.

20.1. THE BASICS

Apache Kafka[1] is designed as a distributed platform that can span multiple data centres and cloud regions. Kafka brokers are accessed by clients to publish new data or consume it. Kafka producers and consumers work around the concept of events. An event is a record or message containing a key, a value, a timestamp, and optionally some metadata. These events are organized into topics. Topics are a logical organization of events. Every event is stored into a topic, in this sense, topics work like folders. Events are stored in the system until they reach the expiration time.

Topics are partitioned across brokers. By replicating events that belong to the same topic into several partitions, Kafka ensures fault tolerance and improves availability and throughput. Figure 20.1 shows a topic split into four partitions. Every square inside the partitions (P0, P1, P2, and P3) is an event which colour corresponds to a different key.

---

[1] https://kafka.apache.org

Depending on the replication policy, events can be replicated across different partitions. Normally there are three replicas of every event. Events with the same key are stored in the same partition and Kafka guarantees they are consumed in the same order they were written.

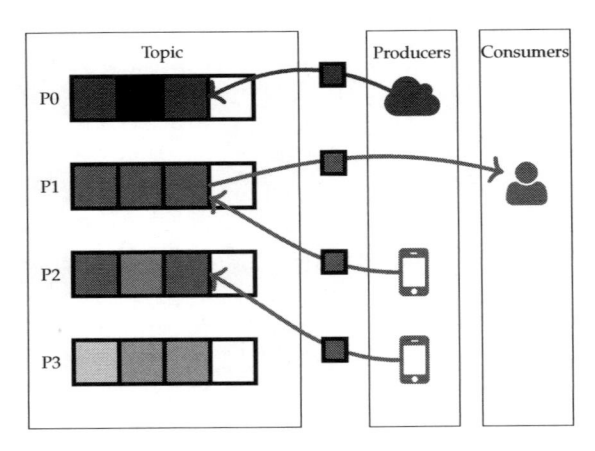

Figure 20.1: Kafka topics and partitions.

Events inside topics are indexed by a consecutive number. When a consumer is subscribed to a topic, she receives an offset with the index of the next event to be consumed. When producers consume events, they increment this offset to get new events if they are available. Different consumers can have different offsets like in Figure 20.2. To ensure that consumers get all the available messages in their order of arrival, consumers can commit the index of the latest message they have consumed. This informs the broker about the current status of the consumer. Kafka by default executes this commit operation automatically although consumers can specify when to commit with the correct configuration.

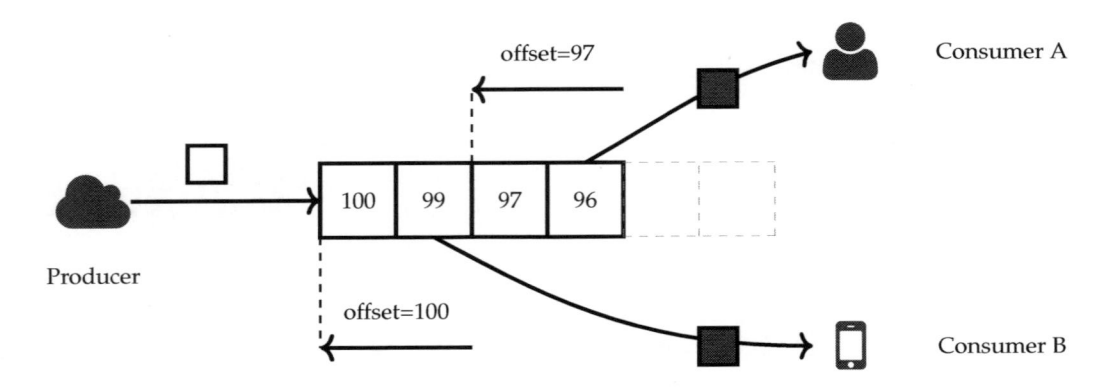

Figure 20.2: Kafka offsets in a topic partition.

There are several Kafka clients implemented in Go. In this Chapter, we explore the official one from confluent[2] and the pure Go implementation provided by Segmentio[3].

The examples described in this Chapter assume a Kafka broker is available and listening at `localhost:9092`. For the examples from Section 20.4 the Kafka API REST proxy must be available at `localhost:8082`. You can deploy a complete virtualized Kafka environment using Docker following the official documentation[4]. A reduced Docker compose solution is provided in the book's GitHub repository.

20.2. Using the Confluent client

The `confluent-kafka-go`[5] is a wrapper around the the `librdkafka` library. This wrapper defines a Kafka client with a producer and a consumer types. Examples 20.1 and 20.2 show standard implementations for a producer and a consumer respectively.

20.2.1. Synchronous producer

The `Producer` type is instantiated using a `ConfigMap` which contains key-value pairs with all the required configuration for the connection[6]. The `Producer` holds a connection that has to be released with `Close()`. For this Example, we send events to the topic named `helloTopic`. Events are defined by the `Message` type described below.

```go
type Message struct {
    TopicPartition TopicPartition
    Value          []byte
    Key            []byte
    Timestamp      time.Time
    TimestampType  TimestampType
    Opaque         interface{}
    Headers        []Header
}
```

The most important field is `Value` which contains the message content in a raw byte slice. `Key` can be used for additional control inside the topic as mentioned before. `Opaque` can be used to pass arbitrary data to the corresponding event handler.

---

[2] https://github.com/confluentinc/confluent-kafka-go
[3] https://github.com/segmentio/kafka-go
[4] https://docs.confluent.io/platform/current/quickstart/ce-docker-quickstart.html#ce-docker-quickstart
[5] https://github.com/confluentinc/confluent-kafka-go
[6] https://github.com/edenhill/librdkafka/blob/master/CONFIGURATION.md

The producer shown in Example 20.1 passes a `Message` to the `Produce` method indicating the partition and the message value. Note that we let the target partition be set by Kafka using the `PartitionAny` policy. The `Produce` function receives a `chan` Event to handle the production of events. Messages are sent to the `librdkafka` which has its own queue of messages. To avoid an overflow, we can wait until the message is sent using the `deliveryChan` channel. This is not the most efficient approach as the production of messages is stopped until a message is processed. The `Flush` function waits for a given time in milliseconds until all the messages have been sent. In the Example it is commented because in our case we are waiting for every message submission.

Example 20.1: Confluent Kafka synchronous producer.

```go
package main

import (
    "fmt"
    "github.com/confluentinc/confluent-kafka-go/kafka"
)

func main() {
    cfg := kafka.ConfigMap{"bootstrap.servers": "localhost:9092"}
    p, err := kafka.NewProducer(&cfg)
    if err != nil {
        panic(err)
    }
    defer p.Close()

    deliveryChan := make(chan kafka.Event, 10)
    defer close(deliveryChan)
    topic := "helloTopic"
    msgs := []string{"Save", "the", "world", "with", "Go!!!"}
    for _, word := range msgs {
        err = p.Produce(&kafka.Message{
            TopicPartition: kafka.TopicPartition{Topic: &topic, Partition:
                kafka.PartitionAny},
            Value: []byte(word),
        }, deliveryChan)
        if err != nil {
            panic(err)
        }
        e := <-deliveryChan
        m := e.(*kafka.Message)
        fmt.Printf("Sent %v\n",m)
    }
    // p.Flush(1000)
}
```

```
Sent helloTopic[0]@30
Sent helloTopic[0]@31
Sent helloTopic[0]@32
Sent helloTopic[0]@33
Sent helloTopic[0]@34
```

20.2.2. Synchronous consumer

Like the `Producer` type, the `Consumer` is instantiated with a `ConfigMap` with its corresponding configuration parameters. Consumers must subscribe to one or several topics matching a given regular expression. The `Poll` function blocks the execution for a given timeout and returns an `Event` or `nil`. Like shown in Example 20.2, using a **switch** statement we can control the execution flow and process messages, errors or other situations.

Example 20.2: Confluent Kafka synchronous consumer.

```go
package main

import (
    "fmt"
    "github.com/confluentinc/confluent-kafka-go/kafka"
)

func main() {
    c, err := kafka.NewConsumer(&kafka.ConfigMap{
        "bootstrap.servers": "localhost:9092",
        "group.id":          "helloGroup",
        "auto.offset.reset": "earliest",
    })
    if err != nil {
        panic(err)
    }
    defer c.Close()

    c.Subscribe("helloTopic", nil)
    for {
        ev := c.Poll(1000)
        switch e := ev.(type) {
        case *kafka.Message:
            c.Commit()
            fmt.Printf("Msg on %s: %s\n", e.TopicPartition, string(e.Value))
        case kafka.PartitionEOF:
            fmt.Printf("%v\n",e)
        case kafka.Error:
            fmt.Printf("Error: %v\n", e)
            break
        default:
            fmt.Printf("Ignored: %v\n",e)
        }
    }
}
```

```
Message on helloTopic
[0]@30: Save
Message on helloTopic
[0]@31: the
Message on helloTopic
[0]@32: world
Message on helloTopic
[0]@33: with
Message on helloTopic
[0]@34: Go!!!
```

The Example above receives the messages from the producer defined in Example 20.1.

Remember that in case the `enable.auto.commit` configuration parameter is set to false, consumers must commit to ensure the correctness of the received messages. This can be done using the `Commit` method as shown in the Example.

20.2.3. ASYNCHRONOUS PRODUCER

Our previous Example of a synchronous producer is not a good idea if we want to get a better throughput for our solution. Actually, Kafka is prepared to receive batches of events to be processed. Normally, producers should send batches of events and wait until they are processed. We can use the delivery channel from the `Produce` function to write a non-blocking handler to observe if everything is working correctly.

Example 20.3 rewrites the previous producer with a goroutine that handles the production process without blocking the execution. In this case, to ensure that we wait until all the messages are sent, the `Flush` function blocks the execution until everything is flushed out.

Example 20.3: Confluent Kafka asynchronous producer.

```go
package main

import (
    "fmt"
    "github.com/confluentinc/confluent-kafka-go/kafka"
)

func Handler(c chan kafka.Event) {
    for {
        e := <- c
        if e == nil {
            return
        }
        m := e.(*kafka.Message)
        if m.TopicPartition.Error != nil {
            fmt.Printf("Partition error %s\n",m.TopicPartition.Error)
        } else {
            fmt.Printf("Sent %v: %s\n",m,string(m.Value))
        }
    }
}

func main() {
    cfg := kafka.ConfigMap{"bootstrap.servers": "localhost:9092"}
    p, err := kafka.NewProducer(&cfg)
    if err != nil {
        panic(err)
```

```
28      }
29      defer p.Close()
30
31      delivery_chan := make(chan kafka.Event,10)
32      defer close(delivery_chan)
33      go Handler(delivery_chan)
34
35      topic := "helloTopic"
36      msgs := []string{"Save", "the", "world", "with", "Go!!!"}
37      for _, word := range msgs {
38          err = p.Produce(&kafka.Message{
39              TopicPartition: kafka.TopicPartition{Topic: &topic, Partition:
                    kafka.PartitionAny},
40              Value: []byte(word),
41          },delivery_chan)
42      }
43      p.Flush(10000)
44 }
```

```
Sent helloTopic[0]@95: Save
Sent helloTopic[0]@96: the
Sent helloTopic[0]@97: world
Sent helloTopic[0]@98: with
Sent helloTopic[0]@99: Go!!!
```

20.2.4. ASYNCHRONOUS CONSUMER

Committing every consumed message is not a good practice because it produces a lot of overhead. It makes more sense to commit after a batch of messages is received. In Example 20.4, a commit is done every two messages in a separated goroutine. The batch size is probably very small and it only makes sense for demonstration purposes. The `Committer` function can detect if the commit fails so we can handle the situation.

Example 20.4: Confluent Kafka asynchronous consumer.

```
1 package main
2
3 import (
4     "fmt"
5     "github.com/confluentinc/confluent-kafka-go/kafka"
6 )
7
```

```go
 8  const COMMIT_N = 2
 9
10  func Committer(c *kafka.Consumer) {
11      offsets, err := c.Commit()
12      if err != nil {
13          fmt.Printf("Error: %s\n", err)
14          return
15      }
16      fmt.Printf("Offset: %#v\n",offsets[0].String())
17  }
18
19  func main() {
20
21      c, err := kafka.NewConsumer(&kafka.ConfigMap{
22          "bootstrap.servers": "localhost:9092",
23          "group.id":          "helloGroup",
24          "auto.offset.reset": "earliest",
25      })
26      if err != nil {
27          panic(err)
28      }
29      defer c.Close()
30
31      c.Subscribe("helloTopic", nil)
32      counter := 0
33      for {
34          ev := c.Poll(1000)
35          switch e := ev.(type) {
36          case *kafka.Message:
37              counter += 1
38              if counter % COMMIT_N == 0 {
39                  go Committer(c)
40              }
41              fmt.Printf("Msg on %s: %s\n", e.TopicPartition, string(e.Value))
42          case kafka.PartitionEOF:
43              fmt.Printf("%v\n",e)
44          case kafka.Error:
45              fmt.Printf("Error: %v\n", e)
46              break
47          default:
48              fmt.Printf("Ignored: %v\n",e)
49          }
50      }
51  }
```

```
Msg on helloTopic[0]@95
: Save
Msg on helloTopic[0]@96
: the
Msg on helloTopic[0]@97
: world
Msg on helloTopic[0]@98
: with
Msg on helloTopic[0]@99
: Go!!!
Offset: "helloTopic[0]
@100"
Offset: "helloTopic[0]
@100"
```

⚠ In the previous example, messages are processed independently of the result of the commit operation. We can continue receiving messages even when the commit fails. We can postpone the message processing until we know that the commit was successful.

```
...
case *kafka.Message:
        offset, err := c.Commit()
        if err != nil {
            // process message...
        }
...
```

As mentioned before, this would generate a lot of overhead. A possible solution is to store incoming messages and process them after the commit in a batch. This could even be done in a goroutine.

```
...
case *kafka.Message:
        append(messages,msg)
        counter += 1
        if counter % COMMIT_N == 0 {
            offset, err := c.Commit()
            if err != nil {
                go ProcessMsgs(messages)
            }
        }
...
```

20.3. Using the Segmentio client

One of the drawbacks of the Confluent Kafka client is the fact that it is a wrapper of a C library. This can be an issue in certain platforms or for those projects where only Go is going to be available. The Segmentio[7] Kafka client is fully written in Go and offers a complete implementation of consumers and producers with additional features such as compression or secure connections.

---

[7]https://github.com/segmentio/kafka-go

20.3.1. The Connection type

The Segmentio client uses a straight forward implementation based on a `Connection` instance. A `Connection` can be instantiated indicating the Kafka host, the topic, and the partition. This connection offers all the methods required by consumers and producers.

Example 20.5 shows the implementation of a producer. The connection uses the method `SetWriteDeadline` to define a timeout for the writing operation. The most basic method to produce messages is `conn.Write` which receives a byte array with the message to be sent. However, for demonstration purposes, we use the `conn.WriteMessages` which receives `Message` instances with more valuable information as can be observed in the definition below.

```go
type Message struct {
    Topic     string
    Partition int
    Offset    int64
    Key       []byte
    Value     []byte
    Headers   []Header
    Time      time.Time
}
```

In the Example, we iterate through all the messages to be sent. However, we could simply pass a collection of messages to be sent. The write operation returns the number of written bytes and error if any.

> ⚠ The `Partition` field from a `Message` instance must not be set when writing messages. It is a read-only field.

Example 20.5: Segmentio Kafka producer.

```go
package main

import (
    "context"
    "fmt"
    "github.com/segmentio/kafka-go"
    "time"
)

func main() {
```

CHAPTER 20. KAFKA

```go
11      topic := "helloTopic"
12      partition := 0
13      conn, err := kafka.DialLeader(context.Background(),
14          "tcp", "localhost:9092",topic,partition)
15      if err != nil {
16          panic(err)
17      }
18
19      defer conn.Close()
20
21      conn.SetWriteDeadline(time.Now().Add(3*time.Second))
22      msgs := []string{"Save", "the", "world", "with", "Go!!!"}
23      for _, m := range msgs {
24          l, err := conn.WriteMessages(kafka.Message{Value: []byte(m)})
25          if err != nil {
26              panic(err)
27          }
28          fmt.Printf("Sent %d bytes: %s\n", l,m)
29      }
30  }
```

```
Sent 4 bytes: Save
Sent 3 bytes: the
Sent 5 bytes: world
Sent 4 bytes: with
Sent 5 bytes: Go!!!
```

The structure of a consumer is very similar to a producer. A `Connection` instance can be used to read one or several messages in batches. Example 20.6 defines a batch of messages with a minimum size of 10 KB and a maximum size of 10 MB. Note that we use a byte array with me minimum size we defined and we populate it until we find an error. Finally, the batches have to be closed.

Example 20.6: Segmentio Kafka consumer.

```go
1  package main
2
3  import (
4      "context"
5      "fmt"
6      "github.com/segmentio/kafka-go"
7      "time"
8  )
9
10 func main() {
11     topic := "helloTopic"
12     partition := 0
13     conn, err := kafka.DialLeader(context.Background(),
14         "tcp", "localhost:9092",topic,partition)
15     if err != nil {
16         panic(err)
17     }
18
```

```
Received 4: Save
Received 3: the
Received 5: world
Received 4: with
Received 5: Go!!!
```

```go
19      defer conn.Close()
20
21      conn.SetReadDeadline(time.Now().Add(time.Second))
22      batch := conn.ReadBatch(10e3, 10e6)
23      defer batch.Close()
24      for {
25          b := make([]byte, 10e3)
26          l, err := batch.Read(b)
27          if err != nil {
28              break
29          }
30          fmt.Printf("Received %d: %s\n",l,string(b))
31      }
32 }
```

20.3.2. Writer and Reader types

The Segmentio client has high level abstraction types named `Writer` and `Reader`. These types are designed to simplify producer and consumer implementations.

Example 20.7 uses a `Writer` instance to send messages to Kafka. The code is very similar to the one shown in Example 20.5. However, note that all the operations are performed using the `Writer` instead of a `Connection` instance.

Example 20.7: Segmentio Kafka high level API producer.

```go
1 package main
2
3 import (
4      "context"
5      "fmt"
6      "github.com/segmentio/kafka-go"
7      "time"
8 )
9
10 func main() {
11     topic := "helloTopic"
12     partition := 0
13     conn, err := kafka.DialLeader(context.Background(),
14         "tcp", "localhost:9092",topic,partition)
15     if err != nil {
16         panic(err)
17     }
18
19     defer conn.Close()
20
```

```
Sent message: Save
Sent message: the
Sent message: world
Sent message: with
Sent message: Go!!!
Producer sent: 131 bytes
```

CHAPTER 20. KAFKA

```go
21      conn.SetWriteDeadline(time.Now().Add(3*time.Second))
22      msgs := []string{"Save", "the", "world", "with", "Go!!!"}
23      for _, m := range msgs {
24          l, err := conn.WriteMessages(kafka.Message{Value: []byte(m)})
25          if err != nil {
26              panic(err)
27          }
28          fmt.Printf("Sent %d bytes: %s\n", l,m)
29      }
30  }
```

The `WriterMessages` method is designed to receive a collection of messages. Observe, that the example is not properly using the method. This is done on purpose to show the function signature. To improve performance, all the available messages should be passed to this method to improve throughput. The `Stats` method returns an instance with the statistics of this writer. The Example prints the total number of bytes written although there is an interesting set of available stats.

A consumer can be implemented using the `Reader` type as shown in Example 20.8. A `Reader` is configured using a `ReaderConfig` indicating the brokers, partition, topic, and group to be subscribed to. The `FetchMessage` method blocks until new events are available or the context expires.

Example 20.8: Segmentio Kafka high level API consumer.

```go
1  package main
2
3  import (
4      "context"
5      "fmt"
6      "github.com/segmentio/kafka-go"
7  )
8
9  func main () {
10     r := kafka.NewReader(kafka.ReaderConfig{
11         Brokers:    []string{"localhost:9092"},
12         Partition:  0,
13         Topic:      "helloTopic",
14         GroupID: "testGroup",
15         MinBytes:   10e3,
16         MaxBytes:   10e6,
17     })
18
19     defer r.Close()
20
21     for {
22         m, err := r.FetchMessage(context.Background())
```

```
Topic helloTopic msg: Save
Topic helloTopic msg: the
Topic helloTopic msg: world
Topic helloTopic msg: with
Topic helloTopic msg: Go!!!
```

```go
23          if err != nil {
24              break
25          }
26          if err := r.CommitMessages(context.Background(), m); err != nil {
27              panic(err)
28          }
29          fmt.Printf("Topic %s msg: %s\n", m.Topic, m.Value)
30      }
31  }
```

In this Example, we commit every consumed message. This produces an unnecessary overhead that can be mitigated by committing several messages at the same time. The `CommitMessages` method has a variadic argument to indicate the number of messages to be committed.

> ⚠ Remember that manual committing is only required when the `auto-commit` configuration parameter in the Kafka brokers is disabled.

20.4. USING THE KAFKA REST API

We have explored in the previous sections how to produce and consume messages from Kafka using the official Confluent and Segmentio solutions. Kafka defines its own protocol over TCP [3] that is implemented by the library `librdkafka` making all the Kafka functionalities available. The Confluent client is a wrapper around this library. Unfortunately, this may not be a convenient solution for all scenarios. On the other hand, the Segmentio client or other implementations may not cover all the Kafka functionalities or simply their approach does not fulfil our requirements. In other scenarios, the utilization of pure TCP traffic may be limited or restricted.

A potential solution is to use the REST API proxy offered by Kafka [8]. By exposing Kafka functionalities through an API REST, any HTTP client can produce and consume messages. In this Section, we explore how to produce and consume messages from Kafka interacting with its REST API using the standard `net/http` Go package.

The examples from this Section assume the Kafka REST API is available at `localhost:8082`. If you are not familiar with HTTP clients in Go, review Chapter 9.

20.4.1. PRODUCER

First, we have to know the REST method for message publishing. After checking the API specification, we find out that we have to use the POST method `/topics/<name>/`

---
[8] https://docs.confluent.io/3.0.0/kafka-rest/docs/index.html

partitions/<number>. Where <name> and <number> are the topic name and the corresponding partition respectively. The message must be attached to the body request. This method expects the encoding format to be specified in the request `Content-Type` header. The API admits data encoding in JSON, Avro, binary, and Protobuf formats. In these examples, we use JSON encoding with the value `application/vnd.kafka.json.v2+json` for our header. On how to specify other formats see the official documentation. The following object contains two messages (records) to be published.

```
{
    "records":
    [
        {"value":{"name":"John","email":"john@gmail.com"}},
        {"value":{"name":"Mary","email":"mary@email.com"}}
    ]
}
```

Note that for simplicity we are only indicating the content of our messages, but other fields such as the key or the timestamp can be set. Check the reference for more details.

Now, we can send this object in the body of a `POST` request to the API like in Example 20.9.

Example 20.9: Kafka producer using the REST API.

```go
package main

import (
    "bufio"
    "bytes"
    "encoding/json"
    "fmt"
    "net/http"
    "strings"
)

const (
    URL = "http://localhost:8082/topics/%s/partitions/%d"
    CONTENT_TYPE = "application/vnd.kafka.json.v2+json"
)

type User struct{
    Name  string `json:"name"`
    Email string `json:"email"`
}

func BuildBody (users []User) string {
```

```go
	values := make([]string, len(users))
	for i, u := range users {
		encoded, err := json.Marshal(&u)
		if err != nil {
			panic(err)
		}
		values[i] = fmt.Sprintf("{\"value\":%s}", encoded)
	}
	result := strings.Join(values, ",")
	return fmt.Sprintf("{\"records\": [%s]}", result)
}

func main() {
	users := []User{{"John", "john@gmail.com"},{"Mary","mary@email.com"}}
	body := BuildBody(users)
	fmt.Println(body)
	bufferBody := bytes.NewBuffer([]byte(body))

	resp, err := http.Post(fmt.Sprintf(URL,"helloTopic",0),CONTENT_TYPE,
		bufferBody)
	if err != nil {
		panic(err)
	}
	defer resp.Body.Close()

	fmt.Println(resp.Status)
	bodyAnswer := bufio.NewScanner(resp.Body)
	for bodyAnswer.Scan() {
		fmt.Println(bodyAnswer.Text())
	}
}
```

```
{"records": [{"value":{"name":"John","email":"john@gmail.com"}},{"value":{"name":"Mary","email":"mary@email.com"}}]}
200 OK
{"offsets":[{"partition":0,"offset":165,"error_code":null,"error":null},{"partition":0,"offset":166,"error_code":null,"error":null}],"key_schema_id":null,"value_schema_id":null}
```

The `BuildBody` function is a helper to generate the body of the request. Note that we set the corresponding `Content-Type` header with the CONTENT_TYPE constant to the POST function. Finally, the program prints the body from the server response. We can see that the body of the server response contains information about the partitions and offsets of every written message.

20.4.2. CONSUMER

Consuming messages from the API REST requires more steps than producing them. To get a message a consumer must: 1) create a new consumer instance, 2) subscribe to a topic and group, 3) fetch the messages, and finally 4) delete the instance if no more messages are going to be consumed. The following Examples are fragments of the same piece of code we have split into chunks according to the mentioned steps.

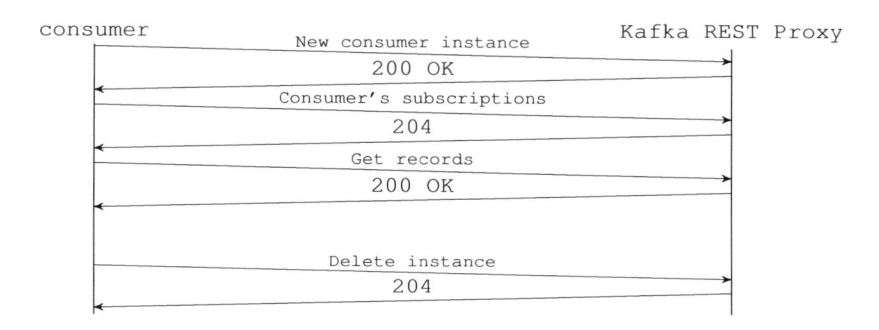

Figure 20.3: Consumer and Kafka REST Proxy communication diagram.

To create a new consumer, we use the `POST` method `/consumers/testGroup` where `testGroup` is the name of the consumers' group. The body request (shown below) contains the name of the consumer (`testConsumer`) and the format to be used by the messages (json).

```
{"name":"testConsumer", "format": "json"}
```

The response body contains the consumer id and the base URI to be used by this consumer. This can be done as shown in Example 20.10. The `DoHelper` is a helper function to fill the `POST` requests.

Example 20.10: Kafka consumer using the REST API (excerpt I, new consumer).

```
1  package main
2
3  import (
4      "bufio"
5      "bytes"
6      "time"
7      "fmt"
8      "net/http"
9  )
```

```go
10
11  const (
12      HOST                = "http://localhost:8082"
13      CONSUMER            = "testConsumer"
14      GROUP               = "testGroup"
15      NEW_CONSUMER        = "%s/consumers/%s"
16      SUBSCRIBE_CONSUMER  = "%s/consumers/%s/instances/%s/subscription"
17      FETCH_CONSUMER      = "%s/consumers/%s/instances/%s/records"
18      DELETE_CONSUMER     = "%s/consumers/%s/instances/%s"
19      CONTENT_TYPE        = "application/vnd.kafka.json.v2+json"
20  )
21
22  func DoHelper(client *http.Client, url string, body []byte ) error {
23      bufferBody := bytes.NewBuffer(body)
24      req, err := http.NewRequest(http.MethodPost,url, bufferBody)
25      if err != nil {
26          return err
27      }
28      fmt.Printf("-->Call %s\n",req.URL)
29      fmt.Printf("-->Body %s\n",string(body))
30      resp, err := client.Do(req)
31      if err != nil {
32          return err
33      }
34      defer resp.Body.Close()
35      bodyResp := bufio.NewScanner(resp.Body)
36      fmt.Printf("<--Response %s\n", resp.Status)
37      for bodyResp.Scan() {
38          fmt.Printf("<--Body %s\n",bodyResp.Text())
39      }
40      return nil
41  }
42
43  func main() {
44      client := http.Client{}
45      // New consumer
46      url := fmt.Sprintf(NEW_CONSUMER,HOST,GROUP)
47      body := fmt.Sprintf(`{"name":"%s", "format": "json"}`,CONSUMER)
48      err := DoHelper(&client, url, []byte(body))
49      if err != nil {
50          panic(err)
51      }
52      time.Sleep(time.Second)
```

Next, the consumer is subscribed to the topic `helloTopic` where the producer sent the messages. The target POST method matches the base URI received in the response from the previous creation of the consumer instance extended with the suffix subscription. In our case, /consumers/testGroup/instances/testConsumer/subscription.

CHAPTER 20. KAFKA

The answer's body contains the list of topics this consumer requested to be subscribed to. The response returns a 204 code indicating a correct response without a body.

Example 20.11: Kafka consumer using the REST API (excerpt II, subscription).

```
53      // Subscribe to topic
54      url = fmt.Sprintf(SUBSCRIBE_CONSUMER,HOST,GROUP,CONSUMER)
55      body = `{"topics":["helloTopic"]}`
56      err = DoHelper(&client, url, []byte(body))
57      if err != nil {
58          panic(err)
59      }
60      time.Sleep(time.Second)
```

Now the consumer is ready to receive records from the topics it has been subscribed to. A `GET` request to the base URI with the `records` suffix will return any available message. In this case, `/consumers/testGroup/instances/testConsumer/records`. Note that the `Accept` header must be set with the corresponding content type we want the incoming messages to be encoded (JSON in this case). The response body will contain the available messages. If no messages are available at the time of sending the request, the returned response will be empty. Additional query parameters are `timeout` to specify the maximum time the server will spend fetching records and `max_bytes` with the maximum size for the returned messages.

Example 20.12: Kafka consumer using the REST API (excerpt III, acquisition).

```
61      // Get records
62      req, err := http.NewRequest(http.MethodGet, fmt.Sprintf(FETCH_CONSUMER,HOST
            ,GROUP,CONSUMER), nil)
63      if err != nil {
64          panic(err)
65      }
66      req.Header.Add("Accept",CONTENT_TYPE)
67      fmt.Printf("-->Call %s\n",req.URL)
68      respRecords, err := client.Do(req)
69      if err != nil {
70          panic(err)
71      }
72      defer respRecords.Body.Close()
73      fmt.Printf("<--Response %s\n", respRecords.Status)
74      recordsBodyResp := bufio.NewScanner(respRecords.Body)
75      for recordsBodyResp.Scan() {
76          fmt.Printf("<--Body %s\n",recordsBodyResp.Text())
77      }
```

Finally, we delete the consumer instance to release resources with a POST request to `/consumers/testGroup/instances/testConsumer`. The body from the response is empty with a 204 status.

Example 20.13: Kafka consumer using the REST API (excerpt IV, delete).

```go
78      // Delete consumer instance
79      deleteReq, err := http.NewRequest(http.MethodDelete,fmt.Sprintf(
            DELETE_CONSUMER,HOST,GROUP,CONSUMER),nil)
80      if err != nil {
81          panic(err)
82      }
83      fmt.Printf("-->Call %s\n",deleteReq.URL)
84      resp, err := client.Do(deleteReq)
85      if err != nil {
86          panic(err)
87      }
88      fmt.Printf("<--Response %s\n",resp.Status)
89  }
```

The program shows the requests and responses between the client and the server during the whole process.

```
-->Call http://localhost:8082/consumers/testGroup
-->Body {"name":"testConsumer", "format": "json"}
<--Response 200 OK
<--Body {"instance_id":"testConsumer","base_uri":"http://rest-proxy:8082/consumers/testGroup/instances/testConsumer"}
-->Call http://localhost:8082/consumers/testGroup/instances/testConsumer/subscription
-->Body {"topics":["helloTopic"]}
<--Response 204 No Content
-->Call http://localhost:8082/consumers/testGroup/instances/testConsumer/records
<--Response 200 OK
<--Body [{"topic":"helloTopic","key":null,"value":{"name":"John","email":"john@gmail.com"},"partition":0,"offset":179},{"topic":"helloTopic","key":null,"value":{"name":"Mary","email":"mary@email.com"},"partition":0,"offset":180}]
-->Call http://localhost:8082/consumers/testGroup/instances/testConsumer
<--Response 204 No Content
```

Note that in this case, we are not modifying the consumer offset. Calling the POST method at `/consumers/testGroup/instances/testConsumer/positions` with the next offset indicated in the body prepares the consumer for the next batch of messages. For our example where the latest record had offset 180, we could send the following body to set the next offset to 181.

```
{
  "offsets": [
    {
      "topic": "helloTopic",
      "partition": 0,
      "offset": 181
    }
  ]
}
```

20.5. Summary

This Chapter explores how to consume and produce data with the Apache Kafka message streaming platform. We analyze different Kafka clients provided by Confluent and Segmentio, and show how they access the same solution from different perspectives. Finally, we demonstrate how using the standard Go library we can easily create our clients without external dependencies using the Kafka API Rest Proxy.

BIBLIOGRAPHY

[1] Apache Cassandra. Apache Cassandra documentation. `https://cassandra.apache.org/doc/latest/`, 2021.

[2] Apache Kafka. Apache Kafka official documentation. `https://kafka.apache.org/documentation/`, 2021.

[3] Apache Kafka. Kafka protocol guide. `https://kafka.apache.org/protocol`, 2021.

[4] ECMA. The JSON Data Interchange Syntax. `http://www.ecma-international.org/publications/files/ECMA-ST/ECMA-404.pdf`, 2021.

[5] GNU. gccgo. `https://gcc.gnu.org/onlinedocs/gccgo`, 2021.

[6] golang.org. Go official documentation. `https://golang.org/doc/`, 2021.

[7] GopherJS. GopherJS. A compiler from Go to Javascript. `https://github.com/gopherjs/gopherjs`, 2021.

[8] Tyler Hobbs. Basic Rules of Cassandra Data Modeling. `https://www.datastax.com/blog/basic-rules-cassandra-data-modeling`, 2015.

[9] IETF. Common Format and MIME Type for Comma-Separated Values (CSV) Files. `http://https://tools.ietf.org/html/rfc4180`, 2021.

[10] IETF. Hypertext Transfer Protocol (HTTP/1.1): Semantics and Content. `https://tools.ietf.org/html/rfc7231`, 2021.

[11] Sobel Jonathan M. and Friedman Daniel P. An Introduction to Reflection-Oriented Programming. `https://web.archive.org/web/20100204091328/http://www.cs.indiana.edu/~jsobel/rop.html`, 1996.

[12] Rob Pike. The Laws of Reflection. `https://blog.golang.org/laws-of-reflection`, 2021.

[13] Russ Cox. Minimal Version Selection. `https://research.swtch.com/vgo-mvs`, 2018.

[14] SemVer.org. Semantic versioining 2.0.0. `https://semver.org/spec/v2.0.0.html`, 2021.

[15] W3C. Extensible Markup Language (XML). `https://www.w3.org/XML/`, 2021.

[16] Niklaus Wirth. *Algorithms + Data Structures = Programs*. Prentice Hall PTR, USA, 1978.

[17] yaml.org. YAML Ain't Markup Language (YAML™) Version 1.2. `https://yaml.org/spec/1.2/spec.html`, 2021.

[18] yaml.org. Yet Another Markup Language (YAML) 1.0. `https://yaml.org/spec/history/2001-12-10.html`, 2021.

LIST OF EXAMPLES

1.1	Save the world with Go!!!	21
1.2	Compilation with go build.	22
1.3	Passing arguments.	22
1.4	Passing arguments output	23
1.5	Sum two numbers passed by arguments.	23
1.6	Sum numbers output.	24
2.1	Third-party package download using `go get`.	28
2.2	Declaration of variables.	29
2.3	Variables declaration	30
2.4	Constants declaration	31
2.5	Enums declaration	32
2.6	Function with two arguments.	33
2.7	Function returning several values.	33
2.8	Variadic function	34
2.9	Functions as arguments.	34
2.10	Functions closure.	35
2.11	Passing values and references to a function.	36
2.12	Zero values during initialization.	37
2.13	`if/else` example.	38
2.14	`switch` example.	39
2.15	`switch`.	40
2.16	`for` loop example.	41
2.17	Example of error handling.	42
2.18	`defer`.	44
2.19	`panic`.	44

2.20	`recover`.	45
2.21	Go runtime initialization order.	46
2.22	Main using `import` _	47
2.23	Package with `init` functions.	47
3.1	Arrays declaration	49
3.2	Slices indexing.	50
3.3	Type differences between array, slice, and item.	51
3.4	Differences between length and capacity	52
3.5	`slice` iteration using the `range` clause.	53
3.6	`map` creation.	54
3.7	`map` access operations.	55
3.8	`map` iteration using range.	56
4.1	Structure definition for a rectangle.	57
4.2	Struct constructor.	58
4.3	Anonymous struct.	59
4.4	Nested structs.	60
4.5	Embedded structs.	61
4.6	Definition of methods for a `Rectangle` type.	62
4.7	Value and pointer receivers.	63
4.8	Embedded methods.	64
4.9	Interface declaration	65
4.10	Interface declaration	67
4.11	Using the empty interface.	68
4.12	Explore the type of an empty interface.	69
5.1	`reflect.TypeOf` with basic types.	72
5.2	`reflect.TypeOf` with structs.	72
5.3	`reflect.TypeOf` with structs.	73
5.4	Recursive struct inspector.	74
5.5	`reflect.ValueOf`.	75
5.6	`switch` using `reflect.Kind`.	75
5.7	`reflect.ValueOf` with structs.	76
5.8	Setting values using reflection.	77
5.9	Setting values using reflection considering unexported fields.	78
5.10	Using `reflect.Makefunc` to create functions on run-time.	79
5.11	Access to field tags using `reflect`.	81
6.1	Creation of goroutines.	85
6.2	Creation of multiple goroutines.	86
6.3	Goroutine using reading channels.	87
6.4	Goroutine using read/write channels.	88
6.5	Channel buffering.	89
6.6	`close` function in channels.	90

6.7	Channel consumption using `range`.	91
6.8	Channels direction.	92
6.9	`select`.	93
6.10	`select` with multi values.	94
6.11	Non-blocking `select` using `default` cases.	96
6.12	`WaitGroup` and several goroutines.	97
6.13	`Timer` and `Ticker`.	98
6.14	`Timer` and `Ticker` management.	99
6.15	Context `WithCancel`.	101
6.16	Context `WithTimeout`.	102
6.17	Context `WithDeadline`.	103
6.18	Context `WithValue`.	104
6.19	Context `WithValue`.	105
6.20	Single actionable variable using `Once`.	107
6.21	`Mutex`.	108
6.22	Atomic access to variable.	110
6.23	Atomic access to `Value` type.	110
7.1	Implementation of a `Reader` interface.	114
7.2	Implementation of a `Writer` interface.	115
7.3	File writing and reading with `ioutil`.	116
7.4	File writing with `os`.	117
7.5	Utilization of file descriptors with `os`.	118
7.6	Writing to standard output with `os.Stdout`	119
7.7	Reading from standard input with `os.Stdin`.	120
7.8	Standard input reading using `bufio`.	120
7.9	Standard input reading using `bufio` scanners.	121
7.10	Standard output writing.	122
8.1	CSV reading.	123
8.2	CSV writing.	124
8.3	JSON marshalling.	125
8.4	JSON unmarshalling.	126
8.5	Custom `struct` JSON marshalling.	127
8.6	XML marshalling.	129
8.7	XML unmarshalling.	130
8.8	XML struct marshalling.	132
8.9	YAML marshalling.	134
8.10	YAML unmarshalling.	134
8.11	YAML struct marshalling.	135
8.12	`Marshal` function for custom encoding using field tags (excerpt).	137
8.13	`Marshal` function for custom encoding using field tags (continues 8.12).	139
9.1	GET request.	141

9.2	POST request.	143
9.3	POST request using `PostForm`.	144
9.4	Other HTTP requests.	146
9.5	HTTP server using `http.HandleFunc`.	148
9.6	HTTP server and handler.	149
9.7	Adding cookies to requests and responses.	150
9.8	Use of `CookieJar` to set cookie values.	152
9.9	Basic authorization middleware handler.	154
9.10	Concatenation of several middleware handlers.	156
10.1	Fill template with a **struct**.	160
10.2	Template **if/else**.	161
10.3	Template **if/else** binary variable comparisons.	162
10.4	Template **range** iteration.	163
10.5	Template **slice** function.	163
10.6	Use of `FuncMap`.	164
10.7	Rendering templates inside other templates.	165
10.8	HTML list with a template.	166
11.1	Single test.	169
11.2	Function test.	170
11.3	Test skipping.	171
11.4	Subtests in practice (part I).	173
11.5	Subtests in practice (part II).	175
11.6	Definition of examples.	179
11.7	Function benchmarking.	181
11.8	Function parallel benchmarking.	182
11.9	File to be tested.	184
11.10	Tests to show coverage.	184
11.11	Profiling of a graph generation program.	186
12.1	Program using modules.	192
12.2	Program documentation.	195
12.3	Documented examples for Example 12.2.	197
13.1	C function called from Go.	200
13.2	C function called from Go with comments.	200
13.3	C function with arguments called from Go.	201
13.4	Casting types between Go and C.	201
13.5	Strings manipulation between Go and C.	203
13.6	Passing arrays from Go to C.	204
13.7	Passing arrays from C to Go.	205
13.8	Passing structs from Go to C.	206
13.9	Passing structs from C to Go.	207
13.10	Instantiating C structs in Go.	208

13.11	Go executing functions from the C math library.	209
13.12	Incorrect definition of Go function to be called from C.	210
13.13	Go function without arguments called from C.	211
13.14	Go functions with arguments called from C.	212
13.15	Cgo function pointers (clibrary.h)	214
13.16	Cgo function pointers (clibrary.c)	214
13.17	Cgo function pointers (main.go)	215
13.18	Cgo function pointers (cfuncs.go)	215
14.1	Proto file `user.proto` defining a `User` message.	222
14.2	Using protos from Example 14.1.	223
14.3	Definition of complex messages.	225
14.4	Utilization of messages from Example 14.3.	226
14.5	User proto definition.	227
14.6	Group proto importing Users proto.	227
14.7	Utilization of protos from Examples 14.5 and 14.6.	227
14.8	`Group` definition with nested `User` type.	228
14.9	Utilization of messages from Example 14.8.	229
14.10	Utilization of type `Any`.	230
14.11	Utilization of messages from Example 14.10.	230
14.12	Utilization of type `OneOf`.	231
14.13	Utilization of messages from Example 14.12.	232
14.14	Utilization of maps.	233
14.15	Utilization of messages from Example 14.14.	234
14.16	Encoding PB messages from Example 14.14 into JSON.	235
15.1	Service definition using gRPC.	239
15.2	Excerpt of a gRPC stub.	240
15.3	User service server.	241
15.4	User service client.	243
15.5	Definition of a server streaming method.	244
15.6	Implementation of streaming method on the server side.	245
15.7	Implementation of a client consuming responses from a streaming server.	247
15.8	Definition of a client streaming method.	248
15.9	Client sending data in streaming.	249
15.10	Server processing client stream and responding.	250
15.11	Definition of a bidirectional streaming method.	252
15.12	Client using bidirectional streaming.	253
15.13	Server using bidirectional streaming.	254
15.14	gRPC services definition with transcoding notations.	257
15.15	gRPC gateway using HTTP (part I).	259
15.16	gRPC gateway using HTTP (part II).	260
15.17	Server interceptor (excerpt).	263

15.18 Client extended metadata (excerpt). 264
15.19 Client interceptor with logging metadata (excerpt). 266
15.20 Server interceptor consuming logging metadata (excerpt). 267
16.1 `log` package messaging. 269
16.2 `log` package messaging. 270
16.3 Logging messages in zerolog. 271
16.4 Set global level zerolog. 271
16.5 Set message context. 272
16.6 JSON tagging and encoding in message logs. 273
16.7 Single error logging. 274
16.8 Stack trace logging. 274
16.9 Stack trace logging. 276
16.10 Customized output with `ConsoleWriter`. 277
16.11 Simultaneously logging to several outputs with `MultiLevelWriter`. 278
16.12 Extensible logging using sub-loggers. 279
16.13 Extensible logging using sub-loggers. 280
16.14 Logger using basic sampler. 281
16.15 Logger using burst sampler. 282
16.16 Integration of contextual HTTP loggers. 283
16.17 Integration of several contextual HTTP loggers. 284
17.1 Basic Cobra CLI 288
17.2 Command receiving arguments 289
17.3 Command with single string flag. 290
17.4 Command with several typed flags. 292
17.5 Command with required flags. 293
17.6 Flag parsing using pointer variables. 294
17.7 CLI with several commands. 295
17.8 Commands using persistent and local flags. 297
17.9 Commands using hook functions. 299
17.10 Command custom help. 301
17.11 Self-documented CLI. 302
17.12 Shell completion command. 305
17.13 Dynamic definition of arguments for a command. 306
18.1 Database connection. 310
18.2 Modifying data statements (excerpt). 311
18.3 Querying data statements (excerpt). 313
18.4 Transaction modifying database (excerpt). 314
18.5 Prepared statement (excerpt). 314
18.6 Basic GORM program. 315
18.7 Embedded structs in GORM. 318
18.8 Belongs to relationship. 320

18.9	Belongs to relationship with custom foreign key.	320
18.10	Has one relationship.	321
18.11	One to many relationship.	321
18.12	Many to many relationship.	322
18.13	GORM creation of records.	323
18.14	GORM queries (excerpt).	324
18.15	GORM queries (continuation).	325
18.16	GORM preload.	326
18.17	GORM preload with single record.	327
18.18	GORM transaction.	329
18.19	GORM manual transaction.	330
19.1	CQL statements for Figure 19.1.	335
19.2	Users and laptops entities.	336
19.3	A user has a laptop relationship using an extra table.	336
19.4	A user has a laptop relationship using a laptop type.	336
19.5	Guarantee that every laptop has a unique user.	337
19.6	A user has many laptops using collections.	337
19.7	Guarantee that every laptop has a unique user.	338
19.8	Users and laptops in a many to many relationship.	338
19.9	GoCQL database connection.	339
19.10	GoCQL data manipulation queries.	341
19.11	GoCQL data manipulation using batches.	342
19.12	GoCQL single result query.	343
19.13	GoCQL multiple results query.	344
19.14	GoCQL UDT struct definition and query.	346
20.1	Confluent Kafka synchronous producer.	352
20.2	Confluent Kafka synchronous consumer.	353
20.3	Confluent Kafka asynchronous producer.	354
20.4	Confluent Kafka asynchronous consumer.	355
20.5	Segmentio Kafka producer.	358
20.6	Segmentio Kafka consumer.	359
20.7	Segmentio Kafka high level API producer.	360
20.8	Segmentio Kafka high level API consumer.	361
20.9	Kafka producer using the REST API.	363
20.10	Kafka consumer using the REST API (excerpt I, new consumer).	365
20.11	Kafka consumer using the REST API (excerpt II, subscription).	367
20.12	Kafka consumer using the REST API (excerpt III, acquisition).	367
20.13	Kafka consumer using the REST API (excerpt IV, delete).	368

List of Figures

11.1 HTML detail for test coverage in Example 11.10. 185
11.2 Memory profile visualization of Example 11.11. 187
11.3 Excerpt of the CPU profile visualization from Example 11.11. 188

12.1 Excerpt of `godoc` Example 12.2 documentation. 198

13.1 Arguments and functions used to call a function with functions as arguments from C. 213

14.1 Steps to define and use protocol buffer. 222

15.1 Summary of elements in a gRPC deployment. 238
15.2 Client-server communication in a server streaming scenario. 245
15.3 Client-server communication in a client streaming scenario. 249
15.4 Client-server communication in a bidirectional streaming scenario. 253
15.5 Summary of elements in a gRPC deployment. 257
15.6 Data flow from client to server using interceptors. 262

19.1 Components of a primary key in Cassandra. 334

20.1 Kafka topics and partitions. 350
20.2 Kafka offsets in a topic partition. 350
20.3 Consumer and Kafka REST Proxy communication diagram. 365

Printed in Great Britain
by Amazon